ROUTLEDGE LIBRARY EDITIONS: DEMOGRAPHY

Volume 15

POPULATION AND THE SOCIAL PROBLEM

POPULATION AND THE SOCIAL PROBLEM

J. SWINBURNE

R Routledge
Taylor & Francis Group

LONDON AND NEW YORK

First published in 1924 by George Allen & Unwin Ltd

This edition first published in 2024
by Routledge
4 Park Square, Milton Park, Abingdon, Oxon OX14 4RN

and by Routledge
605 Third Avenue, New York, NY 10158

Routledge is an imprint of the Taylor & Francis Group, an informa business

British Library Cataloguing in Publication Data
A catalogue record for this book is available from the British Library

ISBN: 978-1-032-53819-8 (Set)
ISBN: 978-1-032-56114-1 (Volume 15) (hbk)
ISBN: 978-1-032-56131-8 (Volume 15) (pbk)
ISBN: 978-1-003-43402-3 (Volume 15) (ebk)

DOI: 10.4324/9781003434023

Publisher's Note
The publisher has gone to great lengths to ensure the quality of this reprint but points out that some imperfections in the original copies may be apparent.

Disclaimer
The publisher has made every effort to trace copyright holders and would welcome correspondence from those they have been unable to trace.

POPULATION

AND THE

SOCIAL PROBLEM

BY

J. SWINBURNE, F.R.S.

LONDON: GEORGE ALLEN & UNWIN LTD.
RUSKIN HOUSE, 40 MUSEUM STREET, W.C. 1

First published in 1924

Printed in Great Britain by
UNWIN BROTHERS, LIMITED, LONDON AND WOKING

To

MY ELDEST DAUGHTER

IDA

IN TOKEN OF HER REAL SYMPATHY

WITH THOSE BORN LESS

FORTUNATELY

CONTENTS

Population and the Social Problem

CHAPTER I

DE CUNICULIS

ONCE there was an island full of rabbits. It does not matter how they came there. The island was overrun with them. Each pair had several litters a year, but as the food they could raise on the island was limited, they died as fast as they were born. In time they had developed some rude sort of civilisation ; which made it a little more difficult to follow the effects of their fecundity. But the number that died directly and especially indirectly from starvation was very nearly equal to the number born, as their means of raising food improved very slowly in comparison. The numbers were kept down by direct starvation ; by deaths, especially of the newly born ; insufficient food ; through disease ; by vice engendered by misery and despair ; and by fighting. The island was divided up into patches, coloured differently on the maps, and they cultivated patch pride as a virtue, and the inhabitants of each patch were always trying to extend their patches at the expense of the neighbouring patches ; and this caused many deaths. They had short and miserable lives, and they knew something was wrong, but having the brains only of rabbits, they did not know what it was.

The Priests said : " You shall give us predominance and food, and we will control you ; for we know all about God. We have created him in your image. He is a big rabbit, and he likes rabbits, so you must breed as many as you can. He is so fond of rabbits that he metes out eternal punishment to most of them, and those alone escape who kow-tow to us and believe what we tell them, and obey their spiritual pastors and masters." Having the minds of rabbits, they gave the priests predominance, and they had their brains warped in their childhood, and were kept in special darkness and misery for thousands of years.

Then a King would be appointed over each patch by the more influential, the ordinary rabbit having no say in the matter ; and the kings robbed, murdered and oppressed, and led their patches to slaughter ; and the working of their sordid and contemptible ambitions was called history.

The Politician said : "Give us predominance and food, and we will talk and flatter your ignorant prejudices, and you shall listen to us, and read about us, and we will give you food, and everything you can want." So the rabbits gave power to the politicians who had the minds of rabbits, the tongues of serpents, and a mendacity not possessed by any of the other lower animals.

Some doe rabbits were hurt because it had been hinted they had the brains of hares ; so they performed all sorts of antics to show that they really had the brains of rabbits, and said that if they were allowed to help in choosing the politicians something good would happen, they did not know exactly what.

The Militarist said : "Our patch is rich, but so is the blue patch next us. Let us attack it and take it ; and we will be twice as rich and twice as large as we are now. When our glorious Empire is twice as rich and twice as large with twice the commerce, you will all be twice as rich, and there will be no poverty. They are thinking of attacking us, so our invasion will be a defensive war. To arms ! You go and kill as many as you can. Many of you will die glorious deaths anonymously, more of you will be crippled for life, all of you will have a foretaste of hell ; and we will inflict as much misery on our neighbours, or I hope much more. I will stay at home and make patriotic speeches, and my name will go down as one who made history. But I will not keep all the credits; those of you whom I select will receive the order of the Golden Eagle or the Zinc Carrion Crow."

The Political Economist said : " I do not want anything from you ; but I have spun out an interesting and complicated study of wealth on the assumption that population is fixed, so that better organisation will put things right. Though I sometimes admit in a footnote that your extreme fecundity upsets my schemes, I generally prefer to deny or ignore its existence. But if you will do without middlemen, adopt free trade, and alter the relations of capital and labour, it will be all right," and he went off to finish a book on the " Double, or Scalp-and-wife Money Standards in the Bungo Islands."

Then it occurred to someone that emigration would ease the stress, so they sent six rabbits to a continent where there was none before. In a few years the six had multiplied into several thousand million ; and they had overrun half the continent. The rabbits on the island thought their population pressure had been eased by several thousand million, instead of six. Most of the several thousand million were dying like the rabbits on the island ; yet only half the continent was occupied by them. It was said that while one half of the continent was vacant and full of rabbit food, it was impossible that the other half should be full of starving rabbits ; and, indeed, it is true that if the rabbits could have been suddenly distributed over the whole continent, they would have been well off, but only for the few months necessary for them to multiply up to the new limit.

The Socialists said : " Some of you are not starving at all, but are rich. This is unfair. Give us front place, and we will divide up and have no rich, so there will be no poor. We will then settle what little work each of you shall do, and you shall have plenty to eat. Instead of each pair bringing up its litters in poverty and difficulty, we will all combine to bring up all the litters collectively, in plenty, ease and comfort, and the more litters there are the more happy rabbits there will be."

The Labour Leader said : " We all do too much work and get too little food for it. All we have got to do is to work much less and eat much more food, and make the rich pay for it."

The Syndicalist said : " Let us all refuse to work ; then the rich will get poor. We are miserable, and we envy and hate the rich. Let us ruin them, and somehow we will be all right. The rich have, in fact, collected all the food somewhere for themselves, and we will get it out of them."

The Philanthropist said : " I will organise a fund to be called after me. You will all subscribe, so that a large portion of you will be kept in demoralising idleness. The more rabbits we support in idleness the less starvation there will be. Carry philantrophy far enough, and you will all be supported by charity, and no one will have to work, and food can always be bought."

The Anarchist remarked—and he had some show of reason : " Some governments say they come from God for our good ; others are elected, and none ever softens our misery. They all say they can and will, so our misery must be their fault, and we would be much better without them." He threw a bomb anonymously and blew the government up ; he dissipated himself too.

One rabbit said : " You are poor because you are prolific." They would not have this at any price, so they reviled him and refused to listen, and said his theory had been disproved ; for his explanation made out that the misery was really their own fault, and it is impossible to get an animal with the brain of a rabbit to realise that its troubles are due to its own faults.

CHAPTER II

THE PRINCIPLES OF POPULATION

ALL kinds of animals continue by having young. If each pair of animals produced two offspring without any failures, and no more, that kind would continue perpetually. If they failed to produce two offspring to each pair, by ever so little, the kind of animal would gradually become extinct. On the other hand, if each pair produced more than two offspring continually, however slightly they exceeded the average, the animals would increase in number without any limit. For example : if each couple produced four offspring on reaching maturity, and then died, the number of animals would double itself in every generation. If the animals matured in a year this would mean that the number would double every year. In ten years the animals would increase a thousand fold, strictly speaking, 1,024 times ; in twenty years, more than a million fold, and so on. It would not matter in this connection how long each animal lived after it had produced its young. To follow this it is necessary to examine the numbers when the state has been in existence one lifetime at least. For example, if each pair of the animals has four young and die at one year old, if one pair is taken to start with, it has four descendants at one year, eight at two, sixteen at three, and so on. If the animals live two years, and two are considered, there are six at the end of one year. At the end of two years two die, leaving four, which produce eight, making twelve. At the end of the next year four die, leaving eight, which produce sixteen, making twenty-four, and so on.

Though death after parentage does not, in the simple case taken, effect the rate of multiplication, death before maturity is a very different matter. If half the animals die before they are old enough to have offspring ; or if, living to any age they have no offspring, the number will remain stationary. In nature it is thus by the immature death-rate that excessive multiplication is kept down. Whether it is the large number of offspring produced by the adults which causes the enormous immature death-rate, or it is the huge immature death-rate that prevents the survival of animals with smaller fertilities than those in existence now is a barren question. The fact is that in the animal world a huge immature mortality is provided for by great fertility of the parents. The term immature mortality is not applicable in the cases of such animals as bees and wasps. To meet all cases " preparental mortality " is a better term. We are, however, mainly concerned with man, and may therefore confine our attention to vertebrates. In this case individuals which reach maturity are all likely to be parents. In the case of civilised man there are special influences at work. The lower the animal, broadly speaking, the greater the fertility of the parents, and with it the greater the immature mortality. Thus a turbot will lay something of the order of fifteen million eggs a year. Many are never fertilised, many are eaten, but tens, perhaps hundreds of thousands of turbotlets come out ; but on the average only two out of all the millions of eggs laid by a parent during her life survive to become parents themselves. The little fish either starve, or are eaten to prevent other animals starving, or both.

Throughout nature we find this great immature or preparental mortality ; and can conclude that great preparental mortality is the condition necessary for the survival of every kind of animal. As the scale is ascended the infant mortality is less ; as the young are looked after by the parents, so that fewer are necessary. By infant mortality is here meant death of the young, not only of those less than one year old.

In the case of turbot we have considered an animal low in the scale, with correspondingly great fertility.

When we come to animals among whom the parents produce, not millions, but a few offspring in their lifetime, we might expect the sacrifice of young to disappear. It is, of course, reduced, but even in the highest animals the natural fertility is still great enough to be coupled with perpetual destruction of young ; and this excess of production is still the necessary cost of permanence. The elephant breeds very slowly ; but Darwin calculated that at their normal rate a pair of elephants would have more than fifteen million descendants in five centuries. At this rate they would pack the surface of the earth in a thousand years.

If a turbot can produce fifteen million young in its life, and those of each sex are equally numerous, the fertility of the turbot may be specified as 7,500,000. On the other hand, if each pair of turbot produced two eggs only in a lifetime, and these eggs invariably hatched out turbot which became parents and reared two more only, the turbot would have a fertility of one. No animal has such a low fertility as one ; if it had, any accidents would reduce the numbers until the animal disappeared.

In the case of man, we might consider as ideal a community in which the men and women are always equal in number, all marrying at 21, each pair having six children, at the ages of 22 to 27. This is certainly not an extravagant view of human fertility under favourable conditions ; that is to say, in the case of thoroughly healthy people living temperately without too severe a struggle. In order to save trouble in calculation it is simpler to consider one sex by itself, and a further simplification in calculation may be made by assuming each female produces three female children at 24. This would mean that the population would be tripled every twenty-four years. In certain favourable circumstances human population doubles in twelve and a half years ; this is equivalent to quadrupling in twenty-five years. We might fairly have taken each woman to have eight children, of which four are females born when the mother is 24. This would mean that the population would double every twelve years. Few people who are not mathematical have any conception of a geometric or logarithmic growth, such as the unchecked increase of population. At this rate a population is multiplied by 256 in ninety-six years, or by 323 in a century, and the present population of the world, say roughly 2,000,000,000, would have grown out of a thousand people in only two and a half centuries.

It may be urged that these rates of increase are excessive. They are excessive in comparison with the rates of increase under ordinary conditions ; because under ordinary conditions people die of starvation, and of disease, and of weakness due to poor nutrition, and they cannot marry as soon as they would like ; and in many cases they limit their families more or less successfully. A rate of increase which doubles the population every twelve years is taken as quite a low estimate of increase from the purely physiological point of view. The people are supposed to be healthy, well fed, and well clothed. Conditions were not very good in England between 1811 and 1821. In spite of this the population of England and Wales increased 18 per cent. in those years. That means a rate of increase of $1\frac{2}{3}$ per cent. per annum ; corresponding to doubling the population in a little more than forty years.

To emphasise the effect of a logarithmic or geometrical growth, which is more generally familiar in the case of accumulation of money by compound interest, a very low rate may be taken ; that by which the population doubles in a century. Assuming that one couple, say Adam and Eve, living six thousand years ago, according to the Biblical notion, were the parents of all mankind, and that at the end of a hundred years there were four people, and so on, the present population of the world would be more than two million billion, or 2×10^{18}, or more than a thousand people per square yard over land and sea. This apparently ridiculous calculation is made to show the real significance of this type of growth. The antiquity of man is so great that the rate of increase of population of the world may be taken as very little above unity ; that is to say, it hardly increases at all. At present there is a perceptible increase in what are known as civilised countries ; but that is a mere incident in the life of the world. There is no time which can be fixed in which the kind of organism we have sprung from had just risen high enough to be classified as human, and there is no reason to suppose we are all descended from two particular individuals out of a particularly advanced group. But, for simplicity, suppose we were all descended from one pair living a million years ago ; the present population of the world would result from a rate of increase of only 0·0023 per cent. each year, corresponding to doubling every thirty odd thousand years. It does not follow in the least that a physiological fertility of 0·0023 per cent. per annum would have been enough to produce the present population of the world. On the contrary, the actual rate of increase is the result of an enormously higher physiological rate, and it is safe to assume that the high physiological rate was necessary to enable the race to survive. For simplicity the round number of two thousand million has been taken as the population of the world. G. H. Knibbs, in his *Mathematical Theory of Population*, published by the Australian Government, gives 1,649,000,000, with a rate of increase of 1·159, that is doubling in 60·15 years ; at this rate, after another period of ten thousand years, the population would be 2 with 5 noughts after it.

There is no reason to suppose the marine population of turbot is increasing ; in fact it is said to be deminishing, yet a female produces fifteen million eggs each year. No doubt this enormous physiological fertility is necessary to fish, and if it were lessened appreciably turbot would soon die out. There is also every reason to believe that the physiological fertility of man, 7 per cent. or so a year, or whatever it really is in fact, was and is necessary for his existence. Whether civilisation modifies the conditions so that a lower physiological fertility would be enough, and whether man, by use of his reasoning powers and will, can control the birth-rate in such a way as to help him, are other questions which will be discussed presently, though they are very difficult to answer.

There must be some age, which may be called the physiological age, to which men and women would live if they were in happy or favourable surroundings, probably about 100, but we may take 70 from the Psalmist, though he was not discussing ideal conditions. If all the inhabitants lived to 70 and then died, the death-rate would be just under 1·43. Any higher rate would show that people died before their time. Thus a death-rate of 2 would, in a stationary population, correspond with a life of 50 years. People do not, in fact, all live to one age and then die, and this way of looking at the death-rate is likely to be misleading. Thus a death-rate of 2, corresponding to a universal age of decease of 50, does not correspond to the case in which one half of the population lives to 25 and the other to 75. But it is not worth while troubling about that here.

As the world is so old, and as man has been on it so long that a rate of increase of the order of 0·0023 would account for the population of the globe, we may discuss stationary populations without falling into appreciable error, as they are much simpler to follow.

In a country where there is no immigration or emigration and a stationary population, the death and birth-rates must be the same. Assuming that men and women are born in equal numbers, and that every woman who marries has eight children, only one woman in four can marry. The other three may die as infants, or may live to any age as spinsters. If every woman who comes of age marries and has eight children, there must be a loss of three-quarters of the women under age. In a stationary population the birth and death-rate is the same ; the figure depends on the ages at which the parents produce, and the ages to which people live. Thus if six out of the eight children died as soon as they were born there would never be any grown-up

people except the parents ; while if all the children lived
to old age there would be four times as many people
as parents, so that the birth and death-rates would be
a much smaller figure. It is simplest in this type of
elementary calculation to consider one sex alone. We
will consider the women as all important, and the men
as disregarded incidents. If we assume that the women
who become mothers bear yearly from 20 to 27, and
die at 27, and that girls are born at 20, 22, 24, and
26, of which the first only survives to become a
mother, the rest dying at birth, we have the maximum death-rate for the ages of the mothers, in this
case 14.8.

In civilised countries we may take the death-rate as
of the order of two. The conditions of the imaginary
example may be altered to reduce the death-rate. Thus,
if all the children, including the mothers, live to a good
old age, the population is increased in comparison with
a given number of mothers. If the mothers have fewer
children the death-rate will fall until the case is reached
where all the women are mothers, each having one girl,
and all living to 50, and the death-rate is 2. If they
all live to 80 the death-rate is 1.25. The low civilised
death-rate of 2 thus means a combination of long life
and few children.

In discussing the case of a stationary or substantially
stationary population, it does not matter for the present
purpose whether we take the death-rate or the birth-
rate. Reverting to the case of a population that
doubles in ten years we have 7 per cent. as the rate of
increase.

Such a population as this differs very widely from an
ordinary civilised population with a birth and death-
rate of from $1\frac{1}{2}$ to 3. The restraint of population is
not due to any voluntary action resulting from a general
understanding of the subject by mankind. The restraint
has been going on for millions of years, but the question
of population has never been discussed seriously at all
until just lately ; that is to say, within the last century
and a half ; and it is generally misunderstood by the

few specialists among the thousands of millions of existing people, and the rest of this public have never heard, thought or dreamed of such a question.

There is a difference between the restraint in the case of the lower animals and man. Thus, in the case of the cod it may be taken that in existing conditions every mature female produces a million eggs a year. If this is, as is probable, the physiological fertility of the cod, that is to say the fertility that would obtain, if the cod led the life most conducive to its health and happiness, the multiplication of cod is kept down mainly by infant mortality, the eggs and the young dying, mainly by being eaten, before they reach maturity. It is likely that the grown-up cod do not live as long as they would in happier circumstances ; so that they do not have their full number of successive broods of a million or so. Considering, for simplicity, the female cod only, and assuming half the eggs are male, it does not matter much whether a given female lays half a million eggs one year and dies, one egg surviving, as a female cod ; or lays three million in six years, one again surviving. In both cases it is essentially infant mortality that keeps the increase down.

In the case of rabbits again ; the females generally produce several litters a year, and the increase, which is astonishingly rapid when it gets any scope, is kept down by infant mortality.

It is possible that the physiological fertility of cod, rabbits, and other animals is less, not more than is found in nature. There are two aspects of this possibility. Thus cod may lay these millions of eggs under stress of competition only, so that if they were put into specially easy conditions their fertility would decrease at once. On the other hand, the fertility being the result of evolution under stress may die away in the course of many generations in favourable circumstances. In human beings we have two temporary phenomena to consider, the greater fertility of the very poor as compared with the rich or those well off, and the real or alleged temporary increase of fertility of the poor in bad times. Permanent changes in fertility in such highly organised and developed animals are exceedingly slow. It has been urged that such development will be modified in cycles of twenty-one thousand years. The discussion of the future alteration of such a character as human fertility is not of practical value. This book is not written with any certainty that it will secure the happiness of thousands of millions of people twenty thousand years hence.

⸲In man, we are so accustomed to the restraint of population that we hardly realise what forces have been raised automatically or by evolution to bring it about. Some of the most obvious may be mentioned. Infant mortality, in spite of efforts of parents, infant mortality due to carelessness, and due to less or more intentional neglect, passing into child-murder ; shortening life through malnutrition and the opportunities given by it to disease, starvation of individuals through poverty, famine, epidemics, such as plagues, other germ diseases, war, poisons, such as opium, alcohol, hashish and to a smaller extent other and modern drugs, and, almost as a class by itself, sexual evils, such as prostitution, all sorts of sexual perversions, such evils as syphilis and gonorrhœa, with a whole ghastly procession of horrible diseases in its train. There are many common but terrible diseases which the public do not know are due primarily to venereal infection. In civilised countries there also appears to be an increase of female sterility due to too much stress in life, and especially in a small and fortunately unimportant class, to mental stress in attempting to do the same brain work as men, which not only lessens fertility, but interferes with the normal, healthy sexual instincts. In civilised life, which is what we are mainly concerned with, as we have no control over savage polity, late marriage, reduced fertility, due to poorer health, to late marriage, and to prudential and purely artificial limitation of offspring play their part.

All these evils are the result of the pressure of population ; they all tend to keep population down, and none of them need exist in an ideal state in which people could marry at the physiological age, and have as many children as their nature dictated. Whether in an ideal state we would have monogamy, polygamy, polyandry, or promiscuity is difficult to say, and discussion of this point would be useless here.

If the ordinary life tables are examined, the meaning of infant mortality is more easily realised. According to the London Table of Simpson, 1728 to 1737, practically half the people born died before they were 3 years old, and more than 65 per cent. before they were 20.

According to Price's Northampton Table, 1735 to 1780, about half grew to 5 years old, and 56 per cent. died before 20. Mylne's Carlisle Table, 1779 to 1787, shows 40 per cent. dying before 20.

The English Life Table, got out by the Registrar General, dealing with more nearly present conditions, shows about 34 per cent. dead before 20, and about 40 per cent. dead before 30. We may take this last case first. If we want to find the physiological rate of multiplication of man, an actual table like this gives figures that are far too low. We may take the rate of increase of the population forming the basis of the table as 1 per cent. Calculations of life and rates of increase of population are very troublesome if made very accurately ; but to save complication we may make some assumptions getting results which are roughly true, and equally likely to be wrong in one direction as the other. Suppose the population, well fed, and looked after carefully, the pre-parental mortality, or the mortality up to say 25 would disappear, or almost disappear.

Suppose 1,000 people are born a year, and their average life is 40, the population is 40,000. Suppose it is stationary ; the birth-rate is then 2.5 per cent., and the death-rate the same. Suppose, to make the calculation simple, the people produce the necessary children at 25 and that 63 per cent. of the people born live to 25. Then 630 produce 1,000 children every year.

It is troublesome to calculate rates of increase in percentages, because we have to make assumptions as to what the population is on which to take the percentage, and we gain no useful information in that way as the parents who go on living after their children's birth do nothing further relevant to the calculation, except form a denominator. But it is clear that if one-third of the people die young, and all the rest marry, each couple produces 3 children at least. Suppose only 75 per cent. are married, the married couples must produce 4 children per couple even to keep the population stationary. This means that if you take the actual population on which the table is based, and prevent child mortality, and provide that the people all marry at 25, and have no more children per couple than in the actual case, each person born is represented by two persons in twenty-five years, in addition to himself ; four in fifty, and sixteen in a century.

If we take the old London table, we are not sure that the population was increasing, or even stationary. It may have been falling naturally, but kept up by country people coming in all the time.

If we take a portion in which 1,000 were born every year, the expectation of life being 19, the population was 19,000. Of these 321 came to 25 without dying. Make the same assumption and we find each couple has 6·2 children. If child mortality were reduced almost to nothing, each man would be represented by three in twenty-five years, nine in fifty, and eighty-one in a century. This is assuming only a portion marry, as in 1728–1737. Suppose that proportion was 67 per cent. ; each couple must have had 9·3, and each person, at the end of a century would be represented by no less than 468, or nearly 500 descendants. This is roughly equivalent to a population doubling in a little more than 11 years ; say 12½ to be on the safe side. Now the adult population of London in the early eighteenth century cannot have been in a condition to encourage the maximum fertility. Many must have been poor, many unable to marry until late, and many unable to marry at all ; yet they coped with an enormous child death-rate. Twelve and a half years for doubling, or approximately $5\frac{3}{4}$ per cent. a year, is therefore not at all an extreme estimate of man's physiological rate of increase.

CHAPTER III

CAUSES OF GENERAL IGNORANCE

THERE is nothing new in the principle that the stress of population is the fundamental fact in sociology ; yet it is never realised even by sociologists. No system of sociology based upon it has ever been put forward. It is quite true there are many people who have an idea of the importance of stress of population, especially among biologists, and people talk vaguely about a prosperous country needing outlets for its surplus population. Such expressions as this are not new. Smith's consciousness of the stress of population is often evident in his *Wealth of Nations*. The ancients also had vague ideas on the subject.

To Malthus is due the credit of first showing that no philanthropic project has any possibility of success, unless it is based on appreciation of the Law of Population. Malthus was a clergyman born in 1766. About the end of that century there was a good deal of discussion as to schemes for reducing or annihilating poverty, and in those days discussions were often carried on by means of pamphlets. On thinking over an impossible equality scheme by Godwin, Malthus hit on what has been called the Law of Population. The more he considered this, the more significant he found it. He therefore read widely, and went about the world to examine the conditions of various peoples ; an undertaking that was very serious in those days. He wrote largely on the subject, and his works gave rise to some discussion at the time, and soon after he interested himself in economics, too, and published a book on that subject, and some correspondence with Say. His *Principles of Population* is hardly ever read now. A new edition has been published quite lately ; but until then it was never to be seen new on booksellers' shelves, and when found, very infrequently, second-hand, it is marked at a low price. Moreover, when Malthus is referred to in books or newspapers he is seldom quoted, sometimes misquoted, and nearly always misrepresented.

It is difficult to discuss the objections raised, as they are all so vague and frequently so absurd that they cannot be examined seriously. They are important, though, as a branch of one of the greatest studies there is : the ceaseless struggle of man against his own good.

One typical view was that Malthus had framed the law of population, and the law was cruel and wicked, and so Malthus was a very iniquitous person. Shelley, Godwin's son-in-law, said he would rather go to Hell than go to Heaven with Malthus. It may be said that Shelley's opinion is of no importance. It is of no value whatever, but it is of importance because he was a well-known man, and the majority of people respect the opinion of anyone whose name they know, even in a very different connection. Shelley's dictum is interesting, as it shows, incidentally, the vanity of the man. He thought that the Almighty might make a mistake in His estimate of Malthus, and that it was a mistake into which he, Shelley, could not fall. His mental powers were so weak that he did not know the difference between a law as a generalisation of phenomena, and a rule of conduct to be enforced. Being without that element of greatness which would have let him realise what he did not know, and what he could not understand, he gave a silly opinion on a matter that was right outside his limited comprehension. No doubt it requires some special form of brain texture to make a lyric poet ; but the rest of the organ may be very poor.

The powers of intellectual darkness were, of course, to the front then as now, the clergy teaching that Malthus' doctrine is inconsistent with the goodness of God. They said we were told to be fruitful and multiply, and things of that sort, and used their pretended special acquaintance with the wishes of the Almighty to prevent the spread of any knowledge that might be good for man.

Another doctrine was, and still is, that children are sent directly as blessings from God, and to act in almost any way so that they do not come, is more or less a kind of murder. If two people marry and have a number of children they cannot nourish or bring up properly, or that are consumptive, feeble-minded or scrofulous ; the children are blessings specially sent by God, and the parents, who are in no way responsible, are to be helped as deserving poor, instead of being punished for their immorality. If the two do not marry and God sends children, the parents are not moral ; they are responsible, and one of them, the woman, should be put into a preliminary hell. If the two marry and, owing to prudence, have no children, they are thwarting an Omnipotent God, and their action is very immoral, in fact almost murderous, while if they do not marry formally and God sends no children they are rather unmoral ; but they are not doing their duty to the community.

Akin to the clerical doctrine was the notion that, though the law of population might explain the multiplication of lower animals, it could not apply to man. Man is a noble animal, walking on its hind legs, though it cannot help swinging its fore-legs while doing so ; and endowed with reason. The multiplication of man is not dependent on anything lower or more automatic than reason. Before a man marries or has offspring he always considers the state of the world in general and decides with unerring precision whether it would be advisable for him to add another human being or not ; and it is the result of this exercise of judgment that there is not and never has been poverty and misery in the world.

The confusion as to the two kinds of law is widespread, and it was quite common in connection with Malthus, and it is in fact still usual to assume that there was no pressure of population until his time, and that, according to, or in obedience to, his law, people are now beginning to increase in such a way that they will eventually crowd one another off the planet.

Another notion is that, whenever the pressure of population began, it has not yet reached any value that matters. People say that there are unoccupied lands that can be further developed, so as to feed more people, and there are still large tracts of country either fertile now, or easy to make fertile, which could support immense populations, and as long as it is possible to increase population there cannot be any pressure. A similar argument is often urged as to existing social systems. If all rich people lived plainly and did not employ others to minister to their comforts ; if all inefficient official employment were stopped ; all unnecessary middlemen abolished, and all overlapping in trade avoided ; and if handworkers saw the folly of limitation of output, and we all worked with efficiency and vigour, two or three times the present population could live well and happily. Therefore there is no pressure of population. Emigration has always been held up as a cure, or at least a practical alleviation.

Some think that the fact that wealth has increased faster than population in some countries, disposes of the law in some way or other, which is not indicated.

Others, again, assume that any pressure there may be is confined to the poorer classes. As the rich are not starving it seems to many that the law of population does not concern them, and the only question of any importance is the improvident multiplication of the proletariat.

A great deal of criticism has been aimed at the illustrations given by Malthus ; a bogus case being made out by taking one drawn to explain growth by geometrical progression and treating it as a statement of the actual increase of population. Malthus had before him the difficult problem of making clear to unreasoning minds what a tendency is. He therefore took simple cases of geometrical progression, such as a people doubling in number every twenty-five years, and he worked out examples. He pointed out that it was quite possible to increase the supply of food on the planet ;

but he argued that the increase of food is not unlimited, while that of population is unlimited as long as it goes by geometrical progression. To take a concrete example he assumed that food might increase with time in arithmetical progression. As a matter of fact a simple arithmetical progression yields an infinite number in time ; but however rapid it is it can always be overtaken by a geometrical progression, however slow. Critics pointed out that food did not in fact increase in any simple arithmetical progression, and that population did not in fact go on increasing in any definite geometrical ratio. Those who are interested in such things often work out the present value of a penny invested 1,900 years ago at 5 per cent. compound interest, added yearly. The calculation is simple, and the answer is seventy-five billion trillion pounds, or 75×10^{36}. That no penny investment has, in fact, produced any such sum does not disprove the law of compound interest, nor the tendency of money invested at fixed or varying compound interest to increase without limit.

Another theory is that though the physiological fertility of natural or primitive man may be very high compared with anything shown by census returns, as man gets more and more civilised his physiological fertility decreases, so that he gradually adapts himself to his environment. The fact that the census rates of multiplication are so much lower than any physiological rate, such as that corresponding to every woman having, say, six children, is itself used as an argument to show that the physiological fertility is reduced. This assumes that such a very highly developed and permanent animal as man alters very much more rapidly than he does. It takes no notice of the millions of years man has existed, and treats the fitful fever of Western life as civilisation. It also involves what may, for short, be called the patch fallacy ; as it forgets that the population pressure in any one country is not independent, but is affected by the pressure all over the world ; as, like that in a fluid, population pressure tends to equalise itself in all directions.

It may be asked what is the Law of Population?

The difficulty in replying is that the answer sounds so obvious as to appear a platitude that must have been plain to anyone with any intelligence as soon as intelligence was developed. It may be put simply: " Man, like other animals, continues by having young." It follows from this, that, like other animals, he must provide more young than just enough to replace each generation, if they all grow up without mishap ; otherwise he could never have continued. Human population, like that of plants and other animals, has, therefore, a physiological rate of multiplication corresponding, as Malthus put it, to a geometrical progression. As man has no rutting season it is more accurately an exponential, or logarithmic growth of the type $N = e^{ax}$ where N is the population, x the time and a a constant coefficient.

Where a is a positive quantity the population tends to increase without limit, slowly if a is very slightly greater than o and fast if it is much greater. If a is o the population remains constant. If a is less than zero, that is, negative, the population decreases by the same fraction or percentage each year ; it is dying out. Real populations do not multiply regularly at a fixed rate, so that a would have to be variable to make the expression fit, and the expression thus becomes meaningless. It is useful to represent the tendency of population, or to denote the physiological law of multiplication which is modified by the actual circumstances of life.

That the Law of Population is so obvious as to be almost a truism, and yet was not discovered, or at any rate stated until man had suffered for millions of years, is extraordinary. It is equally extraordinary that Newton's laws of motion, which are just as obvious, had to wait for Newton to formulate them. But it is much more extraordinary that while everybody who learns Newton's laws of motion assents to their validity at once, the law of Malthus excites the keenest hostility. The reasons for this deserve study and development.

Ignorance of the Law of Population is merely a special case of ignorance about all sociological matters. We may therefore discuss some main causes of this type of general ignorance and then look into the case of population more carefully.

The amount of brain work a man can do in a lifetime is very minute, having regard to the extent of general human knowledge. Most of us dislike brain work any more intense than that necessary for amusement. The result is that, broadly speaking, we are all fools except in one narrow line. Each of us is, as a rule, specially interested and informed in one direction, generally that in which he gets his living. And on all or nearly all other subjects he is not only profoundly but unconsciously ignorant. We cultivate our minds for our professional, or bread-earning work, and we confine the use of our trained faculties to that. We deal with all the other matters with the fallow mind. It is as to subjects outside our special work that we are such fools, because we apply only the fallow mind to them.

An ordinary man in the comfortable classes does his work during the day, competing with others and sharpening his wits, and he has some hours to himself, generally in the evening. These he spends partly smoking— smoking being a seemly way of doing nothing—and browsing on the daily paper. He may read a novel, or he may have some hobby, or absorb as mental pabulum the ephemeral books from the circulating library. We take no interest in matters of grave moment, such as the welfare of our race or of our country, our attention being occupied by party politics, and the stuff daily papers and dreams are made of, which we imagine to be of public importance.

Anyone who is odd enough to study sociological questions is apt to think, not so much that he is wise, as that other people are hopelessly foolish ; but if he tries to compete with other people in any profession he finds he is wrong. Similarly he finds that specialists in sociology cover his knowledge. It does not astonish an engineer who is an expert in, let us say, cotton spinning machinery, to find that most people he meets are ignorant of his subject, and take no interest in making yarn ; but he is continually astonished and shocked at the absence of all elementary scientific and technical knowledge shown by people who are what is called educated, and who go through life without showing the least curiosity about, or the least interest in, the universe, or even in the world in which they live.

What people know or wish to know is largely settled by pure convention. Certain subjects are taught at school and college and they alone are generally valued as knowledge. Thus if a man is well up in Latin or Greek, especially in Greek or in Philosophy, whatever that may be, he is a scholar or a highly educated man ; if he has a still better knowledge of Norwegian he is nothing of the sort. He may be even a French, German or Italian scholar, though as such he ranks lower, but a knowledge of Norwegian carries no credit with it. If he has an encyclopædic knowledge of chemistry he is merely a specialist for his own purposes. He cannot even call himself a chemist, because Parliament is so ignorant as to have enacted that only a man who deals in drugs is a chemist. It might be argued that what is taught at school to the young is selected because it alone is knowledge, or at least because it is the cream of knowledge chosen so as to give youth the very best in a short time. This raises the question: What is the value of knowledge, and what knowledge is most valuable? To say all knowledge is valuable is exaggeration. An intimate acquaintance with the Russian railway time-tables of twenty years ago would be valueless knowledge for two reasons. It would do the possessor of the knowledge himself no good, and, what is more important, it would make him no more useful or helpful to other people. The true value of knowledge can be estimated according to the good it does. Knowledge which enables a man to lead a happier life and to help others to lead a happier life is sound. Knowledge that only flatters a man's vanity because it has a purely conventional value, is spurious.

People do not want to know about sociological matters because such knowledge does not help them individually to earn a better living on the one hand, and it brings no credit, and it has no conventional value. Sometimes the comfortable classes feel a sort of vague *malaise* that life is not what it should be to the great mass of fellow creatures, and they are roused to enough enthusiasm to read an article or two in their favourite newspapers. Such articles are written to please the readers, and to catch more, and they show how all fault lies at the door of the so-called ignorant classes, and how a little common sense on their part, and suppression of the pernicious agitators, would quieten things down and bring either content or resignation and peace. No doubt ignorant agitators do great harm, and cause much bitter discontent and trouble ; but so do ignorant writers of books and articles in high-class papers and magazines. The uncomfortable and miserable classes are woefully ignorant and wrong-headed ; but so are we, and, having regard to our opportunities we are very much worse. This is not due to any inherent folly in our class or innate wisdom elsewhere ; it is because we do not have to bother about our fate as a whole, while the less fortunate have a vague but lively hope of some improvement of their condition by possible social changes. They therefore study such matters more intelligently in proportion to their opportunity and abilities that we do. All the evils in society that arise out of ignorance, especially the ignorance of the poor, are the fault of the richer' and better informed ; we neither try to correct others' ignorance nor to reduce our own.

For the well-being of man, individualism, even of the most enlightened kind is not enough. Thus, to take an elementary example, it is not enough to see that your child gets over some infectious disease, though that is all that concerns you directly ; you should take care that it does not infect other children, though it gives you some trouble. You may combine with others to make a law which imposes penalties on the wanton spread of infection, but such a law does little good, because parents are so selfish they do not try to avoid infection, and this law, like many others, is difficult to enforce against common or individual opposition. A law ought to be a crystallisation of the aspirations of the people, and not a regulation to be broken whenever there is a chance.

What is missing is citizenship, or a true public spirit ; that is, willingness to sacrifice private advantage for the good of others. The highest form takes the good of mankind as its object ; the next only of a country ; below we have a town, a county, a class, a parish, a ship, or a family. Take the case of a town. Do the inhabitants ever take the least trouble to know what would be good for their city? There is a council. Does a councillor study such matters as town planning, drainage, slaughter-houses, clean milk, lighting, rating, or water-supply before becoming a candidate? Or does a highly-trained man who is well up in one or two of these matters give his services? On the contrary, except in rare cases, such as Johannesburg twenty years ago, the capable men of the city will not take the trouble. But any talkative or pushing person who thinks being a councillor will bring him into greater notice, becomes a candidate, and neither he or anyone who votes for or against him ever considers whether he has any qualifications.

In the case of a country there is always widespread patriotism, a phenomenon which demands special study. Whatever patriotism is, it does not involve any consideration of what is really good for the country. A man will give his life, but he will not think for his country. What is to the point with which we are busy is that he will not do brain work over the study of any social question out of patriotism. The most he does is to belong to a party. If his party takes a side in a question, he may study it in order to back his side up, and refute the other side's arguments, but never to learn the truth. Most likely he does not even do that, he reads newspaper articles written for him to show him he is right.

In order that a community should be sensible as such, its members must be sensible as members, and must therefore know something about what is good for the community as a whole. When the knowledge necessary for the community is of no advantage to the individual, he will not take the trouble to acquire it unless it raises

him in the eyes of those round him, or he has the real
kind of unselfishness that makes him work for the good
of others without reward.

The views people have about questions which concern
the community form what is commonly called public
opinion, though it is not really opinion at all.   As a
community, a nation, or, indeed, a world is controlled
mainly by public opinion, it is worth while to see how
it is formed and preserved.   It is very generally assumed
that the chief motive in man is self-interest, and that
his actions are determined by pure selfishness.   The
economic man is a convenient abstraction invented for
the simplification of discussion ; he is akin to the
frictionless machinery which helps one to arrive at the
truth in mechanics.   But the economist does not imagine
that the economic man is real.   The desire to get enough
food to satisfy hunger, or to get house or clothing to
ward off cold may be regarded as the instinct of pro-
longing the life of the individual ; whereas love depends
on the instincts of continuing the life of one's kind.
But these instincts are merely primitive, and do not in
their primary form rule the actions of men.   The true
motive of nearly all our actions is love of approbation.
It is strange that there is no word to cover a universal
motive.   Vanity, pride and conceit are terms of reproach,
used to denote something that is, or is thought, bad.
The meanings are not very clear.   Perhaps vanity might
be defined as the desire that people should think more
of you than you deserve, or at any rate should think
well of you ; conceit as a higher opinion of yourself than
your merit warrants, and pride as a general assumption
of superiority which may be justified, but generally is
not.   It is sometimes admitted that love of approbation
is a good motive, and about the only motive that gives
good results.   But if vanity is defined not as the desire
that people should think more of you than you deserve,
but that people should think well of you, love of approbation is vanity.   But vanity covers a larger field than
desire for approbation, it includes love of distinction of
any sort, such as notice, or notoriety.   It is thus a good,

an indifferent or a bad motive as its results tend to be good, indifferent or bad. We may therefore use vanity as meaning love of distinction, or notice of all sorts ; but it must be remembered that it is not always a bad motive, on the contrary it is generally good.

Many people, perhaps all who are normal, have a strong inclination to do what is right, or rather what they think is right. This is attributed to love of God, sense of duty, promptings of conscience, self-respect, and so on. It is the highest motive of which we are capable. It seems to be a sort of abstract love of approbation not of the actual people round us, but of ideal people. In a way it is an outcome of vanity ; thus vanity in the sense used here is by no means a vice or bad attribute, but the mainspring of the highest motives of which we are capable. There are other forms of high motive, such as love of one's parents, or of any one who influences his or her life. The unselfishness, not to mention the noble self-sacrifice of women for their children, or for others whom they love, seems to be outside and above even the highest type of vanity.

That vanity is generally considered a bad motive is itself the result of vanity. We are apt to dislike another's success in gaining notice or distinction, because it detracts from our own prominence. Generally the qualities we call virtues in other people are those which we think will do us good. Charity, generosity, love of justice, good temper, honesty, gentleness, love, patience, are all of this type. Bravery and courage are good because we think of them as qualities of those around us, who are likely to fight on our side and protect us. It is only grudgingly we admit the bravery of the enemy. He rather is fierce and savage.

In matters of psychology, where one cannot examine the inner workings of other people's minds, it is sound to examine his own, and to assume that others are just like it. Anyone who examines his own motives and actions carefully and impartially will find they are nearly all forms of vanity, generally of very petty vanity. He will be apt to think his own motives are not a fair

sample, because the acts of others do not appear to
have such low and petty sources. But a little thought
will convince him that human motives are pretty much
the same in all. Many may not admit this even to themselves, and certainly not publicly, and they may be able
to assume a position of superiority, but that does not
alter the facts at all. Love of money is often said to be
a powerful motive ; so it is, but it is a form of vanity.
Money gives power and front positions. A man above a
certain modest position does not need more money to
get more food, clothing or other necessaries ; he wants
it to put him in front of other people as much as
possible. A leading barrister, for instance, will spend
most of his working life in a dusty, untidy and comfort-
less office hunting through sheaves of type-written papers
about sordid squabbles of no real importance, and in
law courts where he stands half his time, and sits
crowded up and jostled on a hard seat the rest. He
does this partly because he likes to shine in competition
with other barristers, a feeling which probably is soon
blunted, but chiefly because he makes many thousands a
year, so that his wife has a good position, and has the
pleasant trouble of running a big establishment. He
also has ambitions either to become a law lord or officer,
who is much in the public eye, or at least a judge ; in
which case he will have an assured position in the world,
while he spends the rest of his working life sitting in
draughts, with a railway-rug round his knees, listening
to endless palaver or in Scotland " havers," and giving
judgments to be upset after more palaver in higher
courts. His life may be very useful, or, to a being
outside human sympathies and watching the evolution of
the world, it may be of no more significance than the
career of a periwinkle. But the careers of all those who
make more than the bare existence are much alike. The
object is always the same, social position and consideration ; that is to say the motive is vanity.

  Those who write about them are apt to regard all
people who work with their hands as forming a huge
homogenous class of " workmen." But there are just

as many social strata and distinctions in one class as in another, and there are no sharp distinctions between classes. From top to very nearly the bottom, there is only one great vanity struggle, and there is one long ladder with an almost infinite number of rungs.

Religion is generally considered the source of the strongest motives. A religious man may act in order to secure a definite advantage to himself in the form of a reward after death, or in order to avoid the extreme discomfort of abnormal temperatures. Such a motive is pure selfishness, of course. It was by working on this pure selfishness, combined with extreme credulity, that the Church got hold of Western humanity. Partly, no doubt, the priests gave hope to the miserable by persuading them they would have a bright hereafter of infinite length, so that their unhappiness was just a temporary phase, and they utilised this hope by saying it would not be fulfilled unless the people obeyed their spiritual pastors and masters and put them in control. The doctrine of heaven appears to depend only partially on a simple wish for permanent happiness in the here-after. A man who is not appreciated as much as he thinks he ought to be, and finds people do not think his religious dogmas are correct, and so hurt his vanity in a tender place, may get huge satisfaction by thinking of the time when they will see him elevated in heaven, showing that he is right and is really immeasurably their superior. There is no other form of conceit that approaches anywhere near that of religion.

Through some course of evolution, better understood by those who have studied it, man has a horror of the dark, which he confuses with night ; and the priests found fear a better lever, and invented hell as a means of getting more power. Dying men and women were their special victims. Their minds were weaker, and the dreaded hereafter seemed near. But neither cupidity as to a good place in heaven, or fear of anything un-pleasant in hell ever was a strong motive. Even when men were most credulous they were not in any way better than they are now. Neither heaven nor hell has

ever been real to sane men. The word used in such
connections is that they " believe " in them, which means
that they do not know. When a man says " I believe
so," he means " I am not sure," or more often, " I
maintain that it is so, though we all know that, in fact,
it is not." Again the prospect of the hereafter is too
remote to affect conduct. A man will eat or drink what
he knows will soon give pains outweighing any pleasure,
but the present outweighs the future. This law holds
throughout the region of human folly. Fear of the hereafter, though it now has little or no effect on conduct,
may help to form a conventional morality. Religious
motives are not all so sordid as playing for the hereafter. The good acts of a religious man or specially
woman are ascribed to religion. The same deeds are
done by non-religious people, and it would be more
accurate to say some religious people are good in spite
of their religion. Religion has another important phase,
worship. This has little to do with conduct. In many
cases, especially in women, it seems to be not independent of sexual instinct in some of its curious mani-
festations. Many men, and more women, feel the want
of something stronger to pray to, and to lean upon for
support. Most people are weak enough to want even
human leaders, and are anxious to put themselves under
others for shelter or guidance, and the idea of God as
a big man with human love and human sympathy appeals
to them. The God of the Bible and gods of the
Ancients had every kind of human vice. The God of
the Churches is very amenable to flattery, and most of
the prayers begin with most fulsome praise naïvely laid
on to put Him in good humour to grant the following
requests for specially unjust preference. Some of us
have never suffered want or privation, have known but
one or two real sorrows ; have had nearly all they
wanted and more than they deserved, and neither have
lost a loved one in the war, nor heard a mother crying
in the night. Such a one may feel as if a Superior
Power had decreed : " It shall not come nigh thee,"
and he may long for such a power just to thank Him.

But after all he would be like a sole survivor of a ship-wreck who thinks he was saved specially by a beneficent Providence.

There have been religious wars and religious perse-cutions, which are sometimes laid at the door of religions ; but they are the results of opinions, of which religious opinions are one kind only.

Religion must be taken into account as a great influence in forming public opinion directly. It also forms it indirectly by putting its priests, who as a class have a particular type of mind, into a special position as teachers, and giving them every possible chance of forc-ing their views into people's minds. Our children are taught on their lines, and parents, especially mothers, abuse their children's trust in them by telling them as truths what they know is untrue, or do not know is true, but merely believe. This continual iteration probably deforms a child's brain in some way. Then school and university education is dominated and controlled by the clergy, and has been for centuries, and thousands of sermons are heard every Sunday, and there is visiting and other direct influence throughout the week.

What is generally called an opinion is an unreasoned view or set of views on a matter of which the holder has no knowledge. Thus a man who studies the binomial theorem and finds it sound, even after following the wily fox-pursuer through the thickets of fractional and nega-tive quantities, does not hold an opinion that the theorem is sound. If someone else says the binomial theorem is false, he does not mind at all, as he knows that every competent person will agree with him. If he holds that dogs have souls, and meets someone who denies this, he cannot reason about the matter because he has no idea of what he means by a soul, and he knows nothing more about the constitution of dogs than his opponent. He feels, however, that his opponent holds him in slight esteem on this point, looking down upon him as being wrong. This wounds his vanity. No wound is so deep, or smarts and rankles more than hurt vanity. So the dog-soulist hates his miscreant opponent. He will, perhaps, take the trouble to read all he can about dogs' souls, taking in a weekly paper on the subject, not to find out anything, or to see whether he may be wrong, but to be able to argue his opponent down. As the subject cannot be argued so as to convince, he comes to hate his enemy and is quite ready to injure him. This is the effect of opinion and vanity. An attempt at discussion with someone who agrees with everything you say is dull. But if he disagrees and argues, it causes irritation on both sides, because each feels that the other thinks he is wrong, and therefore inferior, so both their vanities are hurt, and an argument is apt to end in a dispute and mutual contempt.

Religious opinions are most apt of all to lead to quarrel, bloodshed and war, because they are about matters that cannot be settled by any reason. They are about dogmas which are expressed in words so familiar from childhood that people do not realise that they have no meaning whatever. The inquisitor does not torture his victims because he is really anxious about what he calls their souls, and wants to be kind to them ; he does it because the victims hurt his vanity by thinking he is wrong. The martyr again thinks he, or especially she, is right, and rather than admit error, she thinks that if she is burnt it will somehow prove that she was right, and her vanity bears her up. Curiously enough, people are apt to take martyrdom as some test of truth. It is merely a question of obstinacy and vanity, and the martyr is so unbalanced that his or her opinion is most likely to be wrong. People will risk their lives about anything that involves their vanity. Men have lost their lives in Paris in a row about the alleged merit of Wagner's music. But of what value was their estimate? Here was almost as much a question of taste as of opinion. A man who gives out that he likes Brahms, dislikes any one who does not ; taking it as want of respect for his superior musical taste. If his former friend is a musician, the best thing to do is to cite some out-of-the-way composition, and recommend its study ; if he is no musician and sets up his opinion as of equal or superior value, it is specially galling to the Brahmsite, as his only chance is to show that love of Brahms denotes higher musical cultivation. If his opponent admits that he knows nothing of music, peace may be restored. Disputes about matters of taste are always conflicts of vanity. Political opinion in this, and probably in most countries divides the political world mainly into two parties. A man generally belongs to one because his family did, unless he has a type of mind which led him to belong to one party because his family belonged to the other. The two great parties depend simply on difference of opinion. A blue remains a blue, and gives what attention he devotes to the matter to reading papers and listening to speeches which tend to show that he is right, and is therefore superior. If he were big enough to look into the question and see that he might be wrong, his vanity would not let him be known as inconsistent. What is called an inconsistent man is one who holds mutually destructive views not at the same but different times. He ought to be called inconstant. An inconsistent man acknowledges error, and that is very hard on vanity, so that only a great man can afford to be what is called inconsistent. Party government is obviously nonsense, as on any one matter there are generally more than two courses possible, and it is probable neither party urges the best. But as Parliament deals with thousands of questions no one can suppose that one half is always right and the other always wrong when all are equally incompetent. It is much more likely that both parties are generally wrong.

There is generally a third, or a number of small parties. These are dominated not so much by mere unfounded prejudice, kept alive by vanity, as by what they imagine is the interest of their class. Their views may be, and generally are, quite unenlightened ; but they are not pure opinion, they are interested opinion.

Wide-spread popular errors or erroneous ideas are not opinions in our sense. For instance, anyone who thinks the moon affects the weather may be quite ready to alter his views if someone more competent says it does not, and gives his reasons. Gallileo's view about the earth was not an opinion ; but it interfered with existing opinions, as it showed its exponents were wrong, so they very promptly interfered with Gallileo. Party is a phenomenon, difficult to understand. De Stael treats party spirit as one of the passions. The modern study of the Crowd throws a good deal of light on party, and on the question of persistence, and specially of the origin of opinion.

Enough has been said as to how opinions persist ; it is more difficult to see how they arise.

What eventually developes into an opinion is very often started by a crowd and a leader of men. It may originate with the man of the study. Thus the French Revolution is often regarded as a river flowing from Rousseau or Voltaire as source. A small spring is often the reputed source of a large river ; but if the spring is mopped up it makes no difference to the river. It does not matter what is called the source. In such a case as Restrained and Unrestrained Foreign Trade, Adam Smith was a man of the study. It took over half a century for a simple idea to get through some crack in the head of any glib politician, and then it succeeded in penetrating into Cobden. Cobden was a leader of men, and gets as much credit as if he had worked out the principle.

A leader of men is generally not concerned with such a question as foreign trade ; he is rather a talker who talks down to the level of a crowd, and works on its prejudices, its vanity and its passions so as to impose himself on it as a leader. His ideas are generally neither new nor original. His main object, conscious or not, is personal magnification. Elijah prayed that God would show the people that he was the Lord God, and that Elijah was His servant. The last part of the prayer was most important to Elijah. John the Baptist was exceptional, as he did not put himself first. A leader may be quite incompetent and ignorant and still be the cause, or at any rate the apparent cause, of great results. W. Tyler got into trouble with a tax collector and split

him, quite on the spur of the moment. He was immediately a little hero among those around ; his vanity was
flattered, so he headed a movement which became a
rebellion, and lost his foolish life. There is no reason
to suppose he differed from any other component of his
rabble, except that he had the chance of gratifying his
vanity. Joan of Arc, again, had no accomplishment
except perhaps a nice way of feeding the Domremian
pig. She had no qualification. Yet Joan was of great
service. She rode at the head of the army, and the
astute pretended that she led it. Any other girl would
have done just as well, especially if good-looking. A
pantomime-boy would have been best. Her brother
would have been of no use. Joan is typical of many of
the women who are prominent in the feminist movement.
The various leaders of strike movements, labour riots and
such disturbances are of the same kind. They are no
better informed than those they lead, but they have ready
tongues, and it satisfies their vanity to be leaders. In
one sense they are quite sincere in their efforts, and their
conceit is such that they think they are able to do much
good. They work entirely on the discontent and the
prejudices of their crowds ; representing them as down-
trodden, robbed by the rich and unfairly treated, and
urge them to the kind of action that appeals to crowds.
A secondary result is to form a section of public opinion
which finally remains rooted in part of the community.
The leaders of trade unions, of syndicalists, of socialists
and such bodies are of the same type. The particular
ism may have been evolved by some student ; but the
leader is just an ordinary man without any special knowledge of such matters, who has a fluent tongue and
knows how to work on his hearers' prejudices and ignorance, and their natural wish to improve their condition.
Again, he is in a way sincere, and is hardly aware that
his real motive is to gain prominence. This type of
leader also forms or strengthens large masses of public
opinion. The opinion is, like most opinion, mere uninformed prejudice ; but that does not make it any less
important. The absurdity of opinions does not lessen

their importance. A whole nation may, and often does, act upon wholly absurd opinions.

In all the cases discussed the leader of men has taken up a line which he hoped would appeal to as large a number as possible. Vanity generally leads a man to take up a cause that he hopes will be popular. There is a curious sort of vanity which urges its patient to take up a line because it is opposed to those around him. He is conceited as well as vain, and feels he can show his superiority by holding opinions generally unpopular. The same man will be a pro-Boer, a pro-German, anti-vivisectionist, a feminist, a pacifist, a vegetarian, or, according to the times, anything else that will mark him as apart from and therefore superior to the common herd. He will go about London in badly-made tweeds, a soft hat and a red tie to show his superiority to ordinary conventions, and to attract attention. But what he dearly loves is to address a meeting which is broken up, for as long as he gets notice in the papers or elsewhere he does not mind its being unfavourable, because his conceit is greater than his vanity. He is generally called a crank ; he is really merely one common type of self advertiser. He is important, however, because he forms a certain volume of public opinion which is generally specially assertive, and very virulent.

All the types of public opinion discussed leave little chance for the general acceptance of the theory of the pressure of population and its effects. It appeals to no passions, no prejudices, and no self interests, real or imagined.

Public opinion may sometimes descend from the man of the study. The man of the study has not paid much attention to the population question, or to sociology in this country. America is more active in that direction. One branch, Political Economy, has received some attention, and there is, or was, an English School of Economics. Yet economics has practically no influence on British political opinion even about exclusively economical subjects. Political economy and its treatment of the population principle demand a special chapter, but there are reasons why economics has no influence. The first is that, though there is some perfunctory study of some sort of economics for some examinations for some degrees, economics has never been a regular school subject, and it is therefore not regarded as knowledge.

Such subjects as natural science generally, chemistry, mechanics, electricity and medicine are not " knowledge," and a man who is well up in one of them is a specialist. One difference between, say, mechanics and economics is that mechanics helps its votaries to earn their living. It is therefore a live science, and those who know nothing of it, see its results everywhere, and realise that there are men who understand mechanics, and that it is an important kind of information that they do not possess. On mechanical questions the general public, politicians apart, are willing to be guided by engineers. It is the same with all the other sciences that are the foundations of industries.

Medicine is on the border line. It is not the foundation of any industry, but there is much evidence to show the public that there is a body of special medical information. In spite of that there are many otherwise sensible people who prefer the quack to the specially trained expert.

Economics has no prestige as knowledge. It is not an exact or experimental science. It deals almost entirely with tendencies, and most find such ideas very difficult to grasp.

The effect of these causes combined is that the public does not realise that there is any science of economics. The ordinary man is quite sure that he can deal with any problem of practical economics by exercising what he calls his common sense. At most he thinks that if an economic matter is a little out of his depth it can be settled at once by practical business men ; just as a mechanical problem might be solved by engineers. He has, of course, the idea that if anyone knows anything about economics it must be the business man, who knows it in a practical and common-sense way from experience.

The result is that economics has no influence on public opinion.

The public mind is therefore very hard ground for the cultivation of such knowledge as the law of population. In economics, and still less in broader sociological questions, the expert is not consulted, and his existence is hardly suspected. It seems probable that man will continue for many centuries without any rational attempt to understand even the conditions under which he exists.

CHAPTER IV

OBJECT OF THIS BOOK

THE principle of population is quite familiar to biologists and some other groups of scientific men ; but that has hardly any influence on the science of sociology, and none at all on popular ideas, or rather opinions. The principle is also more or less understood by a number of thoughtful and more or less educated people, who seem to think it has no practical application whatever. They imagine that poverty can be prevented or lessened by all sorts of cures which the principle of population exposes as quite useless. Another group, who are more active philanthropists, and much more enlightened, preach the limitation of families to the poor and to the handworkers. At first sight this seems the right and obvious thing to do ; but, though the " Malthusians," as they incorrectly call themselves, are probably doing more good in the world than any other body, their teachings, when followed out thoroughly, will not them-selves get rid of poverty until applied universally. If the people who at present make up the poorer classes in any district have few children, so that there are fewer of them to compete for wages, so that wages begin to rise, and their degree of comfort rises too, handworkers from other places will move into the neighbourhood. To this the answer would most likely be made that preaching " Malthusianism " locally makes the converts better off individually, because each has a smaller family to support ; but that it does not prevent poverty due to others moving in, if it is merely local. To reduce or eliminate poverty in England, it will be said, all that is necessary is to get " Malthusianism " adopted throughout the country. This is an example of the patch fallacy. The idea is that a collection of people with a government of their own is somehow isolated from the rest of the world ; and must be considered as a separate nation with its special colour on the map, and all its special patriotic vanities and ignorances. The patch fallacy comes in in another way, too. Suppose the people in one patch practise "Malthusianism," and get better off, those in other patches will tend to move in. But as the patches are nations with their own governments, patriotisms, and vanities, they will say they want room for expansion, and if the Malthusian patch refuses to admit immigrants, there will be war with outside patches. It is necessary, therefore, to teach " Malthusianism," not only all over Europe and America, but eventually over the whole world ; though not necessarily to inferior races, which will die out by competition in the meantime. To get any grasp of our subject we must, therefore, discuss war ; its apparent causes, its real causes ; its apparent and real effects, and its possible prevention.

There is much more than this to be discussed. In order to understand the position we must see why the principle of population is not generally accepted. We must examine any objections that may be raised and see how far they are sound ; and, what is more important, we must see what schemes for social improvement are put forward, and how far the unseen fact of population pressure upsets them. Such schemes or doctrines need examination for another reason ; people will advocate a policy that looks right if you do not think about it, without thinking about it, or understanding anything of its real effect ; and while they have a popular and, as they think, clear and obvious cure for poverty, they will not look into such questions as population pressure. Before any good can be done the folly of the popular policy must be made quite clear. The difficulty is that we have not to deal with only one popular fallacy, but some dozens.

These various plans to cure or reduce poverty are generally put forward especially to benefit the hand-worker. A few of these are Anarchy, Communism, Doles, Eugenics, Free Trade, Living Wage, National-isation, Nihilism, Profit sharing, " Protection," Social-ism, State Education, State Insurance, Syndicalism and Trade Unionism. In alphabetical order these form a curious mixture. They are advocated by people of very different mental calibre. Out of the whole fifteen, no less than thirteen, including anarchy, involve the gov-ernment. Eugenics may depend on the government, and profit sharing stands alone as a remedy, though it might have to be enforced by government. We must, therefore, see what governments really are, how wise they are, and whether they have any of the power for good which people generally think they have.

There is always a difficulty in dealing simply and clearly with certain subjects, especially those that touch on economics. If a matter is put very lucidly a reader is apt to think it so obvious that he knew it all already and that it is an insult to his intelligence to expect him to read about it. If a simple question is put in a complicated way it is less likely to be understood ; and if it is not explained at all it will generally be over-looked altogether. It might be said that it would have been better to write definitely for the expert economist, and assume a knowledge of economics ; but unfortun-ately the economist has never grasped the law of population, or realised in the least that it is the basis on which his science should be built. It would be no use assuming that the ordinary educated man has any knowledge of economics whatever. He does not realise that there is any such study, and thinks he can settle anything about Currency, India, International Trade, Reparations or Wages or anything whatever the gov-ernment ought to do, right off, without any knowledge, study or thought, merely by his common sense.

There is another curious fact : we are very apt, in studying any matter, to become very familiar with all the twigs and branches, and to know nothing about the roots or main trunk. Thus there are many highly capable steam engineers in charge of large and important power plants who have never grasped the elements of thermodynamics. You will hear a board of directors of a big manufacturing company, all highly efficient business men, saying that the depreciation of foreign money gives foreigners such a pull in the world's market, that we cannot compete with them. I have been told by a highly qualified doctor to coat my knee with powdered potassium iodide or bromide in grease. I could not get hold of his idea of how the salt was going to get into my knee, why it would stay there, or what he thought it would do. Again a captain of a steamer told me he always ran full speed through a fog. A fog got full of steamers because they all went slow. The quicker you went through the less time you were in the fog, and therefore the less chance of collision. Many of our best pianists believe that they can alter the tone of a note apart from loudness, by the way they put the key down. They have never thought of seeing how a piano works.

Perhaps these instances are enough. When it is remembered that practically the whole of the subjects in this book are commonly dealt with only by the fallow and not by the intelligent mind it seems clear that there can be no harm in putting matters in the simplest way possible.

All the important points in our lives are settled by the fallow mind. We are brought up as children by people who have never thought about bringing up children. Our school training is settled by parents who know and care nothing about methods of education. Our governments are run by untrained men elected by people who have given no thought to the matter, and are guided by party spirit and newspaper articles. Our religions and what are called our opinions are held without any thought, and all our unhappiness through disease, poverty, war, government interference and religious intolerance are due to our thinking out nothing except our work for a living ; and deciding on all the really important issues of life with the fallow mind.

It must not be taken that the realisation of population pressure will act as a general cure for poverty and other evils. People are apt to think there is some simple general cure, and to take up some movement with the idea that it, and it alone is to make the world quite different. At present, if all civilised people understood the principle of population and applied it as well as they could, it would not get rid of poverty in the world, because the uncivilised, or less civilised people would emigrate and become the lower layers of the more civilised places. But this does not mean that it is no use understanding a simple matter like this. It may do a great deal of good directly in the near future, by local or temporary reductions of poverty ; but that is not its main value.

All through the world's history there has been the idea, especially among those ill off, that poverty is caused by injustice, and by the greed of the rich, and this idea causes unspeakable unhappiness. To be very poor is bad enough, but it is worse to feel that your poverty is in no way due to yourself, but is put upon you by a set of lucky people who have been born into a different station, and have got you by the throat and will not release you ; and that the poor have been struggling against this for thousands of years and got nowhere.

Practically all the remedies for present misery are based on this kind of idea, and the support of the multitude is got by representing that they are unjustly treated, and that the new cure is to take away their ill-gotten gains from the rich and give them to the poor.

Democracy, doles, labour government, living wage, nationalisation, old-age pensions, poor law relief, relief work, restraint of foreign trade, socialism, sovietism, trade unionism and wages boards are all more or less based on this notion. According to the principle of population they are all quite useless or worse. It is, therefore, worth while to study the theory of population, first to see why all these schemes fail, and then to find out whether any good can really be done.

I have put the good of a knowledge of the population

question very low, when pointing to the difficulties of aliens coming in and forming the lower stratum of a civilised community. It is not impossible that this could be prevented.

Population pressure as the basic principle in sociology has not only not been studied, it has had no attention at all. When it is studied seriously it is quite likely that we may at least find the solution of most of the problems of poverty.

CHAPTER V

POPULATION PRESSURE

THE fundamental conception of the principle of population is that the human race persists by breeding. There is a physiological rate of increase which is, and must be, great enough to secure the persistence of the race in spite of adverse conditions, otherwise the race would not have survived. This means that the physiological fertility of man must be great enough not only to secure persistence in the circumstances of civilised life, or even of savage life as we know it; but it must be great enough to have coped with the most adverse conditions the race has ever experienced during the æons it has existed. It is possible the physiological fertility has decreased, perhaps even during the last few thousand years; but there is no good reason for supposing so. Some local circumstances due to some specially adverse conditions of civilisation might affect the health of a group so that its physiological fertility was impaired; but adverse circumstances might in fact increase it. There is no way of finding this out, as we have no means of knowing what the normal fertility of human beings really is. All we know is that for civilised man it is at least 5 per cent. a year; a rate that is so much higher than the actual rate of increase that it is clear man is, like all other animals, living under pressure of population as the condition of existence.

There is, however, one important difference between civilised man and the lower animals. It is probable that every mature female coddess lays her million eggs each year. Treating the eggs as children, out of the million, only one female cod reaches maturity. It is quite possible that the mature cod do not always live to physiological old age, and do not even lay as many yearly batches of eggs as they would in happier surroundings ; but the main check on population among cod is infant mortality.

Again, in the case of the rabbit ; each doe can have a litter when she is six months old ; she may have four to eight litters of three to eight each in a year, the period of gestation being only a month. Pennant has calculated that a single rabbit could have over a million descendants in four years. In nature it is quite likely each doe does not reach its full physiological age producing young at that rate ; but it produces a great many in its lifetime. Considering does only ; unless rabbits are increasing, each mother doe produces one doe that lives to reproduce. The rest all die one way or another before maturity. Rabbit population is thus restrained substantially by infant mortality.

Whether there is a growing tendency in any of the lower animals to become gradually less fertile by production of smaller number of children per parent, or by longer life, or not, it is clear that some such changes take place, as broadly speaking, the higher the animal is in the scale the greater the age of maturity, and the smaller the number of children annually produced by the female ; and on the other hand the longer the life, and perhaps the longer the period of maturity, and the smaller the infant mortality. The higher you go in the scale the less the physiological fertility ; that is to say, the nearer it approaches unity ; but it never comes down to unity, as that would mean annihilation of the kind of animal in a very short time.

The case of man or at least civilised or partly civilised man is very different. The age of maturity is high, but its period is long. The physiological annual rate of production of the female is about one ; but the physiological period of maturity is of the order of 30 years ; and the physiological age for death is over 70, probably about 100. These are all matters of degree in comparison with the lower animals. The essential difference is that man exercises what is called moral restraint. Women do not generally become mothers until much later than fifteen. They do not generally have children annually for 30 years, and many of them never have children at all ; and of men and women who come to maturity, only a few reach the physiological age for death. These differences, though ascribed to morals, are not generally due to morality in the ordinary sense, nor even to chance, habit or custom. Women do not become mothers as early as they might, mainly because it is not expedient for them to marry before 18 or 20 ; and even 20 is considered in certain classes very young ; many do not marry at all ; or marry late in life. When married they do not have from twenty to thirty children each.

That it is not usual to marry at the physiological age is the direct result of population pressure, as far as men are concerned. Men cannot marry at puberty because they cannot support themselves, not to speak of wives and children. Wives are not so much the difficulty as children. If a boy is living at home, supported wholly or partly by his parents, and marries a girl who is supported by her parents, the wife moving from one house to the other would not increase the total expenses much. It would alter the incidence, unless the parents of the girl subscribed what they would otherwise save by the girl leaving them. In all families, and more especially in poorer families, such an arrangement would be very inconvenient ; even if there were no children ; but the real difficulty is the probable arrival of offspring. This limits the age at which men marry and the number of men and women who marry. It does not limit directly the age at which women marry ; and it is not very clear why the women who do marry do not marry practically at puberty. Women develope quicker than men up to about 18, so that up to about 20 a woman is more completely developed than a man of equal age. As she has been ahead of the man for several years, she has had in addition some experience of adult life. A woman of 20 is thus much older than a man of the same age in everything

but actual years. Among the ill-to-do, who form the
óverwhelming majority, the woman has had to take,
or has taken life much more seriously from childhood.
It can hardly be that women do not marry young
because they are not fit. It is more likely that, owing
to the difficulty of supporting a wife causing some men
not to marry, the competition among women for
husbands gives the older women of something over
20 a better chance, as they have more experience. It
may be, on the other hand, that men generally prefer
to marry girls who are not too young and generally
inexperienced. Men, having had to wait before marrying, may marry girls to whom they have been attached
for some time ; and that tends to increase the age at
which women marry.

That women do not marry as young as they might
is apparently not a direct result of population pressure.
In some climates, and even in the United States, women
develope sooner.

There appears to be a change going on in our ideas
of age. Prince Hal was a great soldier as a young
boy, and Pitt was Prime Minister at 24, or so. The
heroine is steadily getting older. Juliet was 14 ;
Diana Vernon was 18 ; while Anna Comnena was
passée at 29, and had developed into a New Woman.
Maud should have been in the nursery. The heroine of
a modern serious novel is generally much older.

That the women who do marry do not have children
at the physiological rate for the physiological time is
probably due to their health being much poorer than
it would be under favourable conditions. Among the
uncomfortable classes the woman has a hard struggle
from early childhood. She ages quickly. Whether
hard life, and poor, and what is much commoner, in-
correct feeding reduce the fertility of women, or lessen
the time it lasts, it is difficult to say. Some hold that
the struggle against poverty automatically makes the
race not less, but more prolific ; as a sort of special
effort to prevent race annihilation in adverse circumstances. On the other hand, the life of endless anxiety

and hardship, which is the lot of most women, makes them lose their good looks and attraction very much earlier ; and thus tends to reduce the effective period of child bearing. It is not impossible that men are also affected largely by the conditions of civilised life ; and that non-virile husbands are also a cause of reduced fertility of couples.

The greatest difference between modern man and the lower animals is that man is now beginning to limit offspring by artificial means. This has made a good deal of difference within the last thirty years or so, as it seems destined to become a factor of profound importance in due time.

The restraint of population by infant mortality is very much less in man than in most of the lower animals, largely for the reason given.

In such countries as England the infant mortality is high, in comparison with the mortality of moderate ages, but as far as population is concerned, as long as a man or woman has no children it does not make much difference whether death finds its prey young or old.

Population pressure is to some extent analogous to pressure of a gas or vapour in Physics. If a boiler contains water and steam, the pressure may be defined as what tends to increase the capacity of the boiler, or as the tendency of the steam to increase its volume ; that is to say it is the force per square centimetre tending to enlarge the boiler, or pushing the plate outward. But the pressure may also be defined as what opposes the expansion of the steam. Imagine a cylinder set up with the lower end closed and put on a fire or lamp, the cylinder containing some water and having a closely fitting, but freely sliding plug or piston closing the top. If the water is kept at a given temperature by the lamp, the steam will press the piston up. If it is above 100° C. it will press the piston up more than the atmosphere presses it down, and to get equilibrium more force must be applied to the piston. The force on the piston exerted by the steam is the total pressure on the piston. It tends to enlarge the

volume of vapour. It is exactly equal, of course, to the
force exercised by the piston upon the steam. This
force tends to reduce the volume of the steam. If the
piston moves without any friction, an infinitesimal
increase of the temperature will cause the piston to
rise ; while if the temperature is constant an infinitesimal
increase of the external force pressing the piston down
will make it reduce the volume of the steam. That the
volume of the steam is increasing does not mean that
there is more pressure ; and that it is getting less does
not mean that the pressure is less. Thus suppose the
cylinder with the steam and water is taken off the
lamp and covered with a blanket of some material
which will not let any heat pass through it, the piston
will rise if the downward force on it is reduced, so that
we have increasing volume and decreasing pressure.
If, on the other hand, more force is applied, the piston
will go down, reducing the volume, and increase of
pressure then goes with decrease of volume.

Population pressure is, similarly, the stress due to the
tendency of population to increase ; but it is just as
much the stress which opposes the increase of population. Population pressure is, at the same time, the
stress due to the tendency of population to oppose its
decrease ; and it is also just as much the stress which
tends to make it diminish. These are four aspects of
the same pressure. These four definitions of the same
quantity are important, because most writers are
unaware of all but the first, and think the stress of
population is measured by its increase, and that decreasing population has no stress. The fact that the population of France is decreasing is often cited to show that
there is no population pressure there. It proves nothing
of the sort. Without any further facts, it shows almost
nothing. The stress of the population tending to
increase may be less than the stress tending to keep it
down. In the case of the steam analogy it was assumed
that there is no friction ; in society there is the
analogue of friction and of inertia ; so, if the population is changing its rate of increase or of decrease, and

is falling, the expansive stress of the population is less than the restrictive stress tending to reduce it. But there is nothing in the fact that population is falling in France and rising in Germany to show that population pressure is less in France. It might be enormously greater, and the population would still decline if the restrictive tendency were greater still. As a matter of fact such countries as Germany, Austria, France, Italy and Britain are so closely inter-connected in normal times that the pressure is probably sensibly the same. Considering a district as isolated because it has its own government, and its own colour on the map, leads to the " patch " fallacy.

Pressure, for example, of steam, cannot only be defined ; it can be measured. It is most convenient to measure the specific pressure, that is the pounds per square inch, or kilogrammes or megadynes per square centimetre.

In sociology any such accurate measurement is generally quite out of the question ; and it is very difficult to get a clear cut definition, or even very clear ideas.

Population pressure can best be taken as specific pressure ; thus in a large and small country in which the conditions are alike, the population pressure would be taken as equal. Again the population pressure in the United Kingdom is not the sum of the pressures in England, Scotland, Ireland, Wales and the small islands. It is something that can be thought of in terms of one or a few typical people.

The difficulty is increased by enormous differences of condition of people living together as a community. Even in primitive or savage life this difficulty exists.

For simplicity, an isolated community may be imagined in which the individuals are practically all alike in condition. There would be no population pressure if they were all marrying at the physiological rate, and all living to the physiological age. This gives an idea of what constitutes absence of population pressure. Absence of population pressure in the case of man is compatible only with a very rapid increase, probably something of the order of doubling every ten years, or 7·2 per cent. a year. This would generally involve absence of difficulty in getting food and necessaries, and an increase of wealth at the same or greater rate. There is no reason to suppose there has ever been a community with no population pressure, and except for a very short time after a plague, or a famine, or both, such a state has never been possible. Suppose a plague had just carried off half the population of a large island, and the inhabitants abandoned their former habits and customs, and married and reared children at the physiological rate. There would be no population pressure for a short time. As the population approached the value it had before the plague, the population pressure would gradually increase to the old value.

The island population might be experimentally inclined. For instance, they might let every person born reach the physiological age, say 70. The death-rate would then be 1·43. They might make the birth-rate the same. This could be effected in several different ways, or in combinations of them. They might agree, or make and keep a law that only a small percentage should marry ; those that married being allowed to do so at the physiological age, and have the physiological number of children. The majority would then have to suffer celibacy, and the population pressure would be expressed somehow in terms of the percentage who could not marry, and their unhappiness. It is not necessary for the moment to discuss the full effects of forbidding most of the people to marry. Want of homes, unsatisfied longings, prostitution and vice of all sorts are obvious results of population pressure in this case.

The birth-rate being kept the same as the death-rate, so as to keep the population constant, involved in this case a birth-rate of 1·43. In a steady population the births average one per person. If the physiological rate is eight per pair, three-quarters of the people do not marry. If, instead of one-quarter, one-third of the people married, the birth-rate would almost at once go up from 1·43 to 1·9 ; there would then be an increase of 0·66 per cent. At this rate the population would double in about a century or so. This is an important point. A few writers who consider population pressure at all, assume that such a difference in rate increase as from zero to 0·5 means a great difference in population pressure, whereas it is hardly perceptible. Doubling in a century and a half is quite an ordinary rate of increase in practice.

On the other hand, if the number of people marrying were reduced from a quarter to any lower value and left there, there would be a very slight variation of population pressure, but other conditions being the same, population would die out. The slightest reduction of the proportion marrying makes the population die out, while the slightest increase causes the population to grow without limit. Whether the population is increasing or decreasing is no measure of its pressure. To an engineer or a physicist this is obvious, but it may not be so clear to sociologists, or to general non-scientific readers.

Returning to the island example, the people might keep the birth-rate down to the physiological death-rate by allowing all that liked to marry, but only at such advanced age that the birth-rate keeps down at 1·43. The population pressure would then take the form of, or be measured by the unhappiness involved in universal late marriages. The evils of such a way of living would be much the same as in the case last considered.

According to another ordinance, the whole population might marry as young as they liked, but they would all limit their offspring artificially, so as to keep the birth-rate down to 1·43. The pressure would then be measured in terms of the inconvenience and evils bound up with limitation of offspring. Among these are the unsatisfied mother-hunger, and certain injuries to health which are better understood by medical men.

Women, as usual, would be the chief sufferers. But keeping the birth-rate down to the physiological death-rate is not the only way of making the population constant. As an extreme in the other direction, the community might arrange that the people should marry at the physiological age, and have the physiological number of children. The supply of necessaries being assumed constant, the death-rate would soon go up. When equilibrium would be reached, the conditions would be that only a portion would live to marry, and few would live to old age. Lack of necessaries hits infants hardest ; so that the infant mortality would be such that it accounted largely for the extra births. If all that survived the first few months lived to the physiological age, the conditions would differ from the case in which the people all married, but limited their offspring, only in that instead of not being born, all the children above the 1·43 per cent. would die almost at once. The difficulties of existence that would kill off so many infants, would also weaken people so that the average age of death would be lower ; but for simplicity that consideration is neglected in the example, as it introduces confusion without making any difference that counts. In this case the population pressure shows itself in infant mortality, and is to be estimated in terms of the suffering of the infants who die, and of their parents, especially again of the women.

It would make little difference, from the purely arithmetical point of view, whether the extra children died because they could not be reared, or were killed in a lethal chamber, or whether their birth was prevented by limitation methods. As to the ethics of the matter, ninety-nine people out of a hundred would say that the lethal chamber is horrible murder, and is almost unthinkable, and to write about such a thing is disgraceful. Many people again urge that preventive methods amount to some form of child-murder. The only course not open to censure is, therefore, to produce children knowing they cannot be reared. Of course the real difficulty is that the ethics of this question are never discussed with any understanding of the principle of population. The ordinary idea is that the right course is to reduce the infant mortality, and there would be articles especially by parsons and women, pointing out how shocking the infant mortality was, and urging education for the poor mothers, and rearing the children at the expense of the State, so as not to cost anybody anything.

But all that is beside the mark. The position in the imaginary island is that the people can produce necessaries enough for a fixed number, say ten thousand. They know no way of producing more, and the population cannot grow. If the extra children are all reared, a corresponding number of grown people must starve. If the extra children are fed by the State, the extra taxes will press so heavily on the adults that they will be overworked or underfed to the extent necessary to keep the death-rate up to the birth-rate. As pointed out in an earlier chapter, in order to keep the population constant when the adults produce many children, there must be a large pre-parental death-rate. If all that grow old enough to marry, marry at the physiological age, and have the physiological number of children, it does not matter whether they die immediately after or live to old age ; the important point is that only the number of children can grow to be parents which provides the necessary children, the rest must die early. Thus, if eight is the physiological number of children, and all parents have eight, three-quarters of the children born must die before becoming parents.

The inhabitants of the imaginary island may thus have four separate ways by which the population is kept within the means of subsistence. First, full physiological age for all, but only a percentage allowed to marry, and to leave full number of offspring. Second, full physiological age for all, and marriage for all, but at such advanced age that offspring is kept down. Third, full physiological age, and all marrying young, offspring limited artificially. Fourth, parents live to physiological age, all marry who reach physiological age for marriage, and population kept down by infant or pre-parental mortality. The population is kept down to ten thousand in each example ; is the population pressure equal in the four cases? It is very difficult to answer this question, because there is no way of measuring this quantity. The ten thousand people may be divided up into four lots, practising the four methods of controlling the population, each lot being homogeneous, that is to say, consisting of ordinary people in equally good circumstances. The question then is whether people would like to move from one lot into another. The people are supposed to be all alike in circumstances—as nearly average as possible in character. Most likely the different methods appeal to people in different classes, that is to say, with different views of life and of the importance of things. It does not follow that the ten thousand people on the island, with the population kept stationary, would be all poor. It is commonly assumed that population pressure exists only where there is starvation, and that in heterogeneous, that is to say, ordinary circumstances, the pressure exists among the very poor only. The islanders might all have quite a high standard of comfort,; though in real cases no whole population can have a high standard of comfort ; that is a luxury of the higher layers.

The hypothetical islanders differ from a real people in several respects. They are isolated, which means not only that there is neither emigration nor immigration, but that there is no external trade. The greatest differences are that they are supposed to know the principle of population, and to deal with it collectively by agreement or law, and that they are all equally well off.

Taking the last difference first,; if the islanders were a little more like real people, they would not be equally well off. There would be rich and poor and every stage between. It is probable that in that case the various methods of keeping the population constant would appeal most to people of different standing. This increases the difficulty of arriving at any way of measuring population pressure.

5

The most extreme hypothesis, however, is that the inhabitants of the island understand the principle of population, and act intelligently. In real life no community acts collectively and intelligently in dealing with population pressure—or anything else for that matter. Even the few who have some knowledge of the subject do not act from motives of public interest. Nobody considers carefully whether the pressure is such that he ought or ought not to have a child. Provident people do not marry till they think they can afford the expense, or they marry and take care not to have many children. The improvident marry much younger, and as they are generally poorer, their children either descend to a lower social level or, in the case of the very poor, die during infancy.

Having large families does not generally either increase or impoverish particular classes, as all the children need not stay in the class. This is conspicuously clear in the case of the peerage. The eldest son, or the heir succeeds to the title, and the rest of the descendants gradually slip down out of the class. In the professional classes there is a similar state of things. The size of a professional class is not regulated by the numbers of the families in it, it is settled by the demand for the degree of comfort normal for that profession. There is always an interchange between professions, businesses and so on, chiefly on the same level. Though the general tendency in the higher levels is a gradual move downward, a few able men are continually rising into higher classes. It is easy to be misled into what may be called the class fallacy. Error is always arising from considering a class as if it were an isolated, and generally a fixed number of people, whose children grow up into it and replenish it. Probably no one imagines that, for example, the boiler-makers are a hereditary class, fixed in number ; but it is quite common to discuss skilled workmen as if they were a definite collection of individuals whose children all became skilled workmen or skilled workmen's wives.

The interest of the individual is, unluckily, not the

same as that of the community. It does not follow that a man with several children is worse off than another of equal ability with few or none. Of course this depends on what is meant by worse off. A professional man with a large family must live more quietly, and he may fairly be said to live below the standard of comfort corresponding to his ability, and below that of an equally able man who has, say, one son. He may prefer to live that way and bring up a family. But he will also probably be induced to work harder and retire later. Still less does it follow that most of his large family will have to move down into a lower layer. They will have to face difficulties in their youth, and will be brought up to realise what the battle of life is, and when they compete with the single sons of the other professional men, it may end in the large family getting on well and the single sons slipping down. It is also likely that the sons in a small family may have a little money left to them. Nothing injures a young man more than to have an unearned income just large enough to make him independent. It makes it unnecessary for him to work hard at the beginning of his career, and when he wants to marry and finds he has too little, it is too late for him to alter and make up for lost time. In less affluent strata it is much the same. A pair earning thirty-five shillings a week or £90 a year (pre-war standard) may have a family of, say, six without being perceptibly worse off, especially if there is enough difference of age in the children. As soon as they begin to grow up they can earn a little, and when the elder children are earning from four to eight or ten shillings a week each, the family is much better off, as they are all living under one roof, and the children cost little to bring up to the earning age. Many humble parents want a large family to make sure they will have somebody to keep them out of the workhouse in their old age. Going a little further down in the scale of comfort the conditions are similar, except that young daughters are specially helpful. They take life seriously and look after their brothers and help their mother, often releasing them so that they can do outside work. The fact that girls develope quicker than boys, and that they are more serious and less devilish, gives them a sharpness and general ability that lasts all their lives. That is no doubt why women in the ill-off strata are so much more " on the spot " and in ordinary matters generally brighter than their men-kind.

Among wage-earners it is not the custom to save up much before marriage, and the man's wages rise so little that he considers he can afford to marry young as well as older, and having a family does not necessarily press hardly on his wife and himself individually. But his family increases the competition in his group, and though his children may be strong and thrive, their existence involves keener competition, and the throwing out of a certain number into the layer below. In the wage-earning class generally the interest of the individual is thus not coincident with that of the community. Going lower down still, the advent of a child is often a serious trouble to the parents, and especially to the mother, in many cases so serious that maternal instinct does not nearly balance it. Here we have the interest of the individual and of the community the same, but this is among the least provident and least thoughtful of human beings, so it does not help very much.

In a real community there is a gradual change in circumstances from the top to the bottom. A population such as that of a country may be represented by a diagram in which vertical position corresponds with position in the community. A community with many well off and few poor and miserable would be something of the general shape of Africa, India, or South America, but, in fact, real communities are more like South America or Africa inverted.

The figure representing the whole population can be divided up into a number of smaller figures, each representing a class. Each small figure will have a more or less pointed top, and bottom spreading out between, except near the bottom of the diagram, where the figures representing the poorest classes have wide bases. Thus,

to take a very clearly defined class, barristers will have
a point running up very high; perhaps the apex one
unit broad, will represent the lord chancellor, or if he
is married and has a family, his wife and children,
while they are young, may be taken as at the same
height, and the apex will be a few units broad. Then
there will be the past chancellors, chief justice, law
officers, and so on, and less known men with huge
incomes, such as the leaders in special branches of
law. The figure will have a long, narrow neck, as few
barristers are well off, and it will have a wide base
representing the large number who fare very badly at
the Bar.

The diagram cannot actually be drawn with any great
accuracy, even if all possible data were available, because there is a certain vagueness. Thus, though the
Bar is the best defined class, many barristers have private
incomes, others do all sorts of non-legal work, especially
writing, and some are essentially politicians. But there
is a much greater difficulty. It might be simple to
make the height represent wealth, but even that is
vague, because it is difficult to compare a man with a
certain income coming in from invested capital with
another making a yearly salary which is more or less
uncertain. Wealth, besides, is not exactly the quantity
wanted. The idea of the diagram is that people on the
same horizontal level are in the same degree of comfort, of social position, and equally well-off in a broad
sense. Thus the diagram of the Church of England
will be very much like that of the Bar. There will be
a point at the top representing the archbishops, and the
figure will broaden downwards to include the bishops,
deans and so on, and it will have a fairly broad bottom,
representing a number of curates and ill-paid vicars.
The position of the tops should represent the positions
of the Chancellors and the Archbishop of Canterbury.
If they are at the same height, it means that the positions
are equally desirable. Going down to a broader part
of the figures we find vicars of no particular importance
on the same level as barristers of certain poor standing,

and they ought to be interchangeable, so that anybody would as soon be in one position as the other. But this does not mean that people of the same level have the same incomes. A rector of an important parish may have a much smaller income than a successful butcher in the same town, but the positions are not equally desirable. The rector is accepted by society and is treated with respect, out of proportion to his income. Again, a civil servant, earning a thousand a year by real merit, is in a better position than a man of the same age making the same income, allowing for pension, at much the same sort of work outside. The civil servant has the prestige of a government official, and as far as money goes, in some cases, is underpaid for a man in his position. The same man, if he could somehow get a corresponding opening, might earn half as much again outside, the balance is made up by the prestige and the chance of all sorts of honours and letters after his name.

It has been urged already that perfectly justifiable and honourable gratification of vanity is the main motive governing man. Vertical height in the diagram should therefore represent conditions of gratified vanity. This is impossible to measure, or even to estimate, with any sort of nicety. It would be much easier to regard vertical height as representing money position, as after all, if two figures could be drawn accurately by some magic, one according to vanity position, and the other according to wealth in a broad sense, they would not differ very much, and they would be quite near enough for the purpose for which the diagram is imagined.

Each elementary area on the diagram represents an individual; a horizontal line passes through a number of individuals in equally good positions. Each person is struggling to keep his position or to rise, or to fall as little as possible.

All those on a horizontal line are not directly competing with one another, but they are doing so indirectly, and none the less because indirectly. In each group the competition is as keen as possible between those on the same level. Thus, at the Bar there is no real competition between the eminent King's Counsel and the struggling junior. The leader is competing with other leaders of the same standing, and the struggling juniors are striving against one another, not against those above or below them. A solicitor employing counsel balances first the merits of two leaders, then of two juniors. In employing a doctor, the patient chooses between local general practitioners of about the same standing, or if he thinks his case demands more, the choice is between specialists in London. The general practitioners compete with one another, and it is the same with the specialists. The competition is not between the two classes. Going back to the Bar, there is work for only a small number of eminent counsel, if there are too many, the result in the long run will be that they will make less and will begin to fall in the diagram. This will make the scale of fees fall, and this tends to counteract the fall, as litigation will tend to increase if it costs less, and this tends to increase the incomes again. But this increase of eminent counsel is itself dependent on the indirect competition of all the other people on the same level. If the diagram of the Bar is broadened at one place, and the units on this line then fall, people of the ability and position corresponding to that level will not enter the Bar so frequently.

Such adjustments as these will take a long time, and the tendency and real gradual movement towards general equilibrium are always partly hidden by temporary disturbances. Social changes are very rapid just now, at least in Western Europe and America, and parts of Asia, Japan for instance, and in African colonies, but that does not lessen the tendency and real movement towards equilibrium. After all, when the whole time men have been on the earth is contemplated, the rapid changes going on during the last century or two amount to just a very short temporary disturbance. An ephemeral insect of thoughtful tendencies whose life was spent during a typhoon might be forgiven for not realising that water tended to make its surface level and smooth. Even the fact that the sea is never either quite calm or level in no way negatives the statement that gravity always tends to make it quite level and smooth, that is in perfect equilibrium.

In a large town there may be many small grocers. Each has a small shop, and lives in the house over it. They share all the business of the town, and if one does a little better the others do worse, and the small grocers are all competing with one another. An enterprising company then starts a big grocery store. It buys in large quantities on good terms, it provides a better selection, it can deliver goods more quickly, and it does a cash business. It squeezes out most of the small grocers. But this is not really competition of a big concern against little men, it is supersession of the obsolete. If there are several large grocery stores, they will compete with one another. If any small shops remain, it will not be because they can compete successfully with the big store on its lines, but because they supply some wants that the stores do not. They may be open late and cater for women who cannot shop during the day, or feel out of place at the big stores, or cannot find time or tram fares. The little shops will put up their goods in smaller quantities, and will specialise in whatever humbler people like. These humbler shops will then exist, but not by competition with the stores. They will compete with one another, and they will be as numerous as they can be without getting too close together. The small grocers will be represented on a level, cutting the whole population diagram, showing their position, and they will be in competition primarily with the other grocers on the same line, and secondly with all the other people on the same level. If there are too many, that is to say, if the competition is too keen, the number will be reduced gradually. Some grocers will retire sooner and poorer, some will fail, or the town will increase without the grocers increasing in proportion. The store cannot go on the diagram as such. If it is owned by one man instead of a company, he can be placed, of course, and he will be much higher up. If he makes a thousand a year, he will be in competition with people of the same standing. He will compare grocery with other businesses, and will advise one of his to go into it, and the others into something else. If the grocery store is owned by a company, the shareholders may all be men of the same standing as the retail grocers. The store is still not competing with the small grocers, but the shareholders are competing secondarily, not because they are shareholders in the big store, but because they are on the same level.

There will be a very large area in the diagram to represent wage-earners. The group is not very well defined. It is sometimes taken to cover those who are paid weekly. This would include actors and music-hall people, who are supposed to receive king's ransoms every Saturday night. The group might be defined as including those who work with their hands as well as their brains. The group is generally known as the "working men" or "workmen" of the country. These terms are absurd, but they are so largely used that no other name will do as well now. This is a pity, because it does harm to use expressions that tend to encourage this large group in thinking that they alone do the work of the world. "Hand-workers'" may be a better term. The top of the hand-workers' figure will be narrow, and will come up to several hundred a year. The figure will broaden out rapidly as it goes down to about two pounds to thirty shillings a week, and it will come down to the region of starvation wages and so-called sweated labour. It does not include boys earning a few shillings a week, or girls living at home and earning what is little more than pocket-money, as they would be placed on the same line as their parents.

We come here on one of the most wide-spread and mischievous fallacies that ever misled human beings. It is assumed that the hand-workers compete not with one another, but with capitalists, and there is an entirely senseless strife between capital and so-called labour, that is to say, between employers and employed. The idea is that wages are arbitrarily settled by the employers, and that they make their living by paying their men less than they are worth. It is supposed to follow that if the wage-earners can get control, they can settle wages on such a scale that they could get fully paid for their work, and the employers would still have fair remuneration for what they do. If wages really are too low in any group, it is because there are too many competing for the work. This will right itself by the group getting smaller, because it pays men of the right order of ability to go into other groups.

The group of hand-workers is, of course, divided up into smaller groups according to different trades, for instance, miners, mechanics, boiler-makers, masons. Each of these may be divided up still farther before each group is made up of layers that are uniform horizontally, that is to say, a group has to be small before all the people making the same wages are doing the same, and not merely equally good work. Thus the turners earning a given wage are competing with one another. If there were fewer they could command higher wages, but the higher wages would not be permanent. Men of the same ability as the turners would begin to leave other trades to join them, and more boys would go into that line. Thus the turners are primarily in competition with one another, and are secondarily in competition with other hand-workers on the same level in the social system or on the diagram. They are not competing with their employers, and their employers are not competing with them, but with other employers. The employers do not wish to pay low wages, what they want is to get as much work done in proportion to the wages and on-costs as possible. If a hand-worker will do twice as much work, he is worth not double wage, but more, and often much more. If he limits his output he is, of course, worth less, and if he limits his output to a certain small value his services are worthless, because the standing charges are too high in proportion to the work done. The questions of Trade Unions, limitation of output, collective bargaining, piece-work, profit-sharing, strikes, socialism, syndicalism, living wage, employers' federations and labour legislation will be discussed from the population pressure point of view later.

In the real world matters are very complicated, and it is better to work through a simple but imaginary case first.

The island population may now be taken as cut off from the rest of the world so as to be independent, with the population in equilibrium, and still, like ordinary people, ignorant of the law of population. Equilibrium implies that the population is stationary, the death-rate and birth-rate being equal, say 2 per cent. It also implies that there is no invention or technical advance being made which would make it easier to get necessaries. Any such advance would either allow the population to increase, or would improve the standard of comfort, or both. It might be accompanied by an increase of population and a fall in comfort, or an increase of comfort and a reduction of population, as a higher standard of comfort involves a smaller population for a given supply, or a larger supply for a given population.

The population in equilibrium is under pressure from top to bottom. In the upper strata people marry much later than the physiological age, and they have nothing like the physiological number of children. Many of the women never marry. The evil results of the pressure are prostitution, venereal diseases on the one hand, and disappointed lives on the other. But it does not in the least follow that the birth and death-rates are the same in this class, or that they are equal to the average of the whole population. The uppermost layer cannot receive additions from above, and it can and does send a surplus down to the next.

It is often urged that the principle of population cannot be true, because " old families " so frequently die out. This result is not due to the non-existence of the principle of population, but to the ordinary system of names. A man takes his name from his father, and it becomes his name. A woman uses her father's name till she marries, and then takes her husband's, and her male children take the father's name permanently, while the girls take it until they are married. The popular idea about " old families " is, of course, nonsense. Mr. Adam Blueblood has an earlier Mr. Blueblood as father, and his mother is not supposed to count. He is, in fact, descended just as much through his mother as through his father. He has, therefore, half as much Blueblood in him as his father. Similarly he has a quarter as much as his grandfather, and so on. If his descent can be traced up twenty generations to the original Blueblood, he is just as much descended from each of some million other ancestors. So that if the original Blueblood lived a long time ago, that is to say, if the family is very old, its members have so little of the original Blueblood in them, that as far as anything in them goes, any other name would be just as suitable. The old family idea arises out of snobbery and ignorance of the principles of heredity. An " old family " is merely a number of people called by the same name, one selected line of whose descent can be traced back some time. A " family " whose name cannot be traced back is not " old," though, in fact, all human beings are of equally old family. Some day women may have names for themselves. It involves some system of double names. Thus, if the first name denotes the father, and the second the mother, if Mr. Smith-Brown marries Miss Jones-Robinson, their sons and daughters would be called Smith-Robinson, if a Mr. Smith-Robinson married a Miss Scott-Clark, their children would be called Smith-Clark, while if a Miss Smith-Robinson married a Mr. Fitzgerald-Molley, their children would be Fitzgerald-Robinson. The male and female names thus survive continually along their own sides. Such a system of names would upset the old family idea, of course, but would put women on the same level as men as regards heredity, nominally, nothing can alter the fact that they are so in fact. The reason why old families often die out is that masculine nomenclature takes no notice of descent through daughters. In a stationary population there is thus no tendency for a " family " to increase. Some may increase, and others die out. As the " old families " are in the upper layers, they generally send down descendants, and these, if they are along male lines, gradually lose trace of their descent. Even if they did not, the " old families " might be more prolific than the rest of the people, and still many of them would die out.

The motive that prevents fecundity in the upper layers is pride alone. The competition is among people of the same layers, and it is not for food and clothing, but for position in society or in the community.

There is similar competition in each layer, but it is always among those at the same or nearly same level. There is no competition among people in different classes, unless the classes are so near that individuals rise and fall almost insensibly from one to another.

There is a standard of comfort or of living varying with the level. The question of the standard of comfort has often been discussed in connection with hand-workers. Hand-workers are taken, as it were, in bulk, and they are supposed to earn certain wages. Generally the number is taken as constant, and there is supposed to be competition between " capital and labour " which settled the wages, generally in such a way that they are very low compared with what they ought to be if " sensible " ideas were put in practice. Capital is supposed to settle wages, and to make them so low that the hand-workers can only just live, while the capitalists get huge profits by selling at good prices. How it is that the capitalists are not in competition with one another, so that their profits come down to the level below which business cannot pay is not made clear. On the other hand the workmen can combine and, as a body, can refuse to work for less than what they consider fair wages, the idea being that they can then get good wages, and that the products will be sold at the same prices as before, so that they will be well off, while the capitalists lose their enormous profits. But more enlightened writers sometimes apply the principle of population to the labour classes, and they discuss the question of degree of comfort or standard of living. If the number of wage-earners increases they compete with one another and wages come down, and it might be supposed that this would go on until the whole of the class were reduced to the lowest limit, and were permanently on the verge of starvation. In fact, this does not occur. Skilled hand-workers enjoy a certain degree of comfort and social standing. There is no mystery about this. Classes do not multiply their numbers until they starve. Doctors, for instance, do not become so numerous that they die of hunger, and even parsons keep their positions as a class, in spite of the immoral fertility with which the curate is credited. That surprise is caused by the fact that skilled wage-earners keep their position is due to people regarding them as a large " lower class," which is alone affected by the tendency of population to increase. Wage-earners form a large group, and in the diagram the upper part of the area representing them would be fairly high. On a purely income basis it would be well above the lower positions of the figures of clergymen, clerks, doctors, lawyers. Many skilled wage-earners make several hundred a year. The phenomenon of the standard of living is just the same among wage-earners as in other classes. Professional men do not marry and multiply improvidently at the physiological rate. But if they did, most of the children as they grew up would move down to lower levels, and the professional class would remain at the same level as before. The man who makes fifteen hundred a year at fifty, makes very little until he is well on to forty, and he is not able to marry and support a wife in what he considers his proper position, so he does not marry young. When he eventually marries he is careful not to have too many children, not because he considers the question of population, but because they are expensive to bring up, and what is called education is conventionally necessary, while it is extraordinarily costly in proportion to its real value.

Down below the better skilled hand-workers come less skilled, and finally what is called " unskilled labour." The term is vague and unsatisfactory. It is applied to men on a farm, for example. Such men have to do very many various kinds of work throughout the year, and have much knowledge of very special kinds. They are the more highly skilled than most so-called " skilled labour," and their position seems to be anomalous. Going down from stratum to stratum the standard of comfort decreases, and prudence, thrift and economy decrease with wages. Fecundity increases, and the birth-rate is high, and with it the death-rate. There is also a current of descent from the classes above.

Finally we come down to the lower classes of all. Here we have low wages or none. Irregular casual work, and pay to match ; abject poverty, hopeless incompetence and the maximum of misery. This is coupled with irresponsible multiplication of the lowest and worst types, and a high death-rate, especially of infants. To make matters worse, every effort is made to keep the worst and most miserable classes as large as possible by poor-relief, " charity," and government protection.

So far we have been discussing in simplified abstraction an isolated community, living on an island with no external trade and neither emigration nor immigration.

Let us now assume easy emigration and foreign trade. Then, if there are differences between neighbouring communities in the ratio of ability to degree of comfort, people will move from one to the other. Thus, if shoe-makers find that their skill secures better wages or better conditions in another district, they will move. In practice hand-workers generally consider wages only, as men will often prefer an increase in pay, even if the cost of living is so much higher that the extra income does not compensate for it. This is one of the many anomalies due to human foolishness. Broadly speaking, competition tends to equalise the relation of wages, or of comfort to skill and output in each class in a community. If part of a country, say England or Scotland, is considered, this is obvious enough. If England and Scotland are taken as one community, it is still clear. But if Great Britain and another country, say America, are considered, the patch prejudice immediately comes into play, and people think because they are different countries with their own governments, their classes do not come into equilibrium. It is obvious that people cannot be very mobile between Britain and America, but it does not need much migration to bring conditions into equilibrium.

The balance is still more easily secured by trade. Thus, suppose British shoemakers degenerated and did less for their wages than America, and there was no tariff, Britain might import some boots, and export in exchange some goods made by men who did more for their wages than the shoemakers. The balance would probably be made even more simply. Both countries might have been supplying New Zealand with some boots. In that case the American boots would under-sell the British, as the British would rise in price. The effects on the population of the three countries concerned may be followed out. It is assumed, for simplicity, that there are no tariffs. The question of the relation of tariffs to population pressure will be discussed later, in spite of the difficulty that tariffs are, in this country, a question of party politics, people refusing to discuss it with the object of getting at the truth.

The British thus send out fewer boots, and in return get, say, less butter from New Zealand. The demand for shoemakers goes down, so that the competition among shoemakers is rather greater than before, and their wages fall. This makes some shoemakers leave the trade. As less butter is imported, more must be made in this country, so, for simplicity's sake, we may imagine that the ex-shoemakers go on the land. They are not good agriculturists either, so the total produce of the country falls a little, and the result is that it will support fewer people. There will, in fact, be a small but real increase in population pressure, which will cause a small but real decrease of population. In practice such effects cannot be traced, but they are none the less real. There are many streams running into Thirlmere, and it loses by evaporation, supply to Manchester, and overflow. If someone removes a cupful of water, other things being unchanged, he lowers the level of the lake, and lessens the outflow for a short time, but the fact that it cannot be observed or measured does not disprove this, and if other things such as rain, or greater consumption at Manchester alter the conditions, it is still the case that the removal of the cupful of water makes a difference none the less real because untraceable.

As America was already sending some boots to New Zealand in exchange for wool, the exchange just being worth while, she would now send more boots and get more wool. This would make no appreciable difference to her productiveness or population.

As to New Zealand, she would get the same amount of boots, but more of these would come from America, and she would export more wool and less butter. As she exported them both in exchange for boots, they are of corresponding value to her, so there would be no change in the productiveness of New Zealand either.

The net result is that the various classes in different countries are in equilibrium, and any disturbance in any class gradually rights itself. If the workers in any profession or trade do less in return for a given pay or degree of comfort, that profession or trade shrinks locally, and the population decreases.

Equilibrium among nations in contact is brought about by simple changes in external trade, which is very sensitive, by the movement of capital, which is also sensitive, and by migration, which is sluggish. Regarded as a fluid, capital is viscous. It does not find the best openings quickly, and people have all sorts of prejudices. For instance, they dislike foreign investments, they will sink money in a gold mine much more readily than in a straightforward undertaking, and most men who have made money in their own businesses, which they understand, prefer to invest it in outside ventures, which look promising to them because they do not realise the difficulties, while they know the trouble in their own work thoroughly. All the same, small transferences of capital are very sensitive to minute changes of equilibrium, and tend to counteract or prevent any other disturbances.

Migration is slow, but is very effective. Thus German education produced at a low cost organic chemists with little originality, so some of them came over here, where that type of man was not produced. By far the most remarkable case is the migration of large numbers of the inhabitants of Southern and Eastern Europe to America. Some stay there, but many of them come back to Europe with their savings. This tends to equalise hand-worker conditions in the countries where the differences tend to be extreme. That it does not actually equalise them is due to the disinclination to move. " The plant man " tends to live and die where he is born. Migration means leaving home, relations, friends, language and habits, so unless there is a very big attraction elsewhere, a man will not move, either alone, or with his family.

Though we have taken as examples communities that are artificial as to conditions, and simple as to organisation, they are real enough to show how equilibrium can always be reached by slight changes in population pressure, producing changes in population quantity in different classes, or in different localities. There is thus a tendency towards complete balance throughout any community, but as what we call communities are separated chiefly by the purely nominal difference, nationality, there is a tendency towards perfect equilibrium over the whole world. We are arriving at balance so slowly between the United States and Thibet, for example, that little advance is visible in a lifetime;

but when we realise the time of the sojourn of Man on the earth, a few centuries or thousand years is nothing. Yet, as communications are now being developed very quickly, the change towards equilibrium is at last getting rapid.

CHAPTER VI

WEALTH AND ITS DISTRIBUTION

In discussing the constitution of a community it is difficult to find an example that is simple enough for analysis, on the one hand, or is like anything real, on the other. We cannot take the whole world as one large community, because some parts are so much behind that it is not homogeneous, and its discussion would be unwieldly. We cannot take such a country as England, because it is not a self-contained community at all. It is merely an element in the larger community of peoples who trade with one another.

An island whose natural produce is coal, or even gold, could support a population which would live much like their neighbours ; but the dweller in such a place as the Rand would find life very different if a line were drawn round it, over which neither man nor goods might pass. France might be a good case, but it is simpler to take an imaginary community that is civilised, or perhaps like ourselves. This may be considered first as an isolated country meeting all its own wants, with no foreign trade and no migration and at permanent peace with its neighbours. As it has no foreign trade it has no foreign property, if no outsider has property in it. When we have discussed the effects of population pressure in these circumstances, we can trace them when there is foreign trade and foreign capital, when preparation is made for war, and when war comes.

The inhabitants can again be arranged in a diagram in which vertical height denotes the income or even more broadly, position in society, each individual being represented by a minute square. The area of the figure, being the sum of the little squares, represents the number of people. The breadth of the figure at different heights represents the number of people on that level of comfort. The height of the centre of gravity of the figure represents the average income or wealth of the individual, and the product of this height by the area of the figure represents the wealth or income of the community. What height is to mean has been put vaguely, as an accurate diagram is not necessary. To make the matter as precise as, may be, height can be income. As explained in Chapter V, this introduces a difficulty, because then competition is not so rigidly confined to those on the same level ; for instance, an eminent composer of good music, making a very few hundred a year, and that not by composing, is not in competition with the rest of the people who make a similar income. If, given the choice of being a composer of good music, having to earn a precarious living by trying to teach the unmusical sex, or of being, say, an engineer with an income of four figures, he would just as soon choose one life as the other. He thus really belongs to a horizontal line at a height represented by four figures, and he is competing at that level.

What form of diagram represents the best community? Surely we have to consider happiness as our being's end and aim. "The greatest happiness of the greatest number" sounds obvious, but it did not refer originally to a community which is variable in number. Variability in number affects nearly all the hackneyed aspirations of mankind. Thus if there are ten million people, Bentham would consider whether it would be best to have five million with happiness represented by an intensity figure of 2 and five with a figure of ·o, or ten million with a figure of 1. Figures of intensity of happiness are not definite ; if the figure meant income, everybody would agree that ten million people with five hundred a year each would be better than five million with nine hundred and fifty, and five million with fifty pounds a year each. But such discussions belong to sociology as now orthodox, where the number is taken as constant ; the sort of question we have to consider is whether a community of five million people who are happy is better than one of ten million of whom all or many are unhappy.

The first question to be settled, if it could be settled, is rather trite and old. What is happiness? No one can say exactly, but we have broad ideas. It is possible that an impecunious and wholly irresponsible vagrant may be happier than a rich man whose life's ambition to be a member of the Jockey Club is never realised. Again, the fact that life is mainly a struggle for wealth and for what it brings, goes to show that mankind regard wealth as desirable. Wise people point out the hollowness of wealth, but no one else believes them ; most likely they do not believe themselves. The haves always show great ingenuity in trying to persuade the have-nots to be satisfied with their lot, or little, but there is always a suspicion that they are not so much directly concerned with the happiness of the have-nots as with the fear that the have-nots who are the great majority may change the conditions, owing to a desire to have. The struggle for wealth does not itself show that wealth is a good thing. The strife is competitive, and is mainly due to the wish to excel, that is to say, to gratify vanity. From this point of view getting wealthier makes a man happier because he is beating others, and if all got wealthy together, little increase of happiness would come to those that were above the line of misery before. In fact a man would be made happy if he maintained his income while others became poorer. But after all, success in the competition for position generally supplies a very small bit of human happiness. To begin with, there is the happiness of mere healthy existence ; doing a commonplace day's work which has become a pleasant habit, having something to put between the mandibles and a desire for it, being comfortably clad, having time to oneself, and sleeping the sleep of the just pig, are all blessings by no means to be despised. Going higher there is the happiness of friends and of acquaintances. Still higher is the happiness of the home. It is not necessary to wait till a man is dead before calling him happy ; it is much more to the point to see what his wife is like. Then people get a great deal of happiness from other sources than merely succeeding in their trades and professions, but it generally comes from some sort of successful competition. If the struggle for the main success were really the chief object of most people's lives, it must lead to a great unhappiness on the whole, because only a portion can succeed, and very few of us indeed can ever do in their lives what they hope, as young men, or what they think they ought to do. But people get happiness from other sources. Reading for information is largely a form of competition in knowledge. When Johnson said it is annoying to meet anyone who knows more than you do, he spoke loosely. Most people are naturally glad to meet those that know more of their particular subjects, and if they know very much more are proud of their friendship. But there is competition in knowledge, and each likes to know more than others ; and most likely what annoyed Johnson was meeting those who were wrongly supposed by themselves or by others to know more. What is true of reading for information is also true of most acquirements. A man who is fond of painting gets much pleasure, no doubt, during a visit to a good gallery, but in fact he gets more pleasure out of being considered artistic, and he may dress peculiarly on purpose. If he is fond of hunting he will call his house " Tally Ho," to let people know it, while if his fancy is driving good horses, he will wear a short, cylindrical hat. If he is a sportsman he will have stuffed victims of his brutality on show at home. But all these things demand money. Reading is the most inexpensive. The artistic amateur is not content with seeing pictures, he wants to own them and hang them up in his house. It gives him much more pleasure to own one which he has given up looking at than to see any number of paintings. Hunting is enjoyed not

because it is cruel, but largely because it is expensive.
So are driving good horses, fishing, shooting, playing
polo, one style of yachting, various forms of collecting,
and most other hobbies and amusements. Wealth is
therefore a very potent factor in happiness ; and no
moralists will ever prevent the common-sense man
realising how pleasant it is to have money.

These examples all concern the richer classes. They
are obvious to those who are fortunate enough to be
fairly well off ; but it must always be remembered that
the majority are comparatively poor, and only a very
small percentage can indulge in such amusements as
yachting, or collecting pictures. Human nature is the
same in all strata, but the circumstances are different,
and it is very difficult to enter with sympathetic understanding into the lives of those much below or much
above us. The commonest mistake is to assume that
wage-earners form a huge homogeneous class ; whereas
there are just as wide differences in standing among
them as among those who can earn salaries.

Happiness may be co-incident not so much with
welfare, as with its rate of increase. According to this
conception happiness arises out of comparison, probably
unconscious comparison, of the present with the past.
The happy man may then begin with few blessings and
much hardship, but as there is no past to compare his
hard lot with, he does not realise that it is hard. When
one sees children poorly clad and little cared-for,
perhaps hungry, playing in a narrow street, he feels
they ought to be very miserable. Yet they seem to be
in just as good spirits and just as happy as other
children. All the same, our ideal happy man will be
taken from a richer stratum. He has strenuous school-
time, in which he slowly creeps up from bottom to top,
working hard, but successfully. Then as a young man
he has to struggle to make his own way, but he does
make it. His love affair goes badly at first, but he
finally gains the right wife ; as he gets older he
gradually rises, and what is more important his
ambition lessens until he realises he has got practically

all he wants, and more than he feels he really deserves, while his health has gradually improved all the time. He may sometimes find it pleasant to realise that the battle is not to the strong, nor the race to the swift, but to him.

But whatever happiness may be, it is either largely dependent on absolute and relative wealth, or at least wealth is very often a main factor in the production of happiness. Owing to the nature of happiness, it would be impossible to discuss the conditions of the men and women making up a people from the point of view of their happiness, taken one by one or all together. The next best course is to consider their wealth or incomes.

There are difficulties still. For example, would a people made up of families, each making five hundred a year, be happier than one where the incomes ranged from one hundred to five or ten thousand a year, the average being five hundred? If the total income is the same, raising one man to five thousand means sinking, say, eleven men from five to one hundred, and one from five to four hundred. One view is that raising a man from five hundred to seven hundred and fifty, or a thousand would make him happier, at any rate for a time, but that raising him from five to ten thousand would give him but little extra happiness, while reducing eleven people from five to one hundred a year each would cause a great deal of unhappiness which would not be balanced enough to count by the happiness given to the fortunate man. From this point of view, which is of the commonest type, the more evenly the incomes are distributed the better. The example is actually chosen to show up some common illusions. In the example the average was taken as constant, so that the rich man was made so at the expense of others. In real life a man becomes rich by rendering services to the community. He makes a series of exchanges of services for weath, each exchange being good for him, and for the community, else it would not have been made. Hence a rich man's wealth is generally the measure of the good he or his ancestors have done to the community. Of course there are some exceptions, but owing to the smallness of our minds there is a virulent prejudice against the rich, which distorts most of the facts of the case. Thus it is assumed that a manufacturer becomes rich by under-paying his hand-workers, a city merchant gets rich by robbing retailers, a company promoter issues fraudulent prospectuses and robs confiding parsons and widows, and a landlord gets rich by charging exorbitant rents. It is by no means only the ignorant masses who have this idea ; it runs through the literature of economics and sociology. It is a universal or almost universal practice to try to levy taxes in such a way that they fall on the rich rather than the poor. Whether the real incidence is on rich is another matter ; the object and intention is to tax the rich. This chimes in with the prejudice and ignorance of the ill-informed majority, the great aim being to reduce the wealth of the very rich, on the assumption that the possession of great wealth by the few is the cause of poverty of the many, as the wealth must have been taken from the poor. That this sort of ignorance should be common is natural, not only because men are by nature envious, but because it gives a good opening to the demagogue. He can work on such a prejudice and raise himself into notoriety, becoming a people's champion. That it should be common among well-informed writers is more curious. It is probably the result of envy. A man who can write well on, say, economics realises that he has certain ability. He is apt to exaggerate it, because he is dealing with the doings of the public. As has been explained earlier in this book, each of us is seldom wise in more than one direction, that is the direction of his own work, and is quite foolish with regard to the ideas whose bulk or average make up public opinion. A sensible writer on questions which deal with, and therefore generally clash with public opinion, cannot help realising what fools other men are in his own subject, and is apt to forget that anyone who thinks of such matters feels the same, and that he is really not at all cleverer, as he has merely taken up a subject which is not generally studied, and which is commonly assumed to need no study, so that he finds the public saturated with self-satisfied ignorance, and self-confident opinions. Such a writer and thinker probably earns quite a few hundred a year, and he finds business men making thousands. He knows some business men. He finds they talk of nothing but golf, or gardening, or they indulge in what is to him baby-talk, about how the country ought to be governed. In the evening they read newspapers, chosen, of course, to pamper their prejudices, and they smoke, play bridge, read novels, or doze. They can talk about nothing that interests him. As a rule they have no taste for art, music, poetry, or for any branches of book knowledge. He concludes they have no intellects to speak of, and that business is merely making money in an easy way, and that if he went into business he could, with his intellect, make a large income. But if he tries, he finds the despised business man competes with him so that he makes almost nothing. The business man has lots of brains and a special business intellect which it is fashionable to despise. It is there all the same, and it is this same business intellect which is the backbone of civilisation.

This popular illusion as to the rich is not a harmless error, like the notion that the sun puts the fire out ; it is one of the most serious causes of human unhappiness. As far back as history goes we find the poor always in a state of imperfectly suppressed rebellion against the rich. They are kept down for a time, then there is an upheaval or explosion, then an apparent calm while the discontent smoulders, until another outbreak is possible. The fundamental error is always that the poverty of the poor is caused by, or due to the wealth of the rich. The rich have robbed them, or in any case they would be well off if the wealth of the rich were divided among them. In our days we have the absurd feud between capital and labour, which is merely the same nonsense in another form, and we have just the same kind of demagogue flattering the prejudices of the hand-workers, pandering to their ignorance, and climbing into notoriety and place by increasing human suffering.

The greatest harm done by this illusion is not that revolts, revolutions, strikes and other disturbances occur, but that the great mass of humanity is kept unhappy because it is discontented and is always smarting under a feeling of great injustice, while no such injustice in fact exists.

Coming back to the imaginary community, we may consider it as self-contained without external trade or migration of inhabitants, but otherwise like a modern Western people. Whatever the true relation of happiness to money circumstances may be, we will not be far wrong if we discuss the social or money positions of the people as being of importance.

We have then an isolated community, and the diagram is available to represent it. If we examine specimen people selected from different spots on the diagram we find they have, of course, different incomes, and they live in different degrees of comfort. As an example we may take a man in a subordinate position in the office of a city firm, earning five hundred a year. He is in competition primarily with other men of equal ability getting the same salary from other city firms. But he is also in competition with men of similar standing in other professions and businesses. The community being in equilibrium, the competition is just keen enough to prevent his getting more than five hundred a year for his work, and not keen enough for him to have to accept less, or to leave his position. Five hundred a year is the degree of comfort appropriate to this kind‘ of work. The income carries with it the picture of the respectable city man living in a suburban semi-detached house. He goes up to town about nine and reads newspapers and smokes in the train. He is solemn and important at his work, and he comes home about six reading more newspapers, and discussing party politics. In the evening, in summer, he potters about a rectangular garden with a pipe ; in winter he reads novels, plays bridge, smokes, collects stamps, goes to a music-hall or club. Most people would say that population pressure has nothing to do with such a man as this. He is not apparently multiplying rapidly, nor marrying recklessly, nor starving because he has outstripped the means of subsistence. But he is living under keen competition all the same, and this competition is with others in his class or on his level of income. If there were fewer of these, competition would be less and he could claim and get a higher salary.

But with the community coming back to equilibrium after any slight internal disturbance, any particular class or person is not permanently affected by such changes as, for example, a reduction in number of a class. For instance, suppose an epidemic were suddenly to remove a number of people earning five hundred a year in the city ; at first there would be a keen demand, but people from the classes just above and just below would come in, and this would lessen the competition in the class which had been reduced, and would increase it in the neighbouring class. The five hundred a year class, finding living easier, would also marry a little younger or send down fewer to the class just below, and their class would gradually increase in that way until equilibrium was reached again. It does not follow that even in a state of equilibrium each class produces just enough offspring to fill up its own death gaps. It is quite probable that in each class the birth is higher than the death-rate, and that there is a continual flow downwards from every class, until the lowest classes of all are reached. The idea of an epidemic removing a percentage of those earning five hundred a year, and, for simplicity, their families, and the loss being made up by earlier marriage in that small class, sounds rather fanciful. However, the earlier marriage would not be confined to the narrowly defined class at first affected. The question may be looked at another way. If the community of, say, ten million people are living on an island, or are otherwise isolated, and the land just supports ten million in equilibrium, and a certain number are removed suddenly by an epidemic, population will tend to come back to its former equilibrium value. In fact the disturbance would be less local than has been assumed, for the disappearance of a number of families with an income of five hundred a year would affect their landlords, all their tradesmen, and all those who supplied them with anything in return for money. The businesses of their employers would also be put partly out of gear, and the effect would be spread widely, and would be very difficult to trace, but it would be there all the same.

It is difficult to see exactly what determines the degree of comfort corresponding to any particular service to the community, and the degree of comfort must itself be variable, and must depend on the degrees of comfort of other classes. Thus in a country like the old Germany the degree of comfort of a few University professors of history was very much lower than that of an English teacher of equal knowledge and ability. But the degrees of comfort of the people with whom the professors mixed must be taken into account in explaining the apparent difference.

That there must be a particular degree of comfort for each class is clear. Our city man, for instance, must have the right technical knowledge of his work. He must also be presentable ; that is to say he must be able to talk decent English, and to write letters ; and he must have some address and fairly good clothes, otherwise his employers would suffer. He must therefore have been educated as it is called, involving a very expensive process. His family and his associates must also have had the glorious privilege of a conventional education. It would clearly be impossible to get a man to do his work, and to take his place fully, for thirty shilling a week, and it would be of little 'effect gradually increasing an offered salary, until the neighbourhood of five hundred a year was reached. It is thus impossible to know, except by experience, what is the degree of comfort fitting each class in a state of equilibrium, but that need not at all hide the fact that every type of work done for the community commands a particular degree of comfort.

Going from five hundred to a hundred a year or less we get to the class of skilled hand-worker. He has his degree of comfort just as definitely fixed. Apart altogether from any influence of trade unions, a skilled carpenter in a certain district will have a pre-war status corresponding to, say, thirty-five shillings a week. Competition does not bring the carpenter down, to, say, a pound a week, because a pound a week will not produce men of the right training and ability. If the demand for carpenters goes down, very gradually so as not to cause any serious disturbance of equilibrium, all that happens is that fewer men become carpenters ; their standard of comfort does not fall, or it falls inappreciably, but enough to deter the full number of youths taking up carpentry until exact equilibrium is reached again.

At the bottom there is a large class of the submerged which cannot be said to have any standard of comfort at all. Here competition is due not only to improvident fertility of the class itself, but to a never-ending downward stream from and through the classes just above. Generally throughout this book questions are discussed from the population point of view. This is the long view. Movement towards equilibrium brought about by change of birth and death-rates must be slow, as a reduction of the birth-rate to nothing, for example, would not for many years have any affect that could be felt. There are much more rapid movements towards equilibrium after any disturbance, but they are in accordance with ordinary economics, as they occur so rapidly that the population may be considered as constant during the changes. There would be no point in discussing these here, as they have been dealt with very much better and more completely by specialists in economics. They are sometimes touched upon incidentally, but we are for the present concerned with the long view alone.

CHAPTER VII

CIVILISATION AND POPULATION

CIVILISATION has two main influences on population, one to increase and the other to reduce it.

If a district or a continent or the world can support a certain number of people in a given state of civilisation, and advances are made in the knowledge of husbandry of all sorts, and agricultural machines are invented of all kinds, while transport is improved and cheapened, a much larger population can be supported of precisely the same kind as before. The increase of knowledge, with the improvement in plant, thus of itself tends to increase the population that can live on a given area.

But on the other hand, civilisation involves that a small fraction of the community is engaged on producing food, clothing and houses of the simple kind necessary for plain existence. If a country will support a certain population with agriculture in a certain state of development, with 50 per cent. of the people growing food, the rest being engaged on producing clothing, houses and so on, and a gradual change takes place in their ways, so that only 25 per cent. are devoted to getting food, the population must fall a great deal. In the first case, each food producer has to get food for two sets of mouths, his own and someone else's. For simplicity we can consider each food producer as the father of a family, feeding, clothing and housing it. In the second case, he has to provide twice as much food for himself and three others. It is assumed that there is no improvement in agriculture, and that he does not work any harder. He can raise twice as much food as before only by confining his work on

the average to the good ground, which yields double
as much for a given amount of toil.   How much of
this good ground there is, and what it will produce,
determines the population that can be supported.

It is perhaps easier to tackle the proposition the other
way round. Imagine a community living in a country
in a certain stage of civilisation, perhaps a fairly
ancient state, so that we can think of the people as
isolated, and imagine that a certain proportion produces
the food.   The rest are producing other necessities,
such as clothing and houses ; but there are also
soldiers, sailors, politicians, government officials, priests,
amusers, such as authors, actors, musicians, singers,
dancers and painters, and rich men generally, with
direct servants round them, and indirect servants
making all sorts of articles of luxury for them. We
may also imagine a large number occupied in what they
call educating, and the whole population between ten
and twenty doing nothing but being what they called
educated ; also systems of poor law, charity and government support of the thriftless keeping a dangerous
mob of idlers, incompetents and malcontents going.
We may also imagine large, well endowed lunatic
asylums containing, however, only a small portion of
the inhabitants.

In such a country all the ground from which one
man or family can produce enough food for four or
more than four will be in cultivation, but unless there
is a law that each food producer must produce enough
for four, ground will be in cultivation down to the
limit at which it produces only enough to feed one, and
pay for his own necessaries.   But the average must be
four, so a good deal of the land must produce five,
six or more times the food of those that work on it,
to bring up the average.

Suppose the people take to the simple life, and all
set to work to produce only the necessaries for that
life, and suppose there are now twice as many working
at agriculture. Every bit of the ground will produce
more food if more men or families are working on it.

7

More land will be taken into cultivation too. Thus a plot of land which just supported one man or family may now have two men on it. The new-comer, before the simple life came in, may have been a newspaper writer, who grew no food. His supply of food came from some of the richer land. The original producer and the newspaper man now produce more than enough for one, but not enough for two, so that the newspaper man is partly fed by the poor land, and makes a smaller call on the other. It will then pay to take in more land a little poorer, increasing the food supply and with it the population still further.

The result of the change is an increase of food production and a corresponding increase of population.

In this case so far it has been assumed that the land-workers are all living simple lives to start with, and that before the change they were living in the lowest state of comfort, in which they could be good workers. But in the state of civilisation considered, they may have had a much higher degree of comfort, being influenced by the rest of the people. On the general change to the simple life, all example of luxury having gone, the standard of comfort of all may fall below that of the original land-worker. This has two results, it increases the proportion of the people available as food workers, and it reduces the wants of the land-workers. The worker who tilled ground which just kept him may have eaten half the food he grew, and sold or exchanged the other half for clothes and other things. If his wants in these things are reduced by half, land that gives him only three-quarters of the old yield will now support him. More land is taken into cultivation. Without knowing the numerical relations according to the law of diminishing returns one cannot say how much more land would be taken in, and one cannot know how many more the rich land would stand working on it.

Among a civilised people of whom only a small proportion produce food, clothing and so on, the rest are not idle. Most of these are working and very many are working with brains, and working very much harder than the food producers. Their work is sometimes called unproductive, or unnecessary. It is neither really ; it is necessary for civilisation as it produces all those things by which civilisation differs from savagery, or which enables people to live the fuller life. It might be called civilisation work, and all work might be divided into civilisation and bare living. Such terms are very awkward, so civilisation may be called gratular and bare living runcitic work. There is no clear border-line between the two. Every community has some degree of civilisation, and the poorest people have some things they could live without. On the other hand, food may consist of nightingales' tongues or canvas-backed terrapin eaten with the most expensively-labelled wines. Such fare is purely gratular.

When a community is self-contained, growing its own food, it is easy to see that if a change of ideals occurs, which reduces the proportion of gratular, or leads more of the people to do runcitic work, the country can support a much larger population. If the change as to work is rapid, the result will be a great increase of leisure for many years, because the population will not increase effectively for a generation or so. Every civilised community has therefore a margin, in fact a very large margin against anything like general poverty. In bad times all it has to do is to reduce its gratular consumption and increase its runcitic work. It does this after a war, before it gets straight again.

If our community did not grow its own food or produce its own clothing, it would import them from outside. It must export goods to pay for its food and clothes. It is assumed that the people do not own foreign countries, or foreign property enough for the food and clothes to come in as interest without exports. Our community might export nothing but diamonds and rubies to various foreign countries, receiving in exchange necessaries of life from one country. Finding and preparing the bits of carbon and impure alumina would then be purely bread-winner's work, but to the purchasers the goods would be wholly gratular.   If such a community wanted to have the maximum population, it would devote the whole of its work to finding diamonds and rubies and cutting them, and it would send them all abroad in exchange for food and clothing. When it had reached the condition in which the work of hunting for diamonds and rubies corresponded in degree of comfort with that of growing food on ground which supported the worker and his family and left nothing over, and all were down to this degree of comfort, the population would be at its maximum. The diamonds and rubies are purely bread winning as far as the producers are concerned, and purely gratular as to the buyers.

Suppose the community is civilised and grows half its own food and clothing, getting the other half by exporting diamonds and rubies, and suppose the community, though civilised, still to have left some savage instinct, so that they delighted in the bright bits of carbon and alumina, the food producers, by which is meant food producing hand-workers, would be producing what is purely runcitic. Take the case of two jewel hunters, of the same class as the food producers, living in the same degree of comfort and getting the same wages ; the diamonds and rubies of one are sent abroad in exchange for food and clothing, those of the other are bought by rich men and hung on their women. Whether the goods are runcitic or gratular evidently does not depend on their producer, but on the consumer. The producer may grow food or search for diamonds, and both may work to make a poor living.

A civilised community on a given area is thus much smaller in population than it would be if it kept the same knowledge and practice of farming, but lived the simple life. But the knowledge and practice of farming is itself the result of civilisation, and would never have been acquired without civilisation because the science of agriculture is dependent on broader science, and science demands much time and special training, unavailable if all are just able to make enough to keep alive, and agricultural machinery could not be made if it were not merely a branch of machinery in general.

The fact that a civilised society has a large number of people doing gratular work has often been noticed, though not put in quite the same way, and it is discussed on the false foundation that if the consumption of gratular goods, which include all luxuries, and all intellectual pleasures that cost anything were given up, the population would remain the same, and people would be much better off. It is said that if everyone worked for three hours a day, enough food, clothing and necessaries of life would be produced, and thus each person would have, say, eight hours for sleep, three for work, one and a half for eating, and eleven and a half for leisure, intellectual pursuits, games and exercise and amusement.

Others again see that apart from consumption of gratular goods, there is great inefficiency and waste. Thus one economist, without a practical knowledge of business, will urge that the middlemen should be extinguished. Another points out that a terrible lot of grain which might be used as food for man is fermented to make alcohol and waste product, one of these being used for pigs. Many of these theories will be discussed in their proper places, but while we are on this part of the subject it can do no harm to repeat that any such changes would not make the people on the average any richer, or any better off ; it would merely enable more to live on the ground. In a civilised community there is, of course, a huge amount of work done that does not produce either runcitic or gratular results ; it is mere waste due to inefficiency.

Practically all the schemes of social reform which are put forward to enrich the poor, or at any rate to give everyone a fair chance of being comfortably off, are based on the theory that if the consumption of gratular products is stopped, more necessaries can be provided, and the poorer will then be able to live comfortably, while those that like can indulge in intellectual pleasures, which cost little. Reformers are generally content with finding fault with society as it is at present, and think that if they can show what a lot of unhappiness, injustice, misery and vice it causes, that proves at once that some vague scheme they have must be better. Very often the reformer is merely seeking self-advertisement and self-advancement, but that is not at all against his scheme. The very best scheme may be put forward by a pushing man who is concerned only with his own advancement, while a hopelessly bad doctrine, appealing wholly and solely to the envy, vanity and ignorant prejudices of the many may be put forward by a kind, modest, unselfish person, who thinks only of his fellow men. Many of the writers of books and newspaper articles, and of the men who go about talking, rely entirely on the poor man's natural envy of the rich, and they argue that if the riches, which to most of their disciples means hoards of sovereigns, were distributed equally, the good done to the numerous poor would be immeasurably greater than the harm done to the few reduced rich. Thus if one man has £10,000 and ninety-nine men nothing, each of the ninety-nine men will gain more happiness by getting £100 than the rich man will lose on being reduced to £100 ; so as ninety-nine men get £100 the increase in happiness is enormous.

All these superficial schemes are based on two assumptions ; one that the state of society would suit real people, the other that if it came in, population would not be altered. No scheme of reform is worth a moment's thought unless it has an understanding of the principles of population as a basis.

CHAPTER VIII

CAPITAL AND LABOUR

THE common idea is that there is a strong antagonism and difference of interest between capitalists and wage-earners ; that capitalists have a great and unfair advantage in being almost free to settle wages as they like, so as to make great profits out of the hand-workers, who alone are the producers of all value, while the hand-workers by modern methods of trade unions and strikes, coupled with considerable political power, backed by public opinion, are gradually opposing the grinding greed of the capitalists, and improving their own position. Others think or dream that, as the hand-workers produce all there is of value, no one else should get any pay ; in fact capital should earn no interest, and be in the hands of the state, so that its bearing no interest does not deter the state from finding as much as may be necessary for the good of the hand-workers. Brain-workers are left out of account altogether.

At the risk of being tediously elementary we may consider what capital is. It is wealth saved, and in this connection it is wealth saved for investment in industry. The existing capital in the world at any time is like a lot of water in a leaky cistern. It is always running away, and has to be made up all the time.

A man may save money to provide for the future. He may be very cautious, and prefer not to risk lending for fear of losing it, and in that case he buries it. It is not so long ago that people buried money. Naturally a man, let us say Mr. Pepys, who had saved a hundred pieces of gold, would refuse to lend it to an acquaintance to start a small shipbuilder's yard without a special return. He might lose his hundred pieces altogether. The shipbuilder must give him some special payment to cover this risk. If the right payment, including risk, in those times was 10 per cent., the owner of the pieces would be just on the balance of lending or not lending at 10 per cent. If there were no risk at all he would just as soon lend without interest as hide his gold ; the safety being exactly the same. But the mere saving of money to provide for the future is not a quite strong enough motive to make people save as much as is wanted in industry. The shipbuilder would therefore first pay a percentage to cover risk of loss, say ten, and he would have to pay Mr. Pepys some further interest as a special inducement to save. Leaving risk out of account, the mere provision of money for the future is not a strong enough inducement to save to make people save enough to meet the industrial demand for capital. A further inducement is necessary. In our days, in normal times this is a payment of from $2\frac{1}{2}$ to 3 per cent. interest free of income tax ; the interest on a perfectly safe investment. This might be called pure or saving interest. The ordinary thrifty man will now save, and he has two inducements : thrift, that is saving his money for future use, and increase by compound interest ; and the rate he gets, or rather expects, for that is just enough additional inducement to make people save enough for the commercial needs of the public. It is the interest paid by government for investment in what are considered perfectly safe securities. The fact that they are most unsafe is not appreciated, as people have a childish faith in government, though holders of those securities have found out some surprising facts lately.

If the government rate of interest is not enough, when added to simple thrift to induce people to save as much capital as is wanted, the rate of interest automatically rises until there is equilibrium. After a war, for example, when there is a great demand for capital, the rate of pure interest goes up to 5 or 6 per cent. Of course the income tax must be added. It puts up all interest, or depreciates fixed interest stocks.

There is no such thing as a safe investment. Even hiding gold in the ground is unsafe, for two reasons. There is a risk of losing it, as the hider may forget where it is, or may be unable to dig it up when he wants it, or someone may steal it. There is the risk of depreciation of gold, through the gradual increase of the supply, through the development of paying bills and cheques, so that less gold is needed for currency, and through the greater use of paper currency. A young man may buy fifty ounces of gold, and dig up fifty ounces when he is old, he has the fifty ounces of gold, with the same number of sovereigns as before, but if the value of the gold has gone down he is not so well off. He will say that prices have risen.

If he knows of any safe securities which yield, say 3 per cent., he will be so much the better off. But apart from questions of absolute loss, for instance, by repudiation or inability to pay back, the value of the money may be, and nearly always is decreasing, so that he does not really make 3 per cent. If the value of gold is depreciating $\frac{3}{4}$ per cent. a year, he is really getting only $2\frac{1}{4}$ per cent. The investor seldom appreciates this, and he looks upon government securities as quite safe ; so we may take it that 3 per cent. is the extra inducement that will make people save, and that 3 per cent. may be called the saving or pure interest on money. Three per cent. is an outside figure ; consols paying only $2\frac{1}{2}$; but 3 per cent. will be taken as on the safe side.

The thrifty man may have a dash of boldness added to his thrift, and he may therefore prefer an investment that promises a greater return in percentage, coupled with a greater risk of losing his capital. Thus he may prefer 5 per cent. in industrial debentures. The odd 2 per cent. is then insurance against loss of his principal. The investor really thinks the risk less than 2 per cent., or he would not choose that investment. Instead of debentures, he may prefer ordinary shares, which sometimes pay less than 5 per cent., and sometimes more. People are generally optimistic in their investments, and those who choose high percentage returns are more apt to lose their principal than the extra percentage warrants. This does not affect the point that the interest above, say, 3 per cent. is really insurance against risk of loss of principal. That it is not enough to insure fully is another matter.

In industrial investment the interest on capital is generally found to be about 5 per cent., of which 2 per cent. is risk insurance and 3 per cent. pure interest or extra inducement to save ; that is to say, inducement in addition to pure thrift. In new countries, or countries in which rapid progress can easily be made, such as Canada, Australia or New Zealand, the industrial rate of interest is high, because the demand for capital is great, and the owners are largely living in " old " countries. They are then unable to judge which investments are safe, so that the insurance proportion of the interest is very high.

Capital is thus always varying. If more is wanted, that is to say if there is any opening for more, the saving interest rises, and this makes people save more. If there is less demand the saving interest falls, and people enjoy their earnings as they make them. The real saving interest is about 3 per cent. It may vary from time to time, and in extreme cases, such as after a war, it may rise to 6 per cent. or even more.

In industrial use capitalists, on the average, make this 3 per cent. Industrials generally pay on the average about 5 per cent., but the extra two are balanced by occasional losses of capital.

It is thus idle to suppose that capitalists make fabulous sums out of the exploitation of hand labour. Suppose that in some industry a capitalist made 10 per cent. without risk by some system of underpaying his workmen ; other capitalists would soon know, and more works on the same principle would come into being, and would increase until the profits were normal, and then the result would be a further development of that industry with under-paid workmen. We will consider the case of the under-paid workman directly. As regards the capitalists, capital is always in competition with capital, and not with anything else. It is not in competition with the consumer, and it is not in competition with the employed.

The example of the capitalist making money by underpaying workmen is purely fanciful, and was taken because it is a popular idea. Of course, if the workmen were under-paid some of them would leave and go elsewhere, where they could earn more. The whole of the employed could not change easily, as they would often be settled down and attached to the neighbourhood in many ways, so that it would be easier to put up with low pay from week to week than to face a change. But a small portion of the workmen could leave and go elsewhere, and the capitalists would have to offer higher wages to replace them, and that would bring the whole of the wages up to the normal. It might be urged that the employed could not leave and go elsewhere, because wages might be equally low elsewhere. That is a specimen of the kind of statement often made. Of course wages cannot be low as a whole ; low wages are wages that are lower than most other wages ; they can be low only in comparison with other wages. There can be a general comparison of wages at one time with wages at another time, but that is not under discussion. It may be mentioned in passing that it is not generally profitable to pay wages below the normal, as the best hand-workers leave, and inferior work causes more loss than any apparent gain in wages balances, partly because the overhead charges are going on all the time.

The capitalist employer is in competition not with labour, and not with the sellers of raw material, nor with consumers, but with other capitalists. If his business goes well, others come in and compete ; if it goes badly, he loses his capital. On the average capital makes about 3 per cent., and 2 per cent. for insurance ; any business that pays more at once attracts more capital into competition until the profit falls to the normal.

It may be urged that there are many concerns that go on year after year making enormous profits, such as

50 per cent., and that they must be underpaying their hands.

A concern may start a new industry with, say, £100,000 capital, and may do very well and make large profits, not by under-paying hands, as that would merely keep wanted hand-workers away, but by making something new, for which there is a ready market. Suppose after a few years the concern has accumulated large reserve funds, or issued debentures, and is still very well managed. Its profits in relation to £100,000 may easily be 50 per cent., but by the time other concerns are in competition the real profit is down to the normal percentage on the real capital, whatever it is on the nominal. If an investor buys a share on the market he will have to pay say £10 for it, and his dividend will be at the normal rate of 5 per cent. The investors' struggle is always to get chances of high dividends with risks small in proportion.

In discussing questions of capital and labour there is apt to be a good deal of confusion in the case of the capitalist owning and managing his works. The modern tendency is towards factories owned by limited liability companies. In such cases the directors are shareholders, but often rather small shareholders ; and they may be more or less figureheads, the control being really in the hands of a manager or managing director. The discussion is also complicated by costs of raw material and in selling goods. As simple cases are easier to follow, let us take a laundry business. The fact that many of the hand-workers are women makes no difference. Take therefore the case of a modern laundry owned by a limited company and controlled by a salaried manager under a board of more or less inactive directors. The works consists of buildings and machinery. A modern high-class laundry contains a good deal of very ingenious and quite expensive machinery.

Suppose a new district developes very quickly, and the laundry company is formed and starts business with no competition except private home washing. The manager will offer wages just high enough to get people to come and work. Those who think the wages too low need not come ; no one asks them to, and it is no hardship to them that more tempting offers are not made. The wages offered are just high enough to make it worth while for the employed to come and work. The laundry manager fixes the prices for his customers according to his judgment, so as to make the highest profit, not on each article washed, but on the capital. If he lowers the price he gets more custom, but that may need more buildings and machinery, as well as more hands, and the yearly result may be worse. If he raises his price he reduces his turnover. The best price to charge is a matter of careful consideration and compromise. It is largely settled by the cost and trouble and loss of prestige of washing at home. If the result is a great success in profits to the shareholders it does not in the least follow that it is because the manager is paying low wages. He is paying the wages that make it worth while for the hands to work. They are offered wages which they may take if they think the pay good enough, or leave it if they do not. It is quite true that in the district there may be a number of people, mostly women, who are in such wretched circumstances that they are glad to take wages which are too low for them to live comfortably. That is the result of population pressure, not in any way of the new laundry. There may be so many of such people that the manager finds he can fill his works at a rate of wages which is enough to support life in great misery, and nothing more. But if he offers the wages and the hands are glad to take them, there is no reason why he should offer more. Suppose, however, for philanthropic or other reasons he offered higher, perhaps a good deal higher wages, it would not necessarily do the hands any good. The higher wages offered would bring a different class of people along asking for work. The manager would then have the choice of taking on any of a large number of applicants, and he would naturally choose the best of them, not the lowest class ; so that the higher wages would not help the particular people who were ready to work for low pay. A newspaper reader might find that the laundry was now paying its hands very, good wages, and would say that was very satisfactory, because the hands are now well off. It would not occur to him that it was a different set of hands altogether. This point is urged because it is a common mistake in sociology to give a group a name, and to forget that changes of conditions of the group may alter the people forming it, so that though the group has the same name, it is really a different set of people. A very obvious example is the case of the waitresses of a well-known tea-shop company. The company pays very high dividends on its nominal capital, and a retiring philanthropist generally comes forward at the meetings to urge that some of the enormous profits should be devoted to paying the waitresses higher wages. With the greatest sympathy for the waitresses, it must be pointed out that they are a rapidly changing body, and that a rise in wages would mean that the class of girl now employed would be employed no longer ; girls of a better class taking their place. People would then feel satisfied that a deserving class of girl got higher wages, when in fact it was put out of that work.

Returning to the laundry, if the profits are high people with capital would be anxious to invest in the laundry, but shares would be expensive. They would therefore consider the question of starting a rival laundry, and if the district showed chance of success they would start it.

Suppose the two laundries were managed and run in exactly the same way, except that one paid high wages and the other low ; it is quite clear that if the highly paid hands did no more work than the others, the philanthropic concern would pay less, and the other would be able to squeeze it out of existence in time. It is not that one concern is exploiting need or anything of the sort ; it is merely employing a lower class of hands at lower wages to do a given work, and if wages is the determining factor, as in the case taken with its limitations, its rival goes to the wall. It is assumed that the two laundry companies have competed until the charges to the customers are so low that only one of them pays. This would be the natural result of the competition, unless an agreement were made to keep up prices, a condition which we are not considering, and which would tempt a third concern to start. The two concerns would thus come down to offering the same wages. They would be the lowest wages in proportion to the work done. Our sympathy is wholly with the hands who have to work for the low wages, and to be content with them, but the reason why they cannot get higher wages is not that the capitalists are grinding them down, but simply that there are too many of them in competition. The starting of the second laundry and the reduction of prices to the consumers will increase the work to be done, and more hands will be employed. If there are not too many people available the low wages may not attract enough. The laundries will then have to be content with smaller business than the manager would like, or they must offer higher wages. They cannot pay the last comers higher wages than the others, because there are always some other openings, and if the wages were unequal for equal work the lower paid would gradually leave and take other places, displacing those who would then be taken on by the laundries at the higher rate ; or they would threaten to leave unless they got the higher wages.

One condition governing the rate of wages is thus the number of people competing for them. If there are fewer people ready to take low pay in a laundry the wages go up.

The capitalist has wages and cost of plant, salaries, and so forth on one side, and the consumer on the other. He is between them, and the relations to both are similar, but people are so stirred with sympathy for the hand-worker that they look at one side only.

If the laundry charges high prices for washing we never say that the poor have a right to washing at an easy rate, or that the laundries are exploiting the unfortunate because they do not wash for them at prices that do not pay. In this case their product is not taken by the poor, and a laundry is on that ground a bad example to discuss ; but it is a good general example of the employment of capital, as it is very simple and easy to follow. There is plant and salaried employment ; but there is no raw material in the ordinary sense, and payment may be weekly, so that there is no large working capital locked up in wages paid before the revenue comes in, and there is no question of distribution and middlemen. If the business had been a cloth factory we would have had hands who were not wanted, or who would not have accepted the wages offered, marching about with banners, saying they did not want charity, they wanted work, and had a right to a living wage. But it would never occur to the public to parade the streets with banners saying they demanded clothing below cost price because they had a right to a living warmth.

The capitalist, as a cloth factory owner, has to keep his wages down as one factor and his prices up as the other. This does not necessarily mean that he pays low wages. If he has a lot of machinery, so that the interest and depreciation on plant is high, it might pay him to increase his wages 20 per cent. to get 10 per cent. more output. It is well known in many industries that it pays to employ rather better hands than the general run at considerably higher wages. But with regard to each kind of worker it is essential to success that the capitalist makes the best bargain he can, because if he does not make a good bargain a rival capitalist will. But the rate of wages is not determined by the arbitrary will of the capitalist. It depends, among other things, on the relation of the hands available to the hands wanted. On the other hand the capitalist has to sell at the highest price he can get. The reason for getting his hands at the lowest market price and for selling at the highest market price is not in the least that he wants to make profits by swindling hand-workers or by swindling the consumers. He is in similar relations with both. The real consideration is that he is in competition with other capitalists. In the case of the laundries, if he pays higher wages than his competitor he must either reduce his profits, in which case the capital is badly invested, and the laundry will eventually come to grief, or he must raise his prices and lose his custom. It is exactly the same with the prices he charges his customers. He has no wish to screw unwarranted gains out of poor, hard-working people ; he is simply in competition with other capitalists ; he therefore buys at the lowest market price and sells at the highest, and he is controlled in both cases by competition with other capitalists. There is no antagonism between him and his customers, and there is none between him and his hand-workers. Strife between capital and " labour " is just as absurd as strife between buyer and seller of goods. There is internecine strife in a sense between capitalist and capitalist and between labour and labour. In the case of laundry work there is no strife between customer and customer, but in industries where customers are similar, for example, wholesale purchasers of cloth, there is internecine competition between the customers. This is a case of the general law that competition is among likes ; not between unlikes. This is quite clear in the animal world. Each animal is in competition with other similar animals, not with the kind of animal it eats, for example, nor the kind that eats it. It is the same in the vegetable world.

Capital has no power to increase wages out of its own profits.

Capital is potentially unlimited. If more is wanted, interest rises and people are induced to save more. Given time any amount can be raised. Saving can go on without end. The demand for increase of capital is never very sudden, so that there is seldom real difficulty in saving fast enough. On the other hand, when capital is not wanted, interest falls, and people spend their earnings instead of saving, as the motive of pure thrift is not strong enough to keep up the supply. The capital that is in the form of plant of all sorts cannot be spent on enjoyment like saved money, but it wears out, and is being continually worn out, so that if everybody stopped saving, capital would not remain constant ; it would shrink away, quickly at first, and then more slowly.

In the case of the laundries, if one increased its wages because the directors or manager thought the hands had a right to a living wage, and were not getting it, or for any other reason of that sort, if the services given by the hands remained the same, and all the other conditions, that laundry would be under-sold by its rival and go out of business, and would then pay no wages at all.

But suppose both laundries had the same idea, and both increased their wages. The result would be that they would both increase their selling prices. In the case of an isolated town with only two laundries, such a state of things can be imagined ; and the case is typical of certain temporary states that occur in industry. The first result would be that the hands would gradually change, and a higher class would be employed, as already explained. Philanthropic people would say what a glorious thing it was that the laundry hands were making good living wages ; they would forget that the old hands for whom they had sympathy were out and a new set in ; but that is not really the point. The point is that the rise in wages does not come out of capital at all. The laundries raise their prices, and the consumers pay the higher wages, not the capitalists. The capitalist is not so much concerned with the question whether wages in his industry are high or low ; what interests him is whether his wages are higher or lower than his rivals in proportion to what he gets for them. Though each capitalist or capitalistic concern is competing with other similar concerns to make higher profits, the average profits of capital are irrevocably fixed by the psychology of people who can save at a definite figure of approximately 3 per cent. If capital makes more, people are tempted to save more, and more capital comes into competition for the profits that can be divided up ; if it makes less, people spend their money as they make it, and capital decreases until the profits, when divided up, average 3 per cent.

There is no magic in 3 per cent. The number depends on people's thrift and desire to provide for the future, as far as the multitude of comparatively small investors are concerned, and it is they who control the figure. In an old country like England, the ordinary professional or salaried man likes to put by for the future, and a 3 per cent. safe interest in addition is enough to turn the scale and make him save rather than enjoy everything as he makes it.

Capital might be saved by all people in all layers of society. The hand-worker cannot save as much as the leading doctor, and he cannot often save even the same proportion of his income ; but in fact he hardly saves at all. At most he puts a little by as subscription to his benefit fund or to his trade union. This saving is capital, and it may be employed industrially, and is employed industrially, directly or indirectly ; for those that look after the fund invest it in interest bearing securities. Thus a man who pays a few pence a week to his sick club may really be in a small way a shareholder in the company that employs him, and to some extent his own capitalist. But this is not really the hand-worker's idea ; his object is insurance against sickness and unemployment directly, and if a large number joins in a scheme of this sort the revenue and expenditure average out nearly the same, so that a very small accumulation of funds is necessary, and there is no capital saved. Apart from this sort of insurance the hand-worker is very thriftless. Though each could save but little, their number is so large that collectively they might save and possess quite a large share of the capital of the world. It is not suggested that that would do any good directly, because population pressure would not be affected by any such scheme. If hand-workers of a given skill could just preserve themselves in a given state of comfort at thirty shillings a week, and they had saved money so that they got two shillings a week as interest, population pressure working through competition would force them to accept twenty-eight shillings a week. The good would arise indirectly, because if the hand-workers were their own capitalists, even partly, they would realise that the hardness of their lives is not due to capitalists, but to population pressure. They would thus shed the unhappiness due to a rankling feeling of injustice, and to envy of the rich.

In new countries the opening for capital is great in proportion to the local supply, because a large proportion of the local people are not of the kind that save money, and the people of the saving classes are fewer in proportion to the capital wanted than in old countries. Capitalists or investors in old countries are ignorant of the condition in new, and are afraid to invest, so that they will not put money into a venture unless a high risk-interest is given. The development of a new country is thus slowed down to some extent by the ignorant timidity of capitalists at home.

It is often supposed that capital is very astute, or that it is entirely or mainly controlled by hard, far-seeing financiers, whose keen eyes notice every fluctuation of the market, so that capital finds the best interest as water finds its level. In fact, capital is controlled very foolishly, and is wasted enormously. It is largely the savings of professional and business men, and of the rest of the large class of salaried people. They are fully occupied with their own work and follow that with all their strength. They do their own business with the trained, and invest the results of this work with their fallow mind. The waste of capital is enormous in England. A large proportion of it goes in limited liability companies. Some of these are sound business propositions, but the majority, especially of London issues, come to grief in a short time. It is often supposed that the absurd schemes which form the basis of so many companies that are floated appeal to country parsons, impecunious widows, and superannuated army officers ; and that a board consisting of peers, old soldiers, and members of parliament would warn all sensible investors off. But all the same, the investors in such concerns are largely people whose judgment is quite sound in their own business, but is hopelessly at fault outside. It must be borne in mind that the interest or dividend that determines the saving and investment is not what people get, but what they think they are going to get. A man makes apparently high interest in his own business because he understands it, and dovotes his time and attention to it. Properly, much of what he gets is really remuneration that should be classed as salary, not dividends. He makes, say, 10 per cent. in his own business, and it has no further room for capital, or he prefers not to have all his eggs in one basket. He thinks he ought to make, and can make, 10 per cent. in anything he touches, so he puts his money into some scheme which promises high interest, and loses it. It is not suggested that more sensible investment would make the world richer or happier ; it would merely allow more people to live on it in a given state of comfort. The real bearing of this part of the discussion is that capital is invested and lost in schemes which employ hand-workers, so that hand-workers are actually paid out of capital, and the hand-workers to that extent live on consumption of capital. There are thus cases of hand labour battening on capital, but we have so far found none of capital doing so on hand labour. It is not suggested for a moment that this waste of capital in employing hand-workers or anyone else in doing work which does not pay is good for the hand-workers ; it is merely put forward in refutation of the statement that capital exploits hand-workers.

The middle class man of moderate income is the real or controlling capitalist of the world, but he is not at all the conventional type. The capitalists of fiction, and the capitalist of socialistic and similar reforming literature is a very rich man, who spends enormous sums on himself by owning race-horses, steam yachts, and motor cars. Now that cars are fairly common he has to own a pack of them. But this expenditure, profuse as it is, mops up very little of his yearly income. He does not make a mere 3 or 5 per cent., and he does not produce anything in the ordinary sense. He goes to the city every day, and leads a lurid and strenuous life in buying and selling stocks and doing mysterious but decisive deals all day over the telephone, piling up money which is wrung from the hand-worker and the poor. His chief amusement is cornering wheat and running up the prices of necessaries. He generally dies of heart failure at a critical point of his eccentric career ; but what the effect of that is on the poor it is difficult to follow out. Sometimes he finds quite casually that he happens to be ruined. In either case no one knows what happens to his enormous wealth, whether it filters back to the poor again, who really ought to have it, or is handed on to a litter of fresh capitalists who carry on the evil work of the late pig. Another variety of the fiction capitalist makes his huge wealth by paying low wages. Why his hands stay with him instead of going to other works where they can get higher wages is not explained. It is not only ignorant agitators, socialists, and philanthropists that depict these capitalists ; the idea runs through all the conversation and literature of people who ought to know better. It is really based, not on any sympathy with the poor, but on pure and simple envy. A novel writer who makes, say, three hundred a year, but has a reputation which has reached most of the ladies and all the servant maids in the country, feels that he is a great man with a great brain. He finds a wealthy man who goes to the city every day, who never heard of him, and who takes no interest in his novels, nor in any other kind of literature or art. Here therefore is an unknown man of no ability who makes thousands where the writer makes hundreds. This makes the author envious and jealous, and he cannot understand how the money can be made except by robbing somebody or underpaying hand-workers. That the city man has ten times the ability and is ten times as useful to the world is unthinkable. In common conversation, and in newspapers and books, especially story-books, the rich man, especially if he is " self-made," is generally represented as ignorant, and wanting in all ability except cunning. This common foolishness does immense harm, because it adds to the chief cause of unhappiness in the world to-day ; the futile envy of the rich by the poor, and it tends to prolong the unhappiness because it teaches the poor that their un-happiness is not in any way due to their own faults, or preventible by their own actions and conduct, but is due to the misused power of the selfish and cruel rich. Transparent nonsense as this is, it " goes down."

Coming to real life, take the case of a man whose father started a small boot factory, and by the use of good machinery and by good management and organisa-tion developed a large works. As the future of this business looked very promising when the father died, the only son converted it into a limited company, with big capital, of which he holds a large portion of the shares. For simplicity, assume he is chairman with a small fee, but the works is excellently managed by a salaried official. He makes more as dividends than he cares to spend, and it is quite easy for such a man to save. He uses his savings in starting other industries, generally cognate. He may buy a large interest in a tannery, and gets the tannery and boot factory to work together to their common good. He is regarded as a good business man, and becomes leader in a financial group ; and when he makes a good deal on behalf of the group he gets preferential terms. Such a man gets rich, as he deserves. He has really a high ability of a particular kind. But the point is that he can save easily, and though he may generally make more than 3 or even 5 per cent. he would be inclined to save and re-invest his money, even if the rate of interest on perfectly safe investment was less than 3 per cent. This type of capitalist, no doubt, owns a good share of the wealth in the older civilised countries, and a still larger share in the United States. But his influence would be to lower the rate of interest, as he can save more easily. The rate of interest is determined by the class whose saving or non-saving is determined by its rising or falling.

Any idea that the rich can get money out of the poor

by a high rate of interest or profit in industry is thus wrong. The interest payable on the average is determined by the small investor. It is low, about 3 per cent., and not only is no share whatever of this due to the hand-workers as a right, or on any other grounds, but no share of it can be given to them, otherwise the capital disappears and the hand-workers are thrown out of work.

Returning to the example of the laundries, we may imagine the two companies competing on equal terms, giving the same wages for the same work, and getting the same prices from the customers. There is no temptation for a third laundry to start, as the profits are normal. Suppose one laundry gets a new manager who introduces some new machines and re-arranges the work so as to be more economical.

An apology is almost due for bringing a brain-worker into this discussion at all. It is generally assumed that industry is carried on by capitalists and hand-workers, and it is not realised that success or failure depends on the brain-worker. His share has so far been kept in the background in this discussion on purpose.

The manager may charge the same as before, and make more profit, or he may reduce his price and take away some of the custom of the rival concern. Reduction of price is not a tempting course, because the rival concern will reduce too, and will go on making no profit, and then not keeping the plant in order, so that it is a tedious and expensive business to starve a rival out by reducing prices. The laundry with the new manager will then pay higher dividends. Public opinion will claim a share of the higher profits for the hand-workers, but if they are doing the same work for the same wages as before there will be no foundation for the public opinion.

CHAPTER IX

PROFIT SHARING

ONE of the most popular cures for hand-labour troubles is profit sharing, and in many cases it is said to work very well. This result is probably due to the arrangement making the hand-workers feel contented rather than any substantial advance in their earnings.

The popular idea is that capitalists make such huge profits out of hand-labour that they can easily afford to give the men an extra amount, which is a great increase to their wages, but is such a small portion of the profits that the capitalists can hardly feel it.

As already explained, individual capitalists often make very high profits while others lose their principal, and the average profit on capital in industry is of the order of 3 per cent. It comes to equilibrium, because any increase of interest leads more people to save money and therefore increases the competing capital, while any reduction discourages saving. The percentage, above three or so in industry, is risk insurance.

If there are two similar factories in competition, both employing men at two pounds a week to do a particular kind of work, and one can persuade its men to do 10 per cent. more work in the week, that factory can increase its output 10 per cent. If it increases the wages 10 per cent. too, the increased output more than balances the extra cost. This is because wages form only part of the cost. Thus the goods made originally by men earning £100 in wages may involve £50 in material, and £100 at least in management, repairs to machinery and plant, and all other standing charges. £250 has, then, to be charged before there is any profit

at all.   Allowing £30 for cost of selling, and £20 for
profits, which may be 5 per cent. on the capital invested,
the goods " made " by the hand-workers for £100 are
sold at £300.   If the hand-workers do 10 per cent. more
work, and get 10 per cent. more wages, the number of
them may be decreased and the output kept the same,
and this does not help those employed directly.   It
makes them part of a more efficient community, but
that may be disregarded.   The employers in such a case
would not keep the output the same and reduce the
number of hands.   If the number of men is the same
and the output increased to 10 per cent., and the plant
and organisation can cope with the increase without
further expense, the concern sells not £300 worth, but
£330 worth of goods per week, and its cost, instead of
£280 is £295 ; £10 wages and £5 material being
added.   The profit is thus £35 instead of £20.   So that
the increase of wages with a corresponding increase of
work of 10 per cent., increases the profits from 5 to
8¾ per cent., an increase of 75 per cent.   In practice
the other expenses do rise somewhat but not nearly in
proportion, and the selling price has to be lowered a
little to secure the increase of sales ; but an increase of
wages per man, coupled with increased output in proportion, helps both the hand-worker and the employer.
Neglecting the smaller increases of cost, suppose by
increasing the wages 10 per cent. the profit is increased
from 5 to 8¾ per cent., and the 10 per cent. increase
of wages corresponds to 3¾ per cent. on the capital ;
the concern might then put it to the hand-workers that
they would pay them their nominal wages, plus a quarter
of the profits.   This would be taken as a good example
of profit sharing.   It would be said that the firm made
5 per cent. before the change and kept it all, while, on
the profit sharing basis, they make 11¼ per cent. and
share it with their hand-workers, so as to give, roughly,
2¾ per cent. and keep 8½.   The demagogues would argue
that as the profits were all made by the men they should
get the whole of it, while less extreme opinion would
say that, as the hand-workers had increased the profits

from 5 to $11\frac{1}{4}$ per cent., they should have the whole of the increase.

But it is not properly a case of profit sharing at all. The hand-workers are not shareholders, and they take no risks beyond the loss of their extra pay. If the concern makes a loss they do not have to pay anything.

It is really only a kind of " make believe." The employers might just as well say : " If you will work harder, and be contented, and show *esprit de corps*, and enjoy your work, it will cost you nothing, and you will be happier ; and to induce that state of things, which will help us very much too, we will give you an increase of wages proportional to our profits. We will make more ourselves and will beat our rivals and increase our business." The root of the whole matter is that the hand-workers are doing more. If they do not do any more, in the case taken it merely means that the firm raises the wages to an amount that reduces their profits from 5 to $3\frac{1}{2}$ per cent. This means that instead of increasing the weekly pay roll from £100 to £110, it is increased to £105, a 5 per cent. increase of wages.

The concern that is experimenting on profit sharing is supposed to be in competition with a similar house working on ordinary lines. If the rival house makes 5 per cent., and the profit sharing concern $3\frac{3}{4}$ per cent., it is clear the profit sharing concern will eventually go out of business.

Giving a bonus, or a sum over and above their ordinary wages, the sum being in proportion to the profits of the firm is always called profit sharing ; but the expression is misleading. It is not effective from the employer's point of view unless the hand-workers do more per man than before, though they may do less per pound of wages paid. The benefit to the hand-workers is that in the particular firm that gives the bonus they get higher wages. True, they do more work, but that costs them nothing ; on the contrary it may make them dislike their work less, or even enjoy it. But the main effect is that they do not feel that the employers are making large profits out of their work, but they are getting at least some of their own back ; so they are much less discontented, and do not strike or call canny.

But this benefit can exist only as long as competitors do not take up the same system. If all the employers in a given business take up this system of paying bonuses proportional to the profits, they will compete until the actual profits taken by the employers is at the normal rate. This is the fate of all employers or capitalists. One makes an improvement of some sort, and he reaps the benefit only until his competitors imitate him, and adopt it too, or go ahead of him by adopting something better.

If the whole of a trade, say all the wool spinners, adopt the same system of so-called profit sharing, the interest on capital or profit comes down to the average in due course. The question is whether the hand-workers also come down to the ordinary level. If the hand-workers in the wool spinning trade are all making more than the corresponding hand-workers in other trades, these other hand-workers are in competition. The tendency is for the employers to reduce the rate plus the bonus to the normal level. At any time, when a hand-worker leaves or more are wanted, the employer has a number of applicants who are ready to work at the wages common for their degree of skill. They will, therefore, take the work willingly at a wage which, with the bonus, comes to the normal. This is assuming the extra output is neither pleasant nor unpleasant to the hand-worker. If it is somewhat unpleasant, as it probably is in the case now under discussion, the wages will tend to remain above the normal just to the extent that will balance the unpleasantness of the extra work.

Of course the trade union may try to keep the wages up ; that is another question altogether. How far a trade union can really create a sort of privilege in high wages that will be permanent is another question, which is quite separate from that of profit sharing. The trade unions, as unions, generally object to profit sharing. The members individually may prefer it, but they have no voice in the matter. The officials dislike it because it tends to make the men contented, and that outside the work of the officials. These like the men to be discontented, as that gives them something to trade upon, and grievances to foment.

It is not possible to make the hand-worker permanently better off by bonus payments, as population pressure brings the wages down to the lowest that will preserve the degree of comfort corresponding to the kind of work.

A somewhat anomalous case is that of public supply, for instance, of water, gas, or electrical energy. In this case the employer is not in competition with a similar concern. An electric supply company is in competition, not with other electric supply companies—as it has a monopoly of a district—but with gas, candles and oil for lighting, and gas and oil for powers above a kilowatt or two. In such a case, if the hand-workers get more than their market wages, that is to say more than others, equally good, are ready to replace them for, they form a privileged class. If the hand-workers in a public supply have the power of shutting down the supply whenever they like, and if when they do so, neither the company nor the public has any redress, and the public and the newspapers sympathise with them on the ground that they are fighting the capitalist and getting his nefarious profits out of him, while the government makes laws that give them special privileges because the politicians are afraid of losing the hand-workers' votes ; it may be good policy to pay more than market value for the sake of peace and steady working.

Apart from the mere question of costing the employers a little more, this bonus system or so-called profit sharing may have a much more important effect in making the hand-workers happier, and in removing discontent and envy.

People are fond of appealing to what they call justice in these matters. The idea is that the hand-workers make the profits for the owners. It is true that the owners could not make profits if there were no hand-workers, because there would be no output. It is equally

true that there would be no output if there were no purchasers of goods made ; but that does not show that it
is just that the purchasers should have the profits or any
part of them.   According to popular notions of justice,
a stronger case can be made out for the purchaser than
the hand-worker.   The works manager offers a man
£2 to do a certain piece of work.   He can get it
done for that price because many hand-workers are
willing and ready to do it for that sum.   He spends
£2 more on material, machinery, salaries of people
whose work is essential, and he allows £1 for the
capitalists, that being the market value of the use of the
capital.   The hand-worker is not compelled to do the
work, he can take his choice.   If his work is worth more
than £2 he can earn the higher wage elsewhere.   He
sells the work for £2 to please himself only.   The
materials are bought on the same lines ; if the seller
can get more elsewhere he is free to do so.   He sells
at the price to suit himself.   The salaried men are
in the same position, they are paid their market value,
and they give their services in return for payment that
it suits them to accept, and that they accept in their own
interests.   The capitalist get, on the average, the market
value of capital.   If he asks more, other capitalists
will put their money in and undersell him ; if he gets
less he stops supplying capital.

CHAPTER X

TRADE UNIONS

IN the eyes of the public a trade union is an organisation for arranging strikes ; but in fact it is formed with many objects, such as mutual insurance of its members against unemployment, against sickness, and to pay funeral expenses. A union may also be something in the way of a club, or a mutual improvement society.

The trade union is most important as an organisation for collective bargaining with employers as to wages, hours and conditions of working. The strike is the unionist leaders' idea of forcing their will on the employers.

We have to consider whether trade unions do get higher pay for their own hand-workers, whether they reduce the pay of other hand-workers, and if they do get higher pay, who loses or makes up the difference, and especially their effect in the long run when population has time to alter.

We also have to consider the various ways of arriving at, or trying to arrive at, desired results such as limiting output, limiting overtime, limiting piece-work and limiting the number of hand-workers in any trade, and, finally, the effects of strikes of various kinds.

The object of the trade union is really to get round the action of population pressure in each industry. It might be said that the final intention is to get round the action of population pressure in all industries. But the moving spirits in trade unions do not understand population pressure or elementary economics of any kind.

Our province is not so much to criticise either their motives or their knowledge, as to follow out, if we can, the effects of their policies and actions.

In a community in equilibrium in which there are no limitations, so that a hand-worker can change from one kind of work to another if he likes it better, or considers he will be better off, each hand-worker is paid his market value ; that is to say, he gets what he is worth, and no more and no less. The hard part of it is that what he is worth does not depend only on himself and his work, but also on the number of people competing with him. If a few men of great skill are wanted in a particular trade, they can get very much higher wages, until the prospect makes other men train themselves up and compete. The wages then gradually fall off until the men are in the degree of comfort that corresponds to that skill. This is, of course, presuming there are no trade unions. A trade union may be able to prevent the skilled man from earning more than a man of much less value, and in that case his skill is of no value to him, or to anyone else, if he may not use it. The community being in equilibrium, population pressure begins acting throughout the system, and produces the result that each hand-worker gets a wage which keeps each class just well enough off for existence, without falling lower in the scale. Each class is sending down a surplus to the classes below, and at the bottom is a submerged class with nothing to live for but the mere avoidance of death. This is an ordinary civilised community of to-day without labour restrictions of any sort. Each hand-worker gets his market value, or his fair share, or his deserts. It may sound extreme to call wages earned on this standard a man's fair share or his deserts or even the market value of his work. It is not a question of names, but of fact. Population pressure keeps wages down to certain values, and it is idle to say the poor hand-worker ought to have much higher wages. The trade unions step in and say they can procure higher wages.

We can examine their influence broadly, and in detail.

In our case of a community in equilibrium, everybody was producing something. If by some miraculous change everybody could go on producing as before,

and consuming very much more, the extra supply being
due to magic, an increase of population would take place,
and the population would grow until the old balance
was reached ; the only change in the long run being
that the given tract of land would be more highly
peopled with a community in the same state of misery
as before.

But the first miraculous change is not possible. If
the people instead were primitive and not civilised, so
that each family worked its own little plot, it is clear
that the consumption of each family could be increased
only by greater production. If the community is a
little more civilised, and those who have saved capital
enable others to work in a more efficient way, it is still
easy to see that an increase of general consumption
cannot take place without an increase of production.
But as soon as they deal with a civilised community
people get lost in the complications of it, and there are
visions of the State finding unlimited pay at the expense
of the rich, or from nowhere in particular, and of all
sorts of impossible sources of wealth. But it does not
seem very hard to realise that, even in a complicated
society, while production remains the same, general
consumption cannot be increased.

Treating the question broadly again from another
point of view ; it has already been explained how the
individuals in each class are in competition with those
in the same, or in an even class only, and not with
those in classes above or below them. The trade unions
are thus in competition first with similar trade unions,
if there are any, second with non-union workers in the
same industry, and third with workers on the same level
in other industries, whether they are in unions or not.
All these competitors may be in the same community,
but it must not be forgotten that there is certain competition with similar classes in other communities or
foreign countries.

Treating the questions in detail we may revert to
the case of the two laundry companies. Suppose the
market value of the workers is £1 a week, and each

laundry pays £1 a week as wages to each of the hands. For one laundry a union is started. If it includes a proportion of the hands it has not much power. Even a portion of the hands may cause loss by striking, and has more power than if the individuals acted independently. But the union may persuade the majority to join for their benefit, and may threaten to strike unless the non-union hands are thrown out. We will therefore assume that all the hands in one laundry are unionists, while none of those in the rival concern is. The union thinks the wages can be raised 10 per cent., say from twenty to twenty-two shillings a week. These amounts may be wrong for a laundry, but that does not matter. We may assume for simplicity, though that may also be inaccurate, that the year's wages total up to a sum equal to half the capital of the company, and that the company generally pays 5 per cent. In that case a permanent increase of wages, with the same selling price, mops up all the profits. The laundry cannot raise its prices, because the other laundry will undersell it and get all the business. If it refuses the rise in wages the hands will go on strike. The hands probably think that out of every £1 they earn, the company unrighteously makes anything from £1 upwards ; but the fact is that in this case the company's direct loss by stoppage is the profit, namely, about two shillings per pound wages, and the overhead expenses, which are much higher, and are not understood at all by the hands. But the real difficulty is loss of business which will not return. The laundry may refuse the rise, and the strike take place and go on for, say, six weeks. At the end of that time the increase is granted, but the hands have sacrificed £6 each in pay. This has been paid out of the union's savings. But the administration will have cost say £2, so that each hand has lost £8. An increase of pay of two shillings a week will take eighty weeks to repay this ; so with the six weeks of strike the hands do not begin their increase for nearly two years. This is assuming the laundry's trade has not been injured. If the laundry's trade can stand the strike, it must have been in a rising condition, and the demand for more hands would have raised wages automatically. If the strikers have to give in, they have lost £8 each, and the laundry has an injured business which is less likely than before to be able to pay high wages. The result of the strike is in all cases bad. It is loss of money to hands and employers, and that cannot lead to better wages. The only people who benefit are the union officials. They are the movers and instigators, and their positions will be discussed presently.

If we look at the position again at the moment when the union has demanded higher wages, and the manager has to decide, he may consider the hands' conditions sympathetically or he may think only of his company. It makes little difference. He may decide to hold out, on the ground that the wages demanded cannot be paid without injury or death to the company ; or he may conclude that if he gives in, his rivals will soon find their hands demand more wages too. He is in competition with the rival laundries, not with his hands, and a general rise of laundry wages is of little or no importance to him. If he is right, and his grant of increased wages brings on a similar demand in rival concerns, it shows that wages were below the market value. The commercial world is never in equilibrium ; there are continual risings and fallings. A new local industry which wants hands of the same type as laundry hands will make the supply of hand-labour scarce, and a strike is then likely to be successful ; but without a strike the laundries would find it necessary to raise wages to keep their hands.

The union is clearly in competition with the non-union hands, and the great struggle is to swallow up the enemy by getting all the laundry hands into the union. A demand for higher wages is then much more likely to be granted, as it is made in the rival laundries, so that both give increases, and both then charge the consumer more. The capitalists who own the laundries are not directly, or at once, affected. Indirectly, in a short time they may find that customers send less and their business goes down. This means a gradual dismissal of hands until a large proportion of the union is out of work. These hands drift off into other work and drop out of the union. The union, if successful, ends in being a small body of hand-workers having higher wages than they would otherwise have, in a restricted industry.

The laundry, though simple, is not quite a typical instance.

Take the case of bootmakers. Before there is any union there are boot factories mainly in two or three towns, and there are hands of various degrees of skill doing various kinds of work, and wages are fairly settled. Sometimes when business is brisk there is an extra demand for boots which makes a general rise in wages necessary to prevent hands leaving ; at other times there are falls in wages and some unemployment. On the average, of course, the average wages are paid. Suppose a " bootmakers' " union is formed which includes all the " bootmakers," that is to say, all the boot hand-workers. The obvious course of the union would be to limit the numbers so that there is always a shortage of hands. This would be a sort of local counteraction of population pressure. Obvious as this point is, comparatively few unions try to limit the numbers in their trade, and when they do, they are apt to work rather in the dark. The Bar is in a sense a trade union, and it is run by highly educated people for their own benefit ; but as there is no limit in the number of barristers, competition brings the average income down very low. Medicine is another trade union in which the membership is not limited in number. Many groups like accountants, barristers, doctors, parsons, patent-agents, plumbers and solicitors attempt to keep down their numbers by qualifying examinations, but that is all. Many trade unions have rules limiting the number of apprentices in proportion to the journeyman. This is like trying to regulate population by settling how many children, on the average, people may have. If the number chosen is too low the population dies out, if too high it increases —in time—without limit.

Suppose our union formed. They would probably call themselves the " Bootmakers' Union," with the idea that they are the bootmakers, just as the hand-workers in machinery and structural work call themselves engineers. This is not merely a casual error, it is that fitters, turners and so on think they are engineers. They have no idea that anything but capital and their work is involved, and the class of intellect ranging from Watt, or Kelvin, down to the youngest draughtsman is to them nothing, and this error misleads them rather seriously. Suppose the bootmakers' union, consisting of 95 per cent. of the hand-workers, demands a rise and the removal of the 5 per cent. of non-union hands, and gets what it wants, the various makers of boots then raise their prices, so that the return on their capital is normal, for, as already explained, the rise of wages cannot be paid by reduction of interest on capital, or of profits, because any general reduction of profit means a fall in the supply of capital. The extra wages do not come out of the capitalist but out of the buyers of boots and shoes. As everybody uses them, and as the hand-working class forms the great majority, this means that the extra wages come out of the pockets of the hand-workers themselves, including the bootmakers' union. This is just one of the examples of the law that the members of each class are in competition with one another, and not with the members of other higher or lower classes.

The union may argue that there is only a certain definite amount of work to be done, and therefore if each does half as much work, there will be employment for twice as many people ; so that there is room for a union double the size with double the income, and corresponding gain for those that run it.

In bootmaking this particular notion is not easily put in practice, because each man runs a machine. If he ran the machine intermittently so as to give half the output, the employers could not put down a double allowance of machines with a double allowance of men to get the old output. But suppose the union started on their campaign and limited the output of boots and shoes. The wages paid per boot would rise, and the cost per boot owing to the overhead charges would go up more in proportion ; but again the extra cost would not come out of the firm, but out of the public, that is, out of the hand-working classes. In fact a curious result would take place, the factories would make abnormal profits. The demand for boots and shoes is nearly constant, and very insistent, so that a short supply means very great increase of price ; much greater increase of price than that due to the extra cost of manufacture. A sudden restriction of output can thus increase the manufacturers' profits enormously for a time. The natural result is that boots and shoes are imported from other countries. In discussing the subject we may as well assume that other countries have similar trade unions in the boot and shoe trade ; so that the trade union has its way. The increase of demand, giving capital higher interest, will bring more capital into the industry until profits have fallen. There will also be a smaller consumption of boots and shoes. People will wear them out more completely, will have them re-soled and re-heeled more often, and will adopt rubber soles and heels. The final result is that the union becomes a set of hand-workers who are getting more than their market value and are doing less than normal work ; and all this not at the expense of capitalists, nor of the rich, but of the community generally, consisting mainly of hand-workers like themselves. This is still on the assumption that the union limits the number of people permitted by them to enjoy the privilege of working at boots for their living, and it assumes that such power is left in the hands of the union by the law of the land. This is not so ridiculous as it sounds. The union and the public who are paying extra for boots both consider that the extra pay of the union men comes out of the employers' capitalist pockets, and will back the union up in public opinion, and newspaper articles. The government will be controlled by the voters, and the union officials will make the government fear their organised vote. But much more than this, the other hand-workers who are paying high prices for their boots will object strongly to anything being done to render the action of the union illegal ; for they think' the union is making money out of the capitalist, and any law that prevents them relieving the capitalist of his wealth will prevent the other hand-workers from getting what they consider their fair pay, out of their own capitalists' pockets.

We may consider the case of the whole country in which all the trades are in the hands of unions in this way. The first point is that as each union limits the number of its members so that fewer are employed than the trade demands, there are a number of compulsory idlers corresponding to each trade. Chance of work is a monopoly in the hands of a portion of the hand-working class ; the outsiders being not only denied the " right to work " whatever that means, but being denied permission to work by their fellows. The men in unions will be well off, and will marry earlier and have more children, and a few of the children only will get into the unions, the rest being prevented from earning their bread. The result, as far as it is imaginable at all, would be a country in which the population consisted of a small percentage of " well-to-do " people ; a large percentage, say half, of hand-workers and their families, and a large number, perhaps nearly half, of the hand-workers who were non-union, and therefore were forbidden to work for wages. As the production of the country as a whole is less, because the unions limit output, and the union people get all the wages and consume more in proportion to their earnings than the normal, how can the country support all the non-union people? The load cannot be laid on the rich, because they would get poor in a very short time under such a drain. The capitalists could not be made to pay, because capital is always being used up, and replenished by savings, and people will not save unless they get interest. It might be argued that the change might be made very gradually, so that there would never be a number of starving non-unionists. There would be no poor-law, no charity, and no system of State support for the idle, and in that case there would be no idle. It is not that they would exist and starve ; but that they would not exist. But this would mean that the happy hand-workers in their various unions must not multiply ; they must keep the unions less in number by birth regulations. But then you merely have a community in which the law of population is more or less understood, and the unions as such are of no moment. A community in which the members keep the numbers down so that life is easy is thinkable ; but that is a question of birth control, not of trade unions, and is discussed in its proper place.

The bootmaking trade was taken as it employed skilled or fairly highly-skilled hands. Consider such a case as a large class of hand-labourers. A union is formed which includes the majority of the men who happen at a particular time to be employed in a particular but large branch of unskilled labour. They choose the moment when it will put their own and other dependent industries to the greatest possible loss, and strike for higher wages, and get them. When the crisis is over, the wages remain high because the employers cannot reduce them without facing the loss by another strike. If the union is strong and spread over the country, the employers do not mind at first, because they must increase their prices and similar concerns cannot undersell, because their wages are increased to match. The cost of the increase of wages falls on the public ; that is, mainly on the hand-workers themselves generally. In the long run, of course, foreign competition may come in, but if there are corresponding unions abroad, they stop their countries getting any benefits. After some time, if the labourers go on getting steady work and higher wages, it will be said that the action of the union has been splendid ; it has improved the conditions of the workers enormously. But steady, well-paid work attracts a better class of man, so how can it be assumed that the original hand-labourer is any better off at all? The chances are that nearly all the original members of the union are out of it, probably

out of work, too, and the union really consists of a
different set of men altogether, called by the same name.

Whether a trade union, however powerful, can really
raise wages, that is, maintain them above the market
level permanently is very doubtful. The union must be
so strong that it can keep out any men who offer to
work at market rates, and it must have some way of
keeping down its own membership. How is it to settle
the numbers of its members? If the rule is that no one
can join the union unless he is doing union work, it must
be possible for non-union men to compete, and in that
case the wages will be brought down. If no one who is
not already a union man may work, it must take in men
who are not working. In that case numbers will join to get
out-of-work pay, and the extra wages will all disappear.
If it gives no out-of-work pay in these cases, they will
still have a union too large for the work, and the out-of-
work members must get other work, perhaps by joining
another union at the same time. If these difficulties
are solved, as they probably are in fact, another arises
owing to variations of work. In a busy season with a
lot of work the employers will naturally not put up with
a mere flat rate output, and will want more hands.
These presumably join the union. When the rush is off,
the union is too large for the work.

The only way a union can help its members is by
limitation of supply of hands. It must counteract population pressure by some opposing force which limits the
supply. But if successful it would be at the expense of
the hand-workers. Thus, if in a community a small
number of wage-earners can, by some sort of combination backed up by public opinion, which is ignorant of
the real working of the scheme, secure more pay than
their market value without the combination, the final
net result is a community subscribing to make a small
number of their body better off. This makes it harder
for the rest of the people to live, and automatically reduces the number of the community. The community
is on the whole slightly less efficient, and can thus not
support itself so well.

There are a number of cases in which a body of hand-workers has the power of holding the community more or less to ransom. Thus on board an Atlantic liner the wireless operator might not only refuse to send or receive ordinary telegrams, he might threaten to send out distress or other harmful messages unless he was promised a thousand pounds. Or those in control of the engines might refuse to run the machinery unless they had increased pay, shorter hours, and part control of the navigation of the vessel. In such cases the rest of the ships' company and passengers do not discuss the justice of the matter on the lines that as the ship is carrying a million in bullion to America, this must be partly the property of the operator or the engine staff, as the coal is supposed partly to belong to the miners. Neither do they consider whether the operator gets what makes him comfortable in the abstract, or whether the engine men have wives and families. In connection with the sea it has always been recognised that a man is offered a certain piece of work for a certain pay. He can take it or leave it. If he takes it he carries it out, and if he refuses to do his work, choosing a time when he has, for the moment, power in his hands, it is mutiny and he is severely punished. This is only common sense. Almost anybody is able to see that a ship cannot be run on lines which allow anybody on board to hold the whole of the rest up, or to put them all in great danger unless his personal wishes are met. It is generally realised that a ship cannot be successfully navigated or worked on political principles, according to which everything is left to committees of the biggest talkers on board. It is not suggested that autocratic ship-government is perfect ; there are many cases of grossly and cruelly abused power. Still less is this system of discipline suggested as being suitable for a country. It would then have the further disadvantage of being controlled by nothing corresponding to the laws of the country which apply on board ship. But it is suggested that a system according to which anyone on board ship could hold the rest of those on board to ransom when-

ever he likes is just as absurd on land and infinitely
more dangerous. Yet this is very much the way things
go on. A railway company wants signalmen. An offer
is made of so much a week for doing certain work. The
signalman may take the job or leave it ; he is not compelled to take it. He takes it, and in concert with a
number of other signalmen, he says he will stop work on
a certain date unless he gets some concession which he
did not ask for on taking the place. It is not even a
question between the signalman and his employer. The
newspapers discuss the matter, and point out that the
signalman has a hard life, and it would be very nice if
he had a thousand a year and a seat on the board. It is
urged that the railway company is a large concern with
a capital of many millions, so it can easily pay the,
signalman above market values without feeling it. Then
an arbitration board is set to work, and its business is
to settle what wages and hours the signalman ought to
have. The consideration of what the man's work is
worth is left out of account altogether. The vital questions are: " What is a good wage for the man to live
upon, having regard to the high cost of living due to
other people shirking? How much profit ought the railway to be making, and to what proportion of this has the
signalman a right? What are other hands in other
branches of railway work paid, and how far is their work
similar? " There is a fundamental assumption that the
man is permanently and necessarily a signalman, as if
a signalman was a special kind of organism. Being a
signalman he is constrained always to be a signalman.
If he gets low pay he has no redress. If the railway cut
down the signalman's wage to a quarter it is assumed
the signalman would have to go on till he starves, being
quite unable to leave the railway service and do anything
else. It is quite true that anyone who has been a signalman for many years may be a very good signalman, and
cannot easily get work elsewhere. But if the railway
does not treat signalmen fairly, a small proportion leaving, or a reduction of new men to replace those leaving
by superannuation, will force them to change their ways.

The railway signalman's lot is not easy. He has work needing continual attention, and involving enormous responsibility, and it is monotonous and tiring. Everyone would like him, and everybody else for that matter, to be paid well for his work. But population pressure provides that there are so many men who want the work that the market value of this, like other work, is not nearly as high as we would like it to be. But giving the signalman power to get his wages increased at the expense of the community by striking and holding transport up is no cure.

The miners case is even more ridiculous. A man need not be a miner unless he likes. If he thinks the life is the best he can get with his abilities he can have it ; if he thinks he can do better, any other course is free to him. But now it is generally assumed that anyone who chooses to be a miner is to have special privileges. He becomes part owner of the coal he sends up. He has wages settled by arbitrations, coal commissions, politicians, or the government, and the wages have nothing at all to do with the value of his work. They depend on the selling price of coal, on the real or supposed profits of the coal owners, or mining companies, on every man's right to live comfortably whatever he does in return, and an appeal to the goddess of Justice. This lady may be pictured as being clothed in daily newspapers, endowed with the sheep-mind of the crowd ; her eyes wide open looking for the most popular course. That any one set of hand-workers should be able to hold up the industry of the country, on any pretence whatever, seems odd, as one would expect the multitude of hand-workers who suffer would cry out, and the law of the land would protect them. But though, for example, the steel and iron workers suffer when there is a coal strike, and the poor men and women in the potteries are starving, they think the trouble is due to the capitalists, and they sympathise with the strikers and often subscribe to help them with the foolish idea that they are getting their own back from the capitalists. This sounds rather insulting to the intelligence of the hand-workers who form the unions, but it must be borne in mind that the hand-workers, especially the North Country miners, as a whole are much more intelligent than their unions, just as the country is much more intelligent than its government.

The members of a union who go out on a sympathetic strike face great privation out of an almost purely unselfish desire to help another union against the capitalist. Their action may be foolish, but it is very fine, all the same.

The trade union is run by its officials and leaders, and the type is worth study. One type of labour leader often begins as a street preacher. Now an uninformed man with the upbringing of a hand-worker cannot seriously believe that he has any exclusive knowledge that it is his duty to impart by preaching in the street. If he were religious he could attend as a humble and undistinguished member of his local chapel. But this does not suit him. Excessive vanity and conceit drive him to street preaching as he is then much more distinguished. After a time he finds his mouth. He then sees there is a much more popular field for him as a street speaker, and that he can get a crowd of admiring listeners if he makes out that they are all being robbed by capitalists, and goes on to show how he can put things right for them. This type is particularly harmful. In his street preaching he is relying on what he considers facts or truths without any power of weighing them, or any wish to do so. He is in the habit of making all sorts of authoritative statements, not only about the unknowable, but about things that better informed people do know. When he becomes a demagogue he still draws on his wholly ignorant imagination for his facts, and depends on the prejudice, sentimentalism and misinformed emotionalism of a crowd, and that of a very poor type, for his success. He gets into official position in his union. He is ambitious. He wants to make orations to thousands of hand-workers, to be a great power in his union, and eventually to be a " Labour " member in Parliament. His union is really his ladder. He may be, and most

likely he is, sincere ; but somehow everybody is sincere
about opinions which help him on in life. His real
object, perhaps unrealised by himself, is to be a big
trade union secretary, or a leading labour member in
Parliament. But though the politicians treat him as a
kind of workman-statesman, and ministers hold confer-
ence with him, and the papers discuss his policy
seriously, and the hand-workers regard him as their hero,
he is still an ignorant little street preacher, with the same
colossal ignorance of the effects of his proposals, and he
is still guided entirely by his own vanity. It is often
remarked that the wildest labour demagogue becomes
staid and moderate when he gets into Parliament. It
may be that the members of Parliament have such extensive and ample knowledge of all sociological matters,
and such profound grasp of all the intricacies of
economic science that the air they breathe out is so
saturated with godlike wisdom that even a demagogue
is exhilarated and cured by the change. It is possible,
however, that the demagogue is just what he was before,
a very ignorant, incompetent and dangerous person,
entirely out of place ; but that he remains quiet because
he has got what he wanted, and would like to keep it.
Even a prime minister who fomented class hatred to
get into power, lapses back into a demagogue whenever it
makes him more popular for the moment. The successful
demagogue always has to keep up his position, and this
is not easy, because as you look down the union ladder
there are more and more demagogues all struggling to
get up and oust the demagogues above them, and the
lower you go the more irresponsible and extreme are
they. They are also younger and more energetic and
rasher, and at least as ignorant. Once a man has made
a reputation, however, he is at a great disadvantage in
keeping his position. The trade union leader is really
a man of immense importance now. It is a curious fact
that, generally speaking, a public man's importance is
measured entirely by his power of doing mischief, not by
his ability, or his wish to do good. The malign bacillus
that lives upon the festering sores it itself causes at any

rate is not so low as to fatten upon its own kind. It is not insincere. Unless a man's system is out of order, the disease germ cannot flourish. The labour leader, the limehouser or the socialist exists only because socially we are ill.

We have only to imagine the trade union programmes carried out to see their absurdity and realise the harm they do. Take first a community in which all handworkers get their market rate of wages. It is not a happy community, because there is no realisation of the effects of population pressure, and the struggle for life is as keen as it well can be. There are miseries due to poor laws, charity, and the " four gray ladies " Want, Vice, Care and Misery. These are common to both systems. Now imagine the trade unions have had part of their way. Certain activities such as coal-mining, railways, electric and gas supply, as well as posts and telegraphs are under government, and government is controlled by hand-workers who, with no knowledge of economics, do whatever they think will help their own class and hurt all the other classes. A trade union must not be confused with its members. Its members have no real power, it is run by its officials for their own benefit, just as governments are run by politicians. All the hand-workers in government employment get wages which do not depend at all on the work they do, or its value, but on what they think they would like, or what the newspapers think is just. This figure may be anything, say £300 a year each at the pre-war value of currency. The government hand-workers are thus a privileged class. Every hand-worker in the country will want to become a government hand ; how are they to be selected? They must select either the best or the worst, or leave the settlement to jobbing. If they select the best, the first question is whether existing handworkers are to be replaced by better men as the better men offer. The trade unionist would probably say " No." The existing men have the right to work and the right to £300 a year. As they retire or die off new candidates will apply, and they will include much better

men, men in fact who could easily earn much more than
£300 by hard work and taking risks, and who much prefer
to make £300 a year easily with an assured future, and
probably retiring pensions and all sorts of nice things. The
result will be that though the government hand-workers
will be called by the same name as before they will in
fact be people belonging naturally to higher classes, able
to do much better work, and the class that began as government hand-workers will be moved out and excluded
from government work. The third system by which
neither the best or the worst are chosen, means that the
choice will go by favour, and those will be given work at
abnormal wages who have friends in government positions, or who will vote for those in power at the time.
This is simple corruption.

But the impossibility of deciding fairly who are to
enter the privileged circle of highly paid employment is
after all only a detail. When the trade unions have
secured high wages in all government work, the money
being paid by that inexhaustible source of wealth, the
State, the other unions such as the hands in engineers'
works, the steel and iron makers' hands, in fact, all the
hand-workers that can form unions, will demand wages
comparable with £300 a year. The unionists will say :
" Let them have it." Now it is not a question of how
much money the hand-workers are to have. We have
nothing to do with a high cost of living such as that
due to the politicians' debasement of the currency during
and after the war. The point is that the government
hand-workers are to have more and better food, better
quarters, and better living generally. In short, they are
to consume more. But nobody is to produce more,
in fact, if hours are shortened, all the hand-workers are
to produce less. It does not need any deep insight to
realise that the members of a community cannot consume more unless they produce it. The unionist has,
no doubt, some idea that the State can conjure an
unlimited supply of food, clothes, houses, picture-palaces
and what not out of the idle rich, or, at any rate, out
of the rich.

It will be urged that trade unions have, in fact, raised wages. It must be remembered that the value of money has been going down in an irregular sort of way during the times modern unions have existed, so that wages generally have gone up wherever the degree of comfort has been maintained. It is, of course, possible that the trade unions in some cases have educated their members to rise to a higher degree of comfort, and thus to command higher wages. This is very doubtful and outside the present discussion.

The trade unions have two main effects, one physical, and the other, which is much more important, mental.

If we imagine two communities precisely alike, with people all obtaining the market value for their work, and in one trade unions are organised, so that there is discontent and strikes, it will differ in the points that the hand-workers produce less and are off work, striking a certain percentage of their time. The works are therefore run, to some extent, intermittently and uneconomically. If we imagine that the communities are isolated so that there is no competition, the net result will be that the community with the union and strikes will shrink in number, as the land cannot support the population. The population will gradually decline until the increasing return of the resources of the country balances the reduced efficiency of the population. This is not a matter of any importance if there is no foreign competition. If there is, the union community will be much less able to compete. But the real evil of the trade unions is their effect not on the material position of the hand-workers, but on their happiness. It is what newspapers call the psychological effect that is so pernicious. We can imagine a case where the hand-workers, however poorly off, realise that their condition is not due to their being robbed or ill-treated by their employers. They may be proud of their work, taking interest in it and all its details. A bright skilled man can get a great deal of genuine happiness out of doing a really good bit of work. Many of us can remember the old school of millwrights. A millwright was a very skilled fitter, capable of doing wonders with a hammer and chisel, some files and a few other tools. He not only did his work, but he planned it and decided how it was to be done, and was ready to deal with any emergency on his own initiative. The engine-room staff on a modern steamship, making a difficult repair at sea, have a singular satisfaction in their work. But if men have it continually dinned into their ears that they are always being robbed of a large share of their dues, and that everything they do helps their natural enemies, and that the less work they do the longer it will hold out, and if each is persuaded that if he does good work he is injuring his less competent fellows by going ahead of them, there is no happiness to be got out of the day's work. The future looks very drab for another reason. Division of labour is being carried so far, and automatic machinery is coming into such general use, that the skilled hand-worker is getting less and less opening, and what is called mass-production means that a very few skilled men are needed for making some of the producing machines, or the tools for making these machines, but the majority of the work will be done by what is called unskilled labour. What hope is there for hand-workers, where a man does one little bit of work, involving a certain number of bodily movements, over and over again for so many hours a week? Take, for instance, the life of the man with the " grease-gun," whose work is to stand with a sort of oil squirt and lubricate each of procession of cars passing out of a large American factory.

It is not only in engineers' factories that work is getting monotonous, easy and uninteresting. In practically every branch of industry similar changes are taking place. The hand-workers day's work is getting more and more monotonous, and less and less interesting. What we want therefore is that he should enjoy exercising his faculties in making many pieces of work go through his hands, with the best workmanship. Those who have done such work in their young days, as many of us have, know that it is quite interesting to see how many bolts can be turned out in a day on a capstan lathe, and that there is room for study in the arrangement of the tools, in getting the best angles for their cutting edges and so on. But if his trade union makes him believe that the fewer pieces of work he does, the better for him and his fellows ; and the worse the work done the more repair work there will be ; and that all his work is really putting unearned money into the pockets of his enemies the employers, there is nothing in his day's work that he can enjoy. Trades union officials deny that they have any policy of ca' canny,' but their denials cannot be accepted. The basic fallacy of ca' canny is really quite wide. It is that employment is in itself good, and not merely the means of production. In old days and even now, machinery is disliked because it is supposed to lessen employment. Many people advocate hampering foreign trade because they think the restriction increases employment at home.

Trade unions also spread the doctrine that a good workman should not work well or especially fast, because he is then setting the pace for the bad workman who cannot keep up with him. The idea is that all men doing the same kind of work should get the same pay, and that it should be high pay. Consider a class of hand-worker such as a particular kind of bricklayer, whose union insists that the number of bricks laid by each man shall be such that the least competent can lay them easily. As already pointed out, the trade union will try to make the bricklayers a privileged class, earning more than they are worth, at the expense of the capitalists. Any extra wages they can command temporarily, however, do not come out of the capitalists specially, but out of the public in general, including the hand-working classes. But as a trade union has not any power of creating a permanently privileged class, the wages of the bricklayers will come to the level at which it just pays to employ them, that is to say, they will be paid according to the value of their work. As they are all doing the same work and getting the same wages, and the work is that of the worst among them, they will all get the pay of very bad workmen.

Trade unions, though intended to do good to their members, do nothing of the sort as far as raising their wages is concerned. A trade union is really a combination of hand-workers intended to secure higher wages than the market-value at the expense of the capitalists. In so far as it succeeds in getting them, the extra wages come out of the consumers, who are mostly hand-workers. The higher wages throw a number out of work, and they live on out-of-work pay and doles, that is to say, on the other workers. Strikes must in their nature be ineffective, because it is impossible to raise wages generally while things cost the same, as that means greater general consumption with the same production. Occasionally an individual strike is effective, but only temporarily, and the idle time reduces the average wage of the striker. A strike in one trade throws hand-workers out of employment in other trades. The general effect of trade unions is to make the hand-workers, on the whole, less productive, and in the long run this means that it enables industry to support fewer people. Their chief evil is that they foment discontent and cause unhappiness.

CHAPTER XI

THE RAID ON WEALTH

ENVY is a very natural kind of vice. If one makes a certain income and has a certain position among the people in the neighbourhood, it is easy to say that it does not hurt one in the least if others are richer. That is not true. Each one of us feels if other people are richer they do not deserve to be, as they are certainly not better or more able. If the rich people are hereditary peers, or even have inherited their wealth from heads of well-known firms, it is less objectionable ; but there is a tacit understanding that they are not really superior, merely fortunate. That is one reason why the House of Lords is long lived. When a peer is put into a position over a commoner's head, it is acquiesced in, because he was born a peer, and there is therefore no aspersion on the unsuccessful commoner. If two commoners are struggling for a position, each would much rather a peer got it than his rival. The same type of envy and jealousy is naturally more acute the lower down we go in society. The poor man feels a much greater difference between his lot and what he fancies is the lot of the rich, and he is in addition told on all sides that he is the victim of gross injustice, and has been robbed. But the same sort of feeling comes in as has been mentioned as to peers. The poorer classes are chiefly jealous of the small tradesman, or the lower middle classes, and not of the upper middle classes, or " real gentry." This may be partly because envy is wanting not to be in another man's shoes, but to have his advantages added to one's own. It is easier for a poor man to form a picture of himself, with the good things of the life of the class a little above him added to his own, than to imagine himself with the advantages of a duke added to his weekly wages.

Moreover, the people in the class just above him are more like him in manners and outlook, and he feels that they are of his own kind, and this increases his jealousy. Almost everybody is envious and jealous. This does not prevent people getting rich, as we all rather like to be envied, or, at any rate, we like to get rich in spite of any envy it causes.

The main result of envy is that it creates a whole train of fallacies which are very harmful, directly in putting obstacles in the way of development, and still more indirectly by creating a great deal of quite unnecessary unhappiness.

One notion is that there is a certain amount of money in the world, or in the country. This is thought of in a confused way*; sometimes money means current coin, sometimes wealth. This money is unevenly distributed, and the idea is that as the rich have practically all the money, and the poor almost none, the rich have robbed the poor of it, or, at any rate, have somehow got it out of the poor. This idea is akin to the notion that manufacturers make profits at the expense of wage-earners.

It is generally realised that anyone in humble circumstances gets money in return for value given. A bargain is struck between him and his neighbour by which he parts with something or renders a certain service for a certain sum of money. The bargain must be good for both, or it would not be made. To the man the money is more valuable than the service, or the goods*; by the neighbour the services or goods are more prized than the money. The bargain is thus for the good of both parties to it, as far as the man who gets the money goes, he has given the community a trifle more than the value of the money to the community. This is a general rule which applies to all grades of society. When a man makes money he gives the community a little more than he gets. This principle is obscured by people's jealousy, envy and vanity. The invariable answer takes the form of the question : How about the company promoter, the city shark, and the war profiteer? The idea is that most very rich people have made their money dishonestly, and this notion is held largely by even fairly well-informed people, who ought to know much better. The man who makes a thousand a year by working hard at his profession sees a friend making ten thousand a year in the city. His friend seems to have no special ability, and he does not seem to work very hard. Vanity says that the friend is really rather inferior, and jealousy and envy come in, and the obvious and comforting conclusion is reached that the friend is either singularly lucky or he is dishonest. In either case he is making a large income at the expense of the community, including, of course, the poor. There is another friend, who owns and runs a factory for making umbrellas. He also makes a great deal of money. He is really a very good works-manager. He treats his hand-workers well and justly. They like him and work well, and he respects them and pays them well. The works are organised so that his men are never wasting their energies, there is every convenience for handling the material and turning out the goods by mass production. He is a keen buyer of raw material, as he is quite an expert in silk textiles, and he knows all about the material for handles and where to get the best frames at reasonable prices. He is methodical, and pays promptly, and sells only to those who are prompt. He knows how to pack his goods attractively, and he watches the changes of taste in umbrella handles, and actually leads it, so that he is always first in with the latest notions. He knows just when to change the fashion of handles from a bird's head to an organ-stop-knob. He thus makes a very good thing of his business, while every bit of money he earns is in return for services to the community. But when he comes home in the evening, he smokes, reads his trade paper or a novel, and plays golf and some bridge, both badly. He can talk about nothing but umbrellas and politics, and has no taste for any literature or art. He is looked down upon by the professional man, whose vanity says that his umbrella maker, being so inferior, can make all his money in only one way. He sweats his workmen, and he foists bad umbrellas on the public.

The popular idea of a company promoter is that he gets out and advertises a prospectus that is full of plausible lies, and bribes a few men of apparently respectable position to pose as directors. The shares are then subscribed for by poor and innocent country parsons and indigent old ladies. The capital finds its way into the promoter's pocket, and he presently starts another bogus company, and goes on until he is as rich as he wants to be. He then retires, and figures largely in local charity lists, and is finally buried under a beautiful marble monument. It never occurs to people that if company promoting were anything like this, there would be so much competition in the profession that there would be little to go round. A company promoter has, in fact, to be an exceedingly able man, with a great deal of practical and a very useful kind of knowledge and experience. If he is dishonest, the law generally gets hold of him, as company law is very searching. The amount the promoter gets can generally be gathered from the prospectus. The class of directors, generally known as guinea pigs, often peers, or soldiers, are generally ignorant and incompetent ; they are not fraudulent. The capital in limited companies is generally subscribed by hard business men, who are under the common delusion that because they make money easily (to them) in their own business, their money will earn big dividends for them in other ventures. The average limited company gets into liquidation in due course, but the capital does not go into the pockets of the promoters or the directors. It is generally nearly all spent more or less directly in wages for making what turns out to be not worth the cost, and probably most of the money goes as payment to hand-workers. It is not suggested that the payment of hand-workers for making useless products is good. The point is that companies as a rule do not make money for the rich out of the poor in any way, they are more generally machinery for wasting the money of the well-to-do in payment of wages for useless work.

The city shark is difficult to discuss, because the term is more or less indefinite. He is generally supposed to make great sums by buying shares in useless concerns cheap, and selling them at great profits to foolish young men who like to dabble on the stock exchange. But that sort of dealing is not making money out of the poor, it is making it out of fairly affluent fools, who become less affluent and less foolish. But the supply of this kind of fool is too small to feed enough sharks to count.

There is no one more scorned than the profiteer. He is always pictured as a fat and vulgar man with a silk hat on the back of his head. He is largely a political creation. The government, during and after the war, debased its currency to about half its pre-war value. To the public who do not understand currency, as political economy is entirely beyond their ken, this is simply high prices. The government also interfered with equilibrium by all sorts of controls devised without any reference to their economic effects, and thus put up the prices of many goods still further. The profiteer was invented as an explanation of high prices, that took the blame off the government. The idea created was that the sellers of all goods were putting up the prices and taking enormous profits. Why a war should enable them to defy the competition of their rivals in a way that was impossible in peace was never explained. The war created keen demand for some goods, which immediately became valuable and reduced the value of others. The sort of thing that happened was that an ironmonger who had a pre-war kettle marked half a crown in 1914, would re-mark it five shillings in 1918, and someone to whom it was worth something more than five shillings, or she would not have bought it, would hail the unfortunate ironmonger before a profiteering committee, and he would be fined with much obloquy. Another ironmonger, who had no pre-war stock, would buy some kettles from a wholesale house at a figure which would enable him to sell at seven shillings at the lowest, kettles being scarce. He would not be profiteering. The first man really sold at a low price, as money was half its value. When " prices went up " he was expected to sell stock at its pre-war nominal value, but when prices go down the second ironmonger must not charge seven shillings, he must charge half a crown and go bankrupt.

Take a larger instance. It is decided by government to send coal to France, and let the French have it for £2 a ton. There is a coal famine, and the demand is so great that consumers will pay up to £5 a ton for it. There is no way of finding who the consumers would be that would absorb the delivery of coal if it were sold by auction, or what the average price would be, though it would obviously be much over £2. The result is that it is bought for £2 a ton and sold for £5 and there is an outcry about profiteering. Again, if there is a great demand for coal in the country, and the miners either limit the output, or the output is small for any reason, the demand will soar a long way above the extra cost of even extravagant miners' wages. The coal consumers are then willing to pay abnormal prices, and either the coal companies or the middleman must make enormous profits. They cannot help it. The government may step in and seize these profits. But if it is profiteering when it goes into private pockets, it is no less profiteering when the government commandeers the profits. The interference of the government without economic knowledge in the matter of all sorts of controls impoverished many people, ruined others and enriched a smaller but more observable minority. But all this was not robbing of the poor by the rich. It was alteration of values by the war which enriched some and impoverished more, and the unevenness was accentuated by ignorant interference in the way of fixed prices and all sorts of controls. Controls of prices must be distinguished from rationing. Rationing was fundamentally a wise and humane measure.

All these cases, most of them quite trivial, have been

discussed because they represent the ordinary popular notions of those who are supposed to be reasonably thoughtful and fairly well informed. It is on such notions that is based the general idea that the rich are rich at the expense of the poor. The poor are generally taught that the rich are rich by robbing the poor ; as we go up, the idea changes gradually into the milder form, that the rich are so at the expense of the poor. The broad truth is that everybody who is rich has obtained his wealth by service to the community, the service being of greater value to the community than the wealth for which it was bartered. There are exceptions, of course. There are rich people who have made their money dishonestly, but a very small fraction of these have made it out of the poor, they generally make it out of the gullible rich. Against such people must be balanced poor people who are dishonest. Amongst these must be classed not only burglars, habitual criminals of all sorts, but hand-workers who do not give a fair return in work for their wages. Men who ca' canny, who sleep on night-shift, who injure machinery, and have other questionable business habits which need not be given, are all trying to rob the rich, though they really rob their fellows. We might add domestic servants who waste food, break furniture and so on. The waste of food by domestic servants is really quite a large national loss, though it is not intentionally aimed at the rich. The class from which servants come is astonishingly wasteful at home.

It may be urged that a man who owns land or minerals makes much money, without giving anything to the community in return, as he really fleeces tenants. Extremists go further and say that the ground is not really his ; that his ancestors stole it, and that it should not belong to him, but to the extremists themselves.

Suppose the ground of two city plots is put up for sale. Both plots belong to the descendant of some mediæval ruffian, who had the ground given him by a king as a reward for murdering some other mediæval ruffian. Mr. Jones buys one plot for a large sum of money. The other is not sold, and remains in the hands of the man, whose ancestors got it. Mr. Jones is then merely getting a fair interest on his money. He has paid for his ground, and the vendor has spent the money. The State or the community cannot rob Mr. Jones of his property, because it was bought under an absolute, though tacit, agreement with the community that the land, like any other property, became his property when he paid for it. It may be said that the people who have recently bought land might be allowed to keep it, but those who have merely inherited it from the remote past should give it up. But when the two plots were put up, there was an offer for the second, which was very nearly good enough, and the owner had the chance of selling it, but he chose to keep it, also on the agreement with the community that it would remain his. Every bit of land might have changed hands at any time, and most of it has changed hands many times.

It is said that land becomes more valuable automatically, without the owner doing anything ; but when a man buys land he takes that into consideration, and the price paid is for the land, with its chance of growing more valuable. Sometimes it does not become more valuable, and the buyer loses. Again, every time an owner does not sell his land he estimates the chances of rise of value, and sets them against the offer he refuses. It is thus impossible to go back and find any particular time at which land should be confiscated. The increase of the value of ground due to such accident as towns growing is commonly called " unearned increment," and it is said people have no right to unearned increment. All business involves chance, and every investor may lose his money or make more than normal interest ; it is exactly the same in buying land. Another idea is that land should not be owned privately at all. But who should own it? If a square mile of the City of London is to be nobody's, the owners of the buildings are, in fact, presented with the rent. The office rents would remain the same, as people are ready to pay them ; so the owners of the buildings would really become owners of the ground, too, without paying for it. Perhaps it should belong to the parish. But why should the few who make up the parish have it? The City of London would claim it ; but why should the people who now happen to be in the City have fabulous riches, which might be divided among more people? No doubt it will be said all land should belong to the State. Why? Why should the people who happen to be in England now have the land? Why should the few people now in Rhodesia have Rhodesia against the people who will flock there as the place developes? Why should not the whole of the land in the Empire belong to the Empire as a whole? Why have not the natives of India, not to mention the Zulus, as much right to their share of a City site as a British hand-worker? One answer may be, that it is simpler for each country to own its land, so that if the population increases or diminishes naturally or by migration, the land is the property of the people any time in, or rather belonging to, the country. New-comers in Rhodesia would thus get just as much benefit from the land as the people there now, or their children. This arrange-ment would be based on convenience, rather than logic or justice, but it is almost impossible for us to enlarge our ideas of justice beyond the limits of our patches.

But we may imagine that the land is nationalised, that is to say, it is the property of the State, and never of private individuals. The idea, no doubt, is, then, that it is as much the property of the poor as the rich man. In order to trace the effect of the change from the population pressure point of view, we must first settle whether the land has been confiscated or stolen from the present owners, or bought at fair prices. If the land is paid for, the first question is : Who pays for it? A large sum of money would be wanted to pay for the land. It would be raised, people will say, by taxing the rich, including sellers of the land. So that the basic idea of land nationalisation is to take it from the rich, and let them pay one another to make the robbery just.

As a matter of fact, taxing the rich does not mean that the rich lose all they pay. This is one case of real incidence of taxation, a subject which is large enough to be discussed on population principles by itself. If the country steals the land the result is simpler. The revenue from this land reduces or wipes out the other taxes.

Whether it is stolen or paid for, we can now consider the land as owned by the State. What is it going to do with it? If it lets it on lease at suitable rents, the position need be little different. Take the case of the owner of a large estate, with a rent-roll of £10,000 a year. Part of the estate will be used simply as pleasure grounds. We will suppose that if the pleasure grounds were used for farming they would bring in £5,000 more. For simplicity we will assume the rent is 5 per cent. on the value of the land, or the value is twenty years' purchase, the value of the estate is £300,000. It is bought at that price by the State. The farmers or other tenants who paid the £10,000, now rent their land from the State at £10,000. It makes no difference at all to them. The former land owner has £300,000 available. He lends the State £200,000 at 5 per cent. by buying 5 per cent. Imperial Land Bonds at par. He then buys another lot of £100,000 with the rest of his money, this yields him £5,000 a year, with which he rents his old pleasure land. The result is that the farmers are as before. The State is as before, except that it has a new staff of civil servants to pay, and the old landowner is as before. Instead of £10,000 a year from his tenants, he gets £10,000 a year interest on Land Bonds. He has his pleasure land as before, its result balancing the interest on his £100,000 Land Bonds. It may be urged against this that the State can borrow at 3 per cent., so that it would really gain £200,000 by that. Going back to the beginning of the example, the rent of the farmed ground was £10,000. If this is ordinary rent, it may be taken as 5 per cent. on capital, 2 per cent. of this being risk money, which has to balance occasional outgoings, or loss of rent during

changes. If the rent is certain to come in at the rate
of £10,000 a year clear, it should be taken not as a
commercial rent with risks, but as interest on perfect
security, at 3 per cent. The farmed land should therefore be bought for £333,000, and the pleasure land at
£166,000 instead of £100,000.

Those who want municipal trading often argue that
as a town can borrow at 3 or $3\frac{1}{2}$ per cent., while a
company pays 5 per cent., the town has an advantage
of $1\frac{1}{2}$ to 2 per cent. Thus, electric central stations are
5 per cent. business, 2 per cent. being risk insurance.
If a town borrows at 3 per cent., the ratepayers in
the long run pay the other 2 per cent. This is assuming
that the town committee can manage as well as a
company. If it cannot, the ratepayers in the long run
will pay more than 2 per cent. The notion that a
government can make a profit because it can borrow
at low interest is really the same fallacy.

The State, buying the land at fair valuation, and
then letting it, really makes no difference worth talking
about. If the money is raised by taxing the rich, or
by issuing loans, there is merely a sort of shuffling round
which makes no real difference. But if the present
owners become tenants, and the present tenants remain
tenants, which is the simplest way of looking at it, the
only result is that more civil servants are employed, and
there will be waste and mismanagement of all sorts.

It may be said that this is not the object of land
nationalisation. Rich men own large tracts of country,
which are kept idle for the purposes of gratifying the
owners' savage instinct for killing defenceless dumb
animals. For this purpose they will turn tenants out
of their homes, and prevent good land being cultivated.
Suppose the landowner we have just discussed, who
owned the pleasure estate which, if let, would bring in
£5,000 a year, sold it to the State, the State would let
it to various tenants for £5,000 a year. Some of the
land would be very good, farmers would take it, and
live in the same state of comfort as on similar estates.
There would be poorer ground, which would command

less rent per acre. Finally there would be land which could pay a nominal rent only, but would be taken into cultivation. If the land were let in large farms, employing hand-workers in a wise and businesslike way, the tenants would be high-class farmers, and there would be complete organisations of managers, foremen and hand-workers. In this way the estate would support a number of people who would apparently be an addition to the population. The estate was formerly gratular consumption. The owner used it entirely for his own enjoyment. He certainly employed a few game-keepers and other servants, but these may be left out of account. This man now has £5,000 a year instead of his estate. He will presumably spend this on his own enjoyment, too. He may be partly regenerated, and realise that a merely useless amusement is at any rate higher than cruelty, so that he may spend his £5,000 a year on an annual display of fireworks in honour of the League of Nations. He then employs a certain number of firework makers, powder and chemical manufacturers, and so on, producing gratular goods for him. But the net result is that more food is produced in the country, which we will assume, for simplicity, is isolated, so that more people can live. There is, in fact, room for a small increase of population; the common fallacy is to assume that the population is fixed, and that taking more land into cultivation will find livings for some of the poor, so that it makes the people better off; it does not, of course, it merely makes them more numerous, the state of comfort remaining constant, and the population increasing. One argument in favour of land nationalisation is that not only is a great deal of it wasted by being kept unproductive by rich owners, but the land is not used as well as it might be ; our farmers, we are told, are very ignorant and unenterprising, and do not know their business. It is a stock topic among politicians and newspaper writers that the farmer does not study the science of agriculture. He is told to go to Canada or Western America and introduce Western methods of wheat growing in Devon, or to go to France and study the beetroot, then lay down the Highlands of Scotland in beetroot, so as to foil the wickedness of countries who give us cheap sugar by subsidies because they do not understand economics. It does not occur to people that if the farmers are wrong and the prattlers are right, the prattlers could make a much better thing of it by renting farms and running them on Danish, American, or their own lines, and stopping their prattle. The idea that the world would be better if the land were in the hands of government, worked not by farmers, but by irresponsible and ignorant government officials, either elected by vote, or under the thumb of those elected by vote, is not worth serious discussion.

But, if by any machinery we could increase the return from the land, so that more food could be produced, it must be repeated that the result in time would be an increase of population, not an improvement in the average standard of comfort.

CHAPTER XII

NATIONALITY AND ISOLATION

WE are so accustomed all our lives to think of the world as divided up into independent nations or peoples, that it is very difficult indeed to think otherwise than nationally. We think always of what would be just, or what we believe would be good for our country, and we have little sympathy with foreigners. We are apt to regard all foreigners as rivals in business, and enemies, or at least very uncertain friends in war, and we think any commercial success or development of their business is rivalry, which does us great harm. It is exceedingly difficult, if not impossible, to avoid lapsing into this groove, even when discussing matters from the population point of view.

A country is isolated, in fact, by its government. Further barriers are difference of race, difference of language, and above all, patriotism or patch-pride. The language and race barriers are decaying more and more rapidly. This is mainly due to the growth of ways of getting about easily. Trains and steamers have been increasing and improving, and now flying is likely to hurry forward the time when country barriers are broken down. Patch-pride is practically dead as regards counties in England. A man living in Sussex does not regard the men living in Essex as inferior and dangerous foreigners, nor does he think that flourishing Norfolk means poverty to his county. Even in America the various States do not hate one another like the much smaller, less important, Balkan countries.

But as the world is split up into patches, which are strongly individualised, it is necessary to study the effect of the artificial divisions.

If countries were all isolated, with no international trade, each would have its population as large as the conditions allowed. One country, being uncivilised, would have a low standard of comfort throughout. A large proportion of the population would be engaged in producing food, and there would be little gratular production or consumption. The population would thus tend to be large because of the small proportion of gratular product, but it would be kept down, on the other hand, by the backward state of the knowledge of farming of all sorts. Such a country as this would have some external trade ; it would, however, largely be in gratular products. The people would send out camels laden with bright coloured, irregularly, and laboriously made fabrics, and they would come back with all sorts of little bits of mineral, which would be highly valued, because they attracted the eye and were difficult to find. They would also trade in rare herbs, which tasted nice or smelled sweet, or, at any rate, sweeter than the people.

Such peoples would have practically no peaceful communications with their neighbours. Population pressure within would always be active in urging one people to invade another country and carry off food and goods, killing many of the inhabitants and making slaves of the rest. The result of such a conflict between two countries would be that, taking the two countries together, the population would suddenly be reduced, and a large number would be made into slaves, whose misery would be disregarded. The part of the people that was free would then be better off immediately, or shortly after the war. In a few years population would come up again to the original pressure. In the next war this country may be conquered because in the meantime life has been easier and the people may have grown slack.

Consider a modern civilised country cut up into states, provinces, departments, or other large divisions. One province may have coal and iron, and be industrial. Another will grow grain, or meat and dairy produce, and there will be traffic between them. The department that has coal and iron will make more goods than it wants to consume, and will exchange them for food which it wants. It would never occur to the industrial people that it would be better for them to grow their own farm produce under great difficulties, rather than get it by exchanging what they can make easily. Similarly, the more flourishing the farmers were, and the more perfect their systems and the better their machinery, the more business could be done in exchanging iron goods for agricultural produce. The farmer people would call the chance of buying their machinery at prices that to them were ridiculously low the greatest boon, and would be thankful that the iron provinces were in such a flourishing condition, and that the rest of the country also sent them clothes and other goods at prices much below anything they could touch, if they try to manufacture.

The question of government restraint of international trade is fully treated in books on economics, but on the tacit assumption that the populations of the countries concerned remain constant. But in the long run this does not happen. Besides, restraint of outside trade is generally treated only from the internal point of view. It will, therefore, be worth while to investigate the question on the population principle, especially as it is getting more and more mixed up with that of war.

Let us begin with a large area, cut up into districts according to any scheme. Each district may be bounded by zones of latitude and longitude, geographically by rivers or hills, or may be a county. We may imagine something like the United States. For simplicity, we may assume there are only ten States, instead of forty-five, and that the inhabitants trade freely with the people in all the other States, and with the people of the rest of the world outside. It will be noticed that the States do not trade as units at all.; it is the people who trade. For simplicity again, we will assume that the people of each State trade equally with those in all the others. Then each State, by which we mean the traders in it, does one-tenth of its whole external trade with each of the nine other States, and one-tenth with the outside world. Consider for simplicity two States, one of which is good at growing wheat, and bad at making machinery, call it Dakota; another can grow wheat, but is better at manufactures, call it Michigan. The farmers in Dakota then send out wheat to Michigan, and the manufacturers in Michigan send agricultural machinery to the Dakota farmers. The Dakota farmers like it, because they can get tractors and so on cheap. They can grow wheat easily, and make tractors expensively, so it is best for the people of Dakota to devote their energies to growing wheat and not to making tractors. The Dakota people do not look upon Michigan as a hostile rival ; they realise that the more Michigan flourishes, the more wheat they will want, and the cheaper they will supply tractors. The people of Dakota will realise two fundamental facts. First, that they are poorer by wheat sent out of Dakota by the value to them of that wheat, and richer by the value to them of the machinery that comes in. Second, that if they get what is to them a large value in machinery in exchange for a value of wheat, they are all the better off. Goods coming in enrich Dakota; goods going out make it poorer ; but unless it can get in what is more valuable in Dakota in exchange for what it sends out, it will not trade. There will be no trade between Dakota and Michigan unless it suits both. To Dakota the machinery must be more valuable than the wheat; to Michigan the wheat must be more valuable than the machinery. By producing what they produce best in each State, the people are getting the maximum production for their work, and the result is that each State supports the maximum population.

If we consider the whole of the States, the inhabitants of each is working at whatever gives the best production. One State makes a specialty of steel, another of tobacco, a third of meat, a fourth of motors, a fifth of cotton and so on. By this sort of local division of labour, a given amount of work gives the maximum result, so that each State maintains the maximum popu-

lation. There is supposed to be no bar to trading outside the States, so that when people want anything they
cannot get easily in the States, they get it from other
countries in the same convenient way.

Now, let us imagine that Dakota makes up its mind
that, as it has State laws of its own, it is at least as
much an independent country as an ordinary colony, so
it calls itself a country. Immediately a curious mental
fog settles over the question. The newspapers say that
Michigan is dumping tractors, and they should give
Dakotans employment making tractors locally. They
would say that Dakota is made richer by the wheat it
sends out, and poorer by the goods that come in, and
that the more wheat they send out, and the less
machinery they get for it, the better off they will be.
They would also say that the prosperity of Michigan was
a serious menace to Dakota, and that Michigan was
competing unfairly in the markets of the world, especially
if Michigan crippled her external trade by taxing it.
These extraordinary ideas come in only in discussing
a country or colony. No reasonable being thinks an
individual, a house, a firm, a town or a small area on
the map is richer by what it parts with and poorer by
what it receives. In the early part of the reign of
Louis XIV this absurd idea was applied to small places,
now it lingers as regards countries only. The notion,
no doubt, is that if Dakota sends out wheat and gets
no machinery in exchange, she will get money instead,
and be richer. Suppose Dakota sells wheat without buying machinery and gets dollars in exchange. Dollars
will almost immediately be so plentiful in Dakota that
a dollar will buy very little there. In Michigan dollars
will have become scarcer, and will therefore buy more.
The result is that the Dakotans will spend their dollars
in Michigan, and what they buy will be imports into
Dakota. Currency is very small in proportion to the
business it lubricates, and movement of dollars enough to
compensate for any appreciable trade alters the local
value of money at once. The idea of getting rich by
selling goods and hoarding the money is the old

" mercantile theory," which was exploded by Adam Smith about a century and a half ago. The idea that it is a good thing to create employment, even if it is not productive, is another version of the prejudice against machinery. Employment or work is not a good thing in itself. No one likes work generally, and everyone wants either to work as little as possible, or to produce as much as possible with a given amount of labour, mental or physical. What is wanted is production, and work or employment ought to be directed to get the biggest result. In old days, when a machine was invented which did the work of twenty men, with only one to work it, there was an outcry that it threw nineteen men out to starve. Most people now realise that machinery increases production, and does not cause starvation, and that machinery has let the population of this country quadruple in about a century.

The three fallacies : Employment is good, whether productive or not; Goods coming into a country impoverish it; Stopping imports does not stop exports, live only in the case of considering countries or colonies. Nobody supposes that it would be good for the people of Wiltshire to make their own ironmongery or woollens, though it would employ people a good deal, but very unproductively. Neither does anyone imagine that if the Wiltshire folk can buy ironmongery or woollens cheap that they are worse off, nor do they complain that the woollens or ironmongery are " dumped." Nor would anyone suppose that Wiltshire could go on sending out foodstuffs without getting anything in return, or that such a state of things would be good for Wiltshire. It is only when Wiltshire has a government of its own that the curious inversion of common sense occurs.

Going back to Dakota and Michigan. Imagine Dakota puts a duty on machinery. If the duty is not high enough to reduce the imports at all, all that happens is that revenue is raised out of the buyers of machinery, instead of some other way. Apart from questions of incidence this makes no difference. If the duty is high enough to stop the imports, there is no revenue. Revenue is collected only when the duty does not stop imports. If the imports are stopped completely, or to the extent they are reduced, Dakota workmen have to be employed making machinery. What people forget is that they have to be taken off wheat growing. The employment resulting from restraining external trade is inefficient, in exchange for efficient employment, and the effect is less production in Dakota, so that people are at once made poorer, and the State eventually has a smaller population in the same degree of comfort as before. It is often urged that Michigan pays the tax on the imports. If the duty is 10 per cent., and machinery still comes in, the Dakotan farmers have to pay 10 per cent. more for imported goods and for home-made machinery. Taxes in Dakota do not alter the relative value of wheat and machines in Michigan.

We have been discussing two States only ; in discussing the whole ten States and the external world it is still clearer that the Dakota duty will not alter the relative value. Michigan will exchange the same machine as before for a quarter ;—or better, a ton of wheat, as few know what a quarter is ;—because if the relative value began to alter in Michigan, more people would grow wheat and fewer would make machinery.

The machinery coming into Dakota comes in at the normal price, and the duty is paid by the purchaser. If the duty is enough to stop the imports, and to the extent that it stops them, Michigan's output of machinery is reduced, and as they want the same amount of wheat as before, and there is less coming from Dakota, they must put machine makers on to grow wheat. The duty in Dakota thus hurts Michigan just as much as Dakota, as it " gives employment " in Michigan just as much as in Dakota, because it turns people off what they do well and on to what they do badly, and makes them inefficient. Michigan is thus made poorer and able to support a smaller population. It may surprise some to see that a measure adopted by Dakota against Michigan to increase employment in Dakota " increases " employment in Michigan just as much ; that is to say, it increases inefficient and reduces efficient employment equally in both States. It will now be realised that the trade between Dakota and Michigan is flowing round a circuit like liquid in a circuit of pipe. It does not matter whether the flow is reduced by screwing down a valve where the pipe enters Dakota, where it leaves it, or where it enters or leaves Michigan. It may also be surprising to see that a tax on exports has the same effect as on imports. To follow this simply, consider Dakota and the rest of the world, and not Michigan alone. If Dakota puts a very high export duty on wheat and stops the export altogether, that stops the import of machinery, and has clearly the same effect as a protective duty on imports. But suppose it puts 10 per cent. on export wheat. Suppose, before the change, a ton of wheat has the same market value as a machine. It still has the same value outside. Outside people will, therefore, send in one machine for a ton of wheat from Dakota. In Dakota the price of a machine will now be equal to that of a ton of wheat plus 10 per cent., whether the machine is made in Dakota or outside.

If we now consider the ten States all putting on import duties, we have each injuring itself to an extent we may call one, that is to say, it injures the whole of its external trade, and it injures each of the other nine States to the extent of one-ninth and the external world to the extent of one-ninth of the States' trade. So that each State is injured to the extent of two. If the government of one State were eccentric enough to study elementary economics and remove its own restrictions on external trade, its injury of two would at once be reduced to one. It has removed the injury it was doing to the other States, namely, one-ninth to each, and the whole of its own injury to itself. Immediately there would be an outcry from the " fair traders." They would say, " It is conceivable, though we cannot follow it, that Free Trade is good when universal, but it is obviously bad if we alone adopt it." How it is obviously bad is never explained. There seems to be some idea that restraining trade is good for the restrainer and bad for outsiders, so that if they all restrain trade the total injury may be greater than the total good, so that universal freedom may be better than universal restraint. They will say that if everybody agreed to disarm it would be good, but for one to disarm while the others stay armed would be suicidal. But there is no analogy. Restraint of trade hurts each State, and each can get an advantage by removing its own restraints.

If all our States adopt free trade, except with the outside world, instead of each suffering an injury of two made up of one, due to its own action, and one-tenth due to the action of each of the other nine States, and one-tenth due to the external world, they will be much better offs; and the United States is really the biggest free trade community in the worlds; and is an object lesson in the sub-division of labour. That they restrain their external trade means that if the external world also restrains, each State has reduced the evil it caused itself from one to one-tenth, and the whole of the States have reduced the evil external to each from one to one-tenth, the two lots of one-tenth being due to the external world restraint. The restraint of external trade in a large and varied country like the States is quite unimportant in comparison with her own inter-State trade.

Dakota might offer to Michigan to stop taxing Michigan machinery, provided Dakota and Michigan both crippled their external trade with all the other States. There could be no sense in this, but it is the same idea as Imperial Preference. As restraining their external trades hurts Australia, Canada and New Zealand, the sensible course is to stop their restraint with all countries. England would not do the Colonies any good by restraining her trade with the rest of the world. New Zealand may be compared as to population and produce with Somerset. Can we imagine the people of Somerset refusing to let goods come in untaxed, and saying they will stop this if England will stop her own foreign trade? There seems to be some idea that restraint of trade is valuable as something to bargain with. An idiot, when asked why he hammered his head, the tears streaming down his cheeks, replied that he did it because it was so nice when he left off.

Restraint of outside trade is popular largely because it is called " Protection." Thus the machinery trade in Dakota would be called " protected," but such protection does no real good to it. Capital sunk in making machinery in Dakota is in competition with other capital, and makes no special profits, so there is no advantage to the capitalist, especially as there is less room for capital in growing wheat. The hand-workers do not get better wages than they did in growing wheat, and until the population of Dakota has sunk to the number which can live in the State with the smaller production, there is extra poverty and unemployment.

In discussing Dakota and Michigan we saw that a duty on machines going into Dakota increased the price of machinery there. If Dakota and Michigan were alone concerned, Michigan will now have to make less machinery and grow more wheat, so the price of wheat goes up in Michigan. If Michigan takes it into its head that it is a country, it will make things worse by taxing imported wheat.

Michigan, if it thought it was a country, might take another course which would never appeal to it as a State. It might agree that as wheat growing was not flourishing in Michigan, it would be a good thing to subsidise export of wheat. Take Dakota and Michigan again, and suppose they do not restrain their trade, but Michigan subsidises exports or home-grown wheat. Take exported wheat first, and assume she subsidises it so highly that it goes to Dakota. Dakota then has to reduce her wheat growing, and take in wheat, and make machinery for export to Michigan. If the subsidy is not big enough, and is on home-grown wheat, the result will still be to get more wheat grown in Michigan and less in Dakota, so that the workers in both States are made less efficient, and the population therefore falls. The interference of a government with trade, whether it takes the form of restraining it and calling the restraint protection, or bolstering it up by subsidies, reduces the population of its own country, and of the other countries whose trade is modified by the action of the government.

Government interference with trade thus reduces it, and in the long run reduces the population, by making production less efficient. The harm done may be over-rated, because people forget that in most cases the external is only a small portion of the whole trade of a country, and that when a tariff does not actually check external trade, it comes to be mainly a way of collecting revenue, which the public does not mind, as the taxes are supposed to be paid by foreigners.

In spite of difference of government, and in spite of the general idea that each country is improved by throttling its trade with every other country, nations are getting more interdependent every year. In early days each country produces everything it wants, or gets, because communication is difficult. Food is generally apt to perish, and has therefore to be grown near the eater. Now meat is frozen, and food is tinned, and countries tend to specialise in products, so that very soon the different parts of the world will each be producing mainly one thing, in much the same way as the small districts of a county produce each one thing. This change is helped forward by bad internal transport. In many countries the railways are run by the governments, and are therefore run very badly, while in others they are more or less interfered with and crippled by government action. The result is that it often costs more to send goods from one part of a small country to another than to get them across an ocean.

Capital is also moving about freely. At present equally safe investments in out-of-the-way places on the one hand, and America or England on the other, yield different rates of interest, because the lenders in America or England do not know the conditions in out-of-the-way places as well. This is altering rapidly, and in course of time capital will be quite cosmopolitan.

People, however, do not move about much. Tourists who go round beaten tracks have no effect. Men with international business travel about, and tend to break down the artificial nation barriers, and to remove patch prejudices.

In earlier states of civilisation a country like Britain was practically isolated. There was no object in natives of Britain going to France or the Low Countries, as life was just as great a struggle there. The only things that happened were invasions and wars. Thus, if the Danes were feeling the effects of population pressure, a number of them who had a special liking and talent for ruffianism would overrun part of England. Many of both sides would be killed, which eased the situation a little, and if the Danes succeeded, they would be personally better off than if they had stayed at home.

Now the world is gradually turning into one big industrial community. In spite of the curious phenomenon of constraint of international trade, we are slowly, though less and less slowly, coming to the state in which each place produces what it finds it can do best. Districts in which wool and mutton can be grown better than elsewhere, grow more and more wool and mutton, taking in exchange the goods they cannot produce so easily. If it were not for difficulties and cost of carriage, the whole world would soon become specialised. People do not move about nearly so easily. The lower grades of work in some parts of England are often done by unskilled Irishmen ; in America there is a huge floating population of unskilled hand-workers from Southern Europe. In South Africa Chinese hand-labour has been used largely. It is hardly necessary to point to the freed slaves and their descendants in America. They are no longer Africans, they are now a special separate race of Americans.

It is always difficult for men to move about, especially for the ill-to-do. It is easy to talk of hand-workers emigrating, but it is a very serious risk, and a greater plunge into the unknown. Emigration is purposely checked in some cases. For example, a hand-worker cannot make an agreement with an American employer and then go over. He must take the risk. The theory is that he would under-estimate the cost of living, and would agree to come for wages that sounded high to him, and would then find he was much worse off than he hoped. The real object is probably to please American hand-workers by keeping out competitors. The hand-worker, when he does emigrate, generally goes alone, so that the countries he goes to have too many men, and those he leaves have too many women. It is very difficult to get women to emigrate, they are not naturally adventurous. But the hand-worker does not move freely even in his own country. If there is slackness at Leeds and a demand in Lancashire, very few men will move. This is due to the difficulty and cost of moving whole families. Moreover, some of the Leeds family may have work there, while the rest have none. The humbler classes seem to have much more kindness and affection than the more fortunate. They are knit much closer, and more self-sacrificing among themselves ; and a son will stay and take a very poor job, rather than leave his mother and sisters.

If we get away from the patch obsession, and think of the world as occupied by people who are partly separated by sea, mountains, or rivers, and differ also in language, habits and views of life, we can discuss the action and reaction of population pressure in the various places.

We are accustomed now to regard a large foreign trade as vital to a country, and to say that if we do not produce cheaply we will suffer in competition with other nations. We also say that if another nation is flourishing, it must be beating us, and taking our foreign trade away from us. But the ideas are very vague.

If a line is drawn round any part of the earth's surface, whether the part enclosed is a country with a government of its own or part of a country or parts of two or more countries, there will be an exchange of goods across the line. The governments do not matter, unless they stifle trade that crosses their boundaries, and for simplicity we will assume there is no such restriction. The only reason why there is any exchange of goods across our line is that people inside it want something from outside that is more valuable to them than what they give for it, and the outsiders are in the same position the other way round.

If a district produces everything the inhabitants want, so that the relative values are exactly the same as the relative values in a neighbouring district, there will not be any exchange over the line, as it would be of no advantage to the people inside, or the people outside. If there is something, such as tea, which the insiders want, but cannot produce so easily as the outsiders, relatively, they will exchange any of their ordinary products for it. Of course they buy the tea and sell their own products, but the amounts balance, otherwise money would accumulate in the district, or the reverse. For simplicity, we can imagine a gold currency adopted universally. If the district sells goods and buys nothing, gold will get plentiful in the district, and an ounce of it will then buy less than if spent outside the district, while, if gold is scarce in the district, outsiders will find it cheaper to buy goods there.

Our district thus imports first, tea and so on, which it cannot produce locally, and if it can produce other goods at the same values relatively to one another as they are produced outside, it will be a matter of indifference what the people sell.

Our line may happen to have been drawn round a country district where food is grown, and little else. In this case the people exchange food for all sorts of other goods. We might happen to have drawn the line round a big town. In that case the people will exchange all sorts of things for food and other wants. Much of what they give may be services. Two farmers have a quarrel, which they want to get settled, so they go into the town, and legal gentlemen settle it for them, and they retire to the country very much poorer. They really pay the lawyers in food in the long run.

All this is the commonplace of economics, the only difference is that economists generally, if not always, consider only the cases in which the lines are drawn round countries or nations. There is no magic in the boundary of a nation, any more than in that of a country or a district, or a space enclosed by two latitude and two longitude lines. The patch fallacy is apt to come in if countries are considered. Trade has naturally nothing to do with nations, units of government, or anything of that sort. If the line is round a district which can produce various goods, those that it makes with difficulty will be taken from outside in exchange for what it makes easily, unless carriage is too expensive. If a man grows beetroot, and grows it with difficulty, he will give it up, and people will import the beetroot, exchanging, say, oats, which they can grow easily. The beetroot grower will then do other work. But if our enclosure line happens to coincide with a national boundary, a man who grows, let us say, thistles, and grows them very badly, says that thistles should not be imported because that throws him out of work, and thistle growing is a key industry, as the people live on them, and will starve in case of war, if they do not die of starvation in the meantime, because outsiders are sending in thistles so cheap—practically for nothing—that all the thistle eaters are starving because there is no work.

What we really want to discuss is the relations of different districts in such cases as one being inefficient owing to strikes, war, hot climate, or other cause, and to see if we can follow out any changes that might arise from population pressure being greater in one place than another. We also want to discuss some popular ideas, to see if they are sound. For example, we are always told with great insistence, not only by newspapers, but by business men, that Germany has a great advantage over us because her currency is depreciated. As has been explained earlier, the commerce between a district and the world outside is carried on by exchange of goods, not by accumulations of currency or serious depletion. The unit of currency value in the different districts does not matter at all. If a country has a coin which represents ten grams of gold, and calls it an Eagle, and this country issues Eagle notes until all the gold has gone abroad, it has made gold cheap to some extent all over the world. That is not the point. Suppose it goes on printing Eagles till they exchange for only one gram of gold each, it does not alter the relative value of its goods either inside or outside. If depreciated currency gave a country an advantage, we would all follow Russia's magnificent example, and we would all, like Russia, do splendid foreign trade. It may be urged that Russia has taken so many leaps towards Utopia, that we must not ascribe all its success to one of its jumps, but we can think whether our depreciated currency, say just after the war, helped us to trade advantageously with America, or put America at a serious disadvantage.

Returning to our district, it may be almost self-contained, like America, being able to satisfy nearly all its own wants. Next to it there may be another district which also satisfies all its own wants, except in a few lines. It may find it difficult to make paper because there happens to be no good water supply. It will then take paper from our district, giving other goods in exchange, but in order to induce our district to exchange, it will give a little more in other goods than would be obtained for paper inside the district. It does not follow, therefore, that a district exports only what it can produce well. .What it exports and imports is determined just as much by external relative wants as internal.

Each district is certain to have some special wants, as there must be some goods it makes badly or cannot produce at all, or some services that the people cannot render well. It is also pretty certain to do some things better than usual, and these considerations will determine what it sends over the line and what it takes in exchange.

Consider the case of our line being drawn across a large island or continent, it does not matter what, and for simplicity, assume the island area has no external trade. Imagine our line is drawn East and West, and the South district has been partly depopulated by a plague, which is now well over, so that the small population, with capital enough for many more people, is having an easy time. It is easier for them to grow their food, as they now use only their best ground, and similar conditions obtain right through. The North district has had no plague, and population pressure is high, and the people have to work hard and consume little. The first point to notice is that prices will be the same in the two districts, for if they were generally higher in the South, for instance, the Southerner would buy more goods in the North, and gold would move into the North until it became more plentiful there in proportion to the local demands for currency. People would say that prices were rising in the North and falling in the South, until they became equal. The movement of gold might be almost nothing in comparison with the passage of goods across our line.

The next thing to move will be capital. If capital is plentiful in the South, it will command higher interest in the North, and Southern capital will be invested there. The interest will be paid in goods, not money, so there will then be a greater flow of goods South than North over our imaginary line. This is assuming the owners of the capital remain in the South, as they naturally would.

As life is easier in the South, we might expect that people would move down, so that the two populations would have the same ratio to the pre-plague numbers. But men are extraordinarily sluggish in emigration. Some of the young and enterprising, with no home ties, would move, but the migration in similar cases, in fact, is so slow, that it would produce very little effect. The South would remain with low population pressure until population increased, apart from immigration.

Soon after the plague the Southerners, finding all classes relatively better off than before, might realise that each person was in a higher degree of comfort for given attainments, and they might maintain this to some extent by marrying late, and by having no poor-law relief, no doles, and no promiscuous charity, so that there were very few indigent and incompetent dregs at the bottom. In this case we would have neighbouring peoples with different degrees of comfort for the same attainments, and they would trade merely to exchange what they could produce easily for what they could not. Prices would be the same, and there would be four tendencies towards equilibrium; more rapid increase of population in the South, movement of gold South, movement of capital North, and movement of workers South. The first and last being very slow.

There is no sort of trade competition between the people separated by our chance line. There is no real line, and the people are quite unconscious of our investigation. There is just the ordinary competition between people in the same strata that there is in each part of the area. If the whole area, North, South, East and West are all flourishing, whatever flourishing may be, it is all the better for them. If the East flourishes more than the West, it helps the West, because it has more chance of making exchanges, and it may give openings for pushing young men, and for capital. It certainly does not hurt the West. So far we have met nothing corresponding to competition between peoples in the trade of the world.

Each bit of our area is mainly self-supplying, unless we examine very small bits, and they are all exchanging for their own benefit, and the better off their neighbours are the better for them. This is true, whether the area is all as one, or is divided up into parishes, states, counties, or geometrical parts of the surface of the globe. But as soon as it is thought of as divided up into nations a mental fog settles over the whole subject.

Let the plague be a thing of the past, so that everything has settled down again, and our land is in equilibrium, with population pressure everywhere the same. Imagine our line drawn round a district in which coal and iron have been found. The food production and agriculture generally go down, and the people sell coal, iron and iron goods. The neighbourhood becomes a workshop, and gets not only all its food, but practically everything else it wants, except coal and iron, from outside. It can produce so much coal and iron that it can get more food and other things in exchange than it wants, so its population increases. In this case there will be a good deal of immigration, as wages will be high. When equilibrium is reached the district will be very "prosperous," which means that it will be very thickly populated. The individuals in it will not be healthier, wealthier, more moral, happier or in any way better, but the district will be "prosperous."

Suppose there is, somewhere else, another coal and iron district round which we could draw another enclosing line. Both districts will send out coal and iron goods in exchange for food, clothes, and most other things wanted. But the amount they can send out depends on the outside demand. The rest of the area may stop making iron goods altogether, becoming chiefly agricultural. The people will do this only if it pays them, that means if their population can increase. Take the whole area, it will raise the maximum amount of runcitic products in accordance with its state of civilisation, and this amount will regulate the population of the area. The whole of the people will need a certain amount of coal and iron goods, and if the two coal and iron districts can produce more, they are in competition, and each tries to give as much coal and iron in exchange for a given amount of other goods as it can. If our whole area considered is a country, let us say like England and Wales, one of our lines may enclose the black part of Warwickshire, and the other the corresponding part of South Wales. The localities are in competition, and if the only demand for their goods is in England and Wales, they are competing for English and Welsh trade, but if we consider two districts in relation to the world, they are competing for world trade. Competing for world trade is thus just a grand name for exchanging some things we produce for others that we want more. Our iron-workers are not a people or a community, they are merely an important class in our district. The various iron-workers in Warwick are competing with the other iron-workers in Warwick, and easy carriage and communication puts them in competition with the various iron-workers in South Wales. This is merely an instance of the fact that competition is among similar people. If communication is good all over the world, each member of each class is competing with all the other members of that class,; to localise classes and call them districts, and say the districts are competing for world trade, is a far-fetched notion, arising from the patch obsession.

It is easier to think and write of an area as producing different goods, and no harm is done if the real meaning is borne in mind. Many districts are purely workshops as regards industry. Towns again naturally have no agriculture, other areas are almost entirely farms and so on, and the more easily they can sub-divide their work and exchange their produce the greater the population that can thrive on each.

Between the men involved in any two or more areas that produce anything particularly well, such as machinery, there is thus direct competition. Each area is in the first place trying, not to send out as much as it can, but what is more important, to get in as much as it can by sending out, the idea being that the individuals get rich. They do not necessarily get rich, they merely increase the population of the area, though, of course, some of the inhabitants get richer. External trade of any town, district, area, country, nation or continent is thus merely parting with some things it can make well and can spare for what it wants.

A district or a country may be practically a workshop or a farm,; and a country, that is to say, a district which happens to have its own government, may be a workshop or a farm. Denmark is largely a farm, while Great Britain is mainly a workshop. Other countries are also farms or workshops of one kind or another, and they purchase what they want by sending out what they want less. If two districts are both farms, for instance, they will both want manufactures, and in order to get them they will send out farm produce. They are then in competition for the trade of the world in newspaper language. If one of them does not grow things as well as the other, its population will gradually fall until the increased returns enable it to balance. Thus it is in equilibrium while it produces, say, enough farm produce for itself and 10 per cent. extra, which it uses to exchange for manufactures ; and if another area comes into competition, and gives a little more farm produce for a given amount of manufacture, our area must in future exchange at the same ratio. If it sent out as before and got in less, this would put its internal consumption out of proportion ; if it sent out more, it would shorten its own food supply ; it must therefore decrease in population until it can produce more farm stuff per man and get the proportion right.

Another area may be, as an extreme case, almost a bare rock, populated by people working in factories. If another district under-sells it, it cannot adapt itself by reducing its population, because there are no increasing returns in such a case as there is no dependence on the land. Capital will not take the place of land, because capital is always wasting away.

Generally speaking, the idea of nations all competing for the trade of the world, and being dependent on it, arises largely from a false estimate of the relative volumes of home and external trade. Areas, whether nations or smaller or larger, merely take in what they cannot make well themselves, and send out as little as they can in exchange. The less the better for them. If an area, say a manufacturing area, gets its work upset by trade unions, strikes, and so on, the net result in the long run is that it will support fewer people : any sort of inefficiency such as government waste, large armaments, poor relief, expensive but ineffective education, costly clergy, or municipal extravagance acts to reduce the population.

Any area, generally speaking, is better able to do outside business if outside areas are flourishing, because there is then more external demand for exports and more to choose from in the matter of imports. The population in any area is thus better able to grow, if it is growing outside. The only exception concerns any outside area that competes in our area's exports, or creates a rival demand for its imports. The demand for the imports is generally overlooked, but it is just as important. Thus, if Warwickshire makes iron ware and sends it out in exchange for, among other things, woollens, and South Wales also sends our iron wares; if South Wales sends out cheaper, it will compete with Warwick, and Warwick will have to send out more iron ware or take in less woollens, or both. It is affected by a rival exporting area. If Kent wants woollens badly, and increases her export of cement, getting in more wool, the price of wool goes up, and Warwick has either to take in less wool, or send out more iron, or both. The real rivals of an area are thus those other areas which want the same imports, and those which are ready to send out the same exports. Subject to those two cases, the more external places develope the more demand there is for our area's exports and the more choice of cheap and good imports.

It is, of course, the imports that are valuable. Warwick does not get any good directly by sending out iron goods, quite the reverse, it is poorer by every ton that goes over the boundary. What it wants, and the only thing it sends out its iron for, is the imports.

Similarly Devonshire does not want to part with farm produce, because it is an evil thing; it wants iron goods, so it parts with farm produce to get them. The more iron goods it can get for a given amount of farm produce the better. The Devonshire people think that the better the bargain they make the richer they become. This is true of the whole county, but it allows the population to increase.

It is always individuals, or groups of individuals, who are competing with other individuals or groups doing the same or equivalent work. The idea of districts, towns, counties, nations, or continents competing is very misleading, because it does not bring the true meaning of competition home. Thus, if a particular class of hand-worker in one country works short hours or limits output, it cannot prevent competition by making the practice uniform throughout a district or a country. There is competition with the corresponding classes all over the world, and if they are more efficient, our particular class will get behind.

This type of competition is difficult to trace, and it is disguised or loaded. Thus, if the marine boiler-makers on the Clyde secure high wages or short hours or small output compared with the same men on the Tyne, it will not increase the price of Clyde compared with Tyneside built ships perceptibly, because the boilers are a small part of the cost, but the competition is there all the same. In this case, in time a few boiler-makers will move from the Tyne to the Clyde, and this will weaken the hands' position there, and make it easier to get high wages on the Tyne. The union will, there-fore, make the Clyde and Tyneside boiler-makers act in unison. But this will not prevent competition with the boiler-makers in America, France or Germany. The trade unions are trying hard to work in concert over the whole industrial world, but their efforts are to secure not reduced competition, but imaginary wealth out of the non-existent funds of capitalists.

The question of restricting foreign trade may seem unimportant from the population point of view, as throttling exports and imports primarily lessens the efficiency of the people who do it, and reduces the population both in the district that checks its external trade and the outside districts that might have traded with it, and that does not seem to be a matter of great import-ance. The main importance of the subject is in con-nection with war. People do not think of preventing local exchange between districts under the same govern-ment; restriction of trade is concerned with countries or nations, that is to say, with the fighting units of the world, and it tends to keep up patch-pride, and to keep people separated as nations, and thus to preserve the state in which we are all ready to slip down into war.

CHAPTER XIII

WAR

In primitive times war was plainly a direct development of population pressure. A tribe multiplied until food was scarce, or food supply decreased, and the tribe got hungry without necessarily having increased ; and the simple and obvious course was to attack a neighbouring tribe, kill as many as possible, making the rest slaves, and steal their food. Taking the two tribes together, the death of many in battle eased the pressure, and the extremity of further suffering was inflicted on the remains of the conquered tribe, and any starvation or extra hard work was allotted to them. There was thus a temporary reduction of population pressure on the whole community, and the portion of it which was victorious was very much better off until it multiplied up again. If the invading tribe retaliated, and conquered the invaders, the position was merely changed as to which groups in the two tribes became comfortable for the time. In the case of a mere unsuccessful invasion both tribes had their population pressure reduced temporarily, and therefore the war did good to both from that point of view.

As civilisation advanced, war grew expensive in several ways. Keeping up a standing army of trained soldiers for offensive and defensive purposes was a drain on the tribe or country. An offensive war meant paying soldiers, providing equipment, and often means of conveying them into the enemy's or victims' country. Then a large auxiliary army had to be raised and equipped, and this took men away from agriculture and flock and herd work, so that the food supply went down. But whether there should be a war was determined by the few controlling a country that might invade another. There were three main sets of motives, the sordid, the politic and the purely savage. The sordid consideration was that they were obliged to keep some standing army and a trained population to protect themselves against invasion, and as this was a perpetual expense, and it did not cost very much more to invade a neighbouring country, a successful invasion would pay. The invaders would lose men ; this did not matter, as each of them individually then felt sure he would get through all right, and promotion would be general. This is a simple view which assumes free people. In ancient times people were mostly slaves. This fact is not commonly realised, and overlooking it makes it very difficult to understand many of the happenings of ancient days. The sordid temptation was stealing food and property, and getting more slaves. The politic motives were the self-glorification of the politicians who were often soldiers. Successful soldiers were very popular, so when there was a wave of extra population pressure and therefore of discontent with the government, a war, or at least a war in which they took the offensive, made militarists popular. The purely savage motives were the natural cruelty of man, who delights in killing or maiming his fellow men, even now in some proportion in being a beast to women, and in plunder and general destruction, not only of ordinary property, but of works of art or religion. Primitive wars were carried on to get food and goods, and of course to kill, but not to get territory ; that is a later development. The Romans enjoyed exterminating enemy inhabitants.

Pride naturally came into the question. The population of a country, including those that did not fight, liked to prove that they could beat another country.

Religious wars were largely engineered by priests, whose object was to increase their own power. It is difficult now to understand why people should willingly go and fight and lose their lives on behalf of a dynasty, or of a particular variety of dogma. In the case of a dynasty a war would be arranged by a government, or a faction. This would be organised in such a way that the soldiers had no say in the matter. Each one would have to fight because the others did ; no individual could start a mutiny, as he would be alone against an organisation. But he would also suffer from the government fetish, and would think that if his lot won, he and all the others would be very much better off. He would expect, if of rank in the army, to get lands or offices allotted to him, and even as a common soldier, he would look forward to plunder of all sorts. He would also like to show that his side was right, and that he was one of an army who were better and braver soldiers. Then the crowd influence of his side would affect him.

In the case of a religious war the influences are not very different. The organisation that uses him is anxious to increase its power, and he again is merely a tool. He may in this case be an element of a crowd which believes some particular creed is right. Crowd vanity then makes them feel very bitter if people do not believe their creed, as other people then do not think much of them. To be little thought of hurts their vanity so terribly that they willingly risk their lives to break the heads of those who do not admit they are right. A religious war is thus really largely a war of vanity.

Coming to modern times, the apparent causes of war, or the excuses and the real causes, are difficult to follow. The first cause of war is population pressure, but it does not follow that a war eases the pressure, even in the case of the nominal armies. One of the most difficult factors to understand is patriotism. It is essentially patch-vanity. All the people who live on a particular patch persuade themselves that they are better than people living on other patches. This conceit is not so offensive as personal conceit, because it does not belittle those the patient meets, as they belong to the same patch. If a man shows that he thinks that he is better than a friend he talks to, the friend objects to his assumption of superiority. If a man says that people on his patch are very superior, his friend is included among the superior people and likes it. It is when people of different patches meet and each praises his own patch and thus shows the other that he does not think much of him, that vanity is hurt. Patch-pride is thus merely a form of individual vanity or conceit which is complaisant enough to include a number of associates. There is more than this in it, though, as people are always anxious to belong to particular classes, and to label themselves to show it.

Patch-pride might include pride in being on the earth instead of on some other planet or star, but though this would be ridiculous, class-pride in being a human being is quite common.

This absurd form of patch or rather group-pride is shown in the notion that the universe exists solely for the benefit of our solar system, that the solar system exists solely for the good of one of its planets, and that the planet and everything on it exists entirely for the good of one particular part of the organic growth on this planet at a particular time of its development. Man's past history is a mere moment in the history of the universe, and his future is no more. Though the past history of the universe, by which is meant the history before man developed, is supposed to have been designed to lead up to man, little is heard as to whether the rest of the history of the universe, that is to say, the history after man has disappeared, is somehow preordained for his benefit. This is probably owing to the difficulty of imagining a universe going on for æons without man. Such is man's pride, and his want of reverence.

Patch-pride generally begins in relation to a country or an empire. It is one part of the basis of patriotism. A man will be proud of being white. This pride will show as a contempt for coloured people. Whether coloured people ever have a contempt for whites is another matter. Whites being so much more powerful makes this doubtful. He will be proud of being a

European or an American and of being a Scotchman
or a Welshman. If he belongs to a small country he
will do all he can to keep up its language and customs.
But patriotism goes far beyond mere patch-pride.
People think that it is a fine thing to do anything they
can for their country, or to suffer for it, and especially
to die for it. It is very difficult for an old man who
stayed at home comfortably during the war to write
dispassionately. He cannot help remembering that
younger men threw up their careers and prospects,
risked and often lost their lives, or came home crippled,
maimed, or permanently injured, after suffering four
years of Hell on earth ; and it is almost impossible
to write detachedly, and to the extent that he does so,
his words appear insultingly ungrateful. Patriotic
military spirit seems to be largely a crowd phenomenon.
The soldier puts his active mind into his purely
technical work as a soldier, and he deals with such
matters as probable death or injury, or the general
effects of war with his fallow or crowd mind, or with
his fallow crowd mind if there is such a thing. A
gunner will have accurate logical ideas about all the
scientific technicalities of gunnery ; he will know how
to inspire his men with enthusiasm, he will show the
highest qualities of intellect and character as a soldier.
Ask him what he is fighting about and his fallow mind
answers that we must beat the Germans. What the
war is for he does not know. He has a vague idea that
the Germans wanted to take Belgium, France, Italy and
England. That they would, if not resisted, have treated
the whole of these countries as they did Belgium and
the parts of France they overran, and that all the
women in these countries would have been violated, and
all the men turned into various kinds of slaves. If
he sat down to think the whole matter out quietly he
would have much trouble in finding any real sense in
his conduct. He would realise that if he had not
volunteered for the front, people would have regarded
him as a coward, and not being anything of the sort
he could not well have stayed at home. He might

think he was fighting for his country. But what does that mean? He might have a sweetheart or wife, or parents, sisters and brothers to fight for, and he might realise that his help affected their safety only by one in a few million, while his own safety was jeopardised to very different odds, so that fighting for his country is not rational on a low basis. His neighbour may have the morals of the old woman who lived in a shoe, the manners of a smoker, and the wisdom of the man at the other telephone : why fight for him? Beyond his own family and circle, why should he fight for the inhabitants of his country? He would not give his time gratuitously to serve his country in peace, nor would he give his wealth if he had any. But in the artificial excitement of ‚War he is ready to give his life anonymously, and to risk being maimed or being maltreated for years in a German prison.

The crowd spirit at home is just as remarkable. The idea is that the world was at rest, without any idea of war, until suddenly Germany, after preparing secretly for a couple of generations, broke out. But all the other nations were more or less armed. Decently informed people knew that Germany was preparing for what she called world-conquest. Even some of the politicians knew it, but did not see how it would advance them to act upon their knowledge. ‚We had our Navy in good order, and a small army ready, and other countries were more or less ready, or were getting various schemes through. If a lot of nations are armed, it means that they are ready to fight. In early days, when men out ‚West in America generally carried revolvers, there was plenty of shooting, but those who went about unarmed did not get mixed up with this. To be armed was to court fighting. A contingent of armed nations is like a lot of savage dogs who develope a complicated and furious general dog-fight without its being clear which began it. What they fight about is of no moment, they fight. More dogs join in, and eventually they stop through pure fatigue. All the dogs are maimed, torn and bleeding ; they have all suffered, and not one has gained anything at all. They have merely yielded to their savage nature without any sense whatever.

A League of Nations to secure peace is an absurdity. A nation is a lot of people organised for war, not for peace. We do not form a League of Thieves to make locks unnecessary.

Patriotism is a curiously spotty virtue. On one hand we saw young men throwing up and spoiling their careers and joining up, enduring years of hardship and misery, while they wrote cheery letters home, and risking life and limb over and over again. Many older men gave up their businesses to do war-work gratuitously or at nominal salaries. Many women devoted their whole time and energies to unpaid war-work with no uniform, no man's dress, no meeting with young officers, no excitement, no reward and no recognition. On the other hand, when the Government issued loans, high interest had to be given and people thought they were patriotic in subscribing for them. In order to get them to do the work the country needed, handworkers and women had to be ridiculously over-paid, and young men who were badged, that is to say, whose work at home was necessary, instead of being grateful for their release, demanded exorbitant pay.

The whole attitude of the public was, and is, devoid of any sort of gratitude to those who saved and protected us. We actually paid the men in the trenches less than the young women employed in France. The war was utilised as a means of advertisement. At one period there would be half a column in the papers about what was being done, followed by long accounts of actors and singers who were giving performances to the soldiers. Using the war for purposes of self-advertisement was so common that the term " Limelighters " came into use to denote culprits. The idea that military service was nothing was very clearly shown by the honours lists. Politicians, newspaper men, business and professional men who sat on Government Committees, and all sorts of people who may have done work that was useful in its way, but not dangerous, were made into various kinds of peers, privy councillors and what not. The *Globe* of April 28, 1919, gave a list of hereditary honours only, granted between December 1916 and that date. There were one hundred and twenty-six, of which one went to a sailor. Then there were knighthoods and damehoods galore for people who had done good, but not dangerous work, for people who had talked, and for people with social influence ; in fact a new order had to be made to provide innumerable distinctions for those who did not fight. A glance at Whitaker's Almanac of 1914 and 1920 will give some idea of the extent of this absurdity. Many of the recipients of these honours were of military age and were exempted to do some particular work.

Then the general attitude towards money and the country was instructive. As already mentioned, workmen and munitions women had to be overpaid and flattered to get the work done. But higher up were women, mostly girls, getting high wages as clerks in government offices. Daughters of well-to-do parents would draw several pounds a week for inexperienced services whose pre-war market value was not more than a few shillings, and they really took credit for helping the country and doing Women's War Work.

In the much more important relations between contractors and the government, though patriotism showed itself at first, there soon was striving on the contractors' part to make as much as possible. This, no doubt, partly arose from a common confusion of mind. Contractors and controlled firms dealt with government officials who were generally eager and energetic, but were often not very competent. Sometimes the officials were stupid, obstinate and difficult to deal with as jacks-in-office. In such cases when friction arose, a contractor would feel that the government was trying to stop him and to rob him ; he therefore did his best against it. In practically all such cases the contractor confused the government official with the government, and the government with the country.

There was the same sort of manifestation in connection with the income-tax. At the beginning of the war people paid willingly enough, as they felt the country wanted money. But as the tax began to increase and money became scarcer, the usual friction soon developed again. The methods of collecting income-tax are complicated and unfair, and the officials who deal with it demand more than they are entitled to, hoodwinking the victim, and often give a great deal of unnecessary trouble; and the taxpayer is, no doubt, very apt to act as if the only questions were between him and a hostile government official, and to forget that it is his country that wants the money. He also has the irritating feeling that the money is being wasted in all sorts of bids for popularity among the hand-workers, and in paying for government departments, which are not merely useless, but interfere with industry in all sorts of ways. But in spite of that, it might be expected that patriotism would be the controlling motive. The soldier felt that campaigns are largely controlled by politicians, and that he might be sent on some futile expedition to gratify the vanity of some minister who had a pet scheme, or wanted to make his policy popular with the ignorant at home, but though the real or apparent incompetence or folly of those who control matters affected him ever so much more, his patriotism overcame all, and he did his best with no reservations.

After the war a Royal Commission was appointed to settle claims made by inventors. There seemed to be no signs of patriotism among the claimants. Numbers of people did their best, putting their inventive brains at the service of the country, and naturally little has been heard of them ; but on the other hand, there was a stream of claimants, generally with exorbitant demands for rewards for inventions of little or no merit. Many of these were men in the fighting services, and others were of military age, but had been exempted.

Patch-pride is a form of group-pride, a kind which has many fields and is generally admired and cultivated. At school the boy is taught to take pride in his form and his house, as well as his school, and to look down on boys in other forms or houses. This is at base a simple way of promoting good conduct. By getting all the boys to behave well for the credits of all the different divisions they belong to, a good result is easily gained. Group-pride at school is worked in conjunction with a sort of elementary militarism in games. This is intended to give boys discipline and to teach, unselfishness, and the better kind of schoolboy honour. Militarism is connected very closely not only with patch-pride, but with all the smaller forms of group-pride. Group-feeling makes people do good for the credit of their group, but it seems to be inseparable from group-pride, which tempts people to be proud of being in a particular group. Thus if the inhabitants of a town take delight in laying it out well, and having worthy buildings and good water and other services, so much the better for those in the town ; but when it prevents a district which is looked upon as two, having something good which the parts cannot have separately, merely because they are in two parishes or districts, or have different names, the common foolishness of patch- or group-pride comes out. This sort of nonsense is not confined to the lower classes. The inhabitants of two little neighbouring blots on the map are often too proud to visit across the boundary. Group-pride comes out in the assumption made by barristers, that they are a kind of superior creation which can be approached only through solicitors, and should have little or no contact with such people as clients or witnesses. The manners of a leading counsel to his employers in an ordinary King's Bench case are an amusing study in group-pride. The same thing is seen in the government civil servant, perhaps more especially as you go down. It is notorious that it is impossible to get a government official of any kind to realise that he is the servant of the public. Group, patch and similar forms of pride may do a great deal of harm or a great deal of good. Probably on the small scale the balance is very much on the good side. The group-pride that has led to

most bloodshed in the past has been that of opinion
groups. The most prominent and virulent group
opinions are connected with religion and politics.
Opinions, by which are meant ignorant prejudices
founded on little or no knowledge, are held by most on
religion and politics, because people feel or have felt
concerned in those subjects. The less knowledge there
is as a basis for opinion, the more chance there is for
quarrelling, bloodshed and murder. There is no bitter
enmity between those who embrace the doctrine of
Relativity and those who do not, because the subject
can be discussed, more especially by those who understand it, and relativists do not feel that others have any
sort of contempt for them, and their opponents also
find nothing that hurts their pride. But in politics,
and especially in religious matters, there is no common
basis for discussion. Through our edcuation we feel
great pity for the early Christians, especially the
martyrs, and we picture women martyrs as all young
and beautiful with golden hair hanging pathetically
down. We do not realise how their exasperating
conceit irritated the public. Martyrdom itself was
really a curiously stupid form of pigheaded conceit.
Someone of no account, whose opinion on the unknowable was just as valueless as anybody else's, would insist
that he and a few like him were right and everybody
else wrong, and finally they would become so obnoxious
that force seemed the only cure. In the end they were
told they must be quiet or they would have to be
burned. They preferred being burned, and this was
subsequently taken as a proof that their opinions were
correct. The martyrs used not to wait patiently until
they were burned ; they raised as much trouble as they
could, and if that did not excite enough hostility they
asked the authorities to come and burn them. That
people could think martyrdom proved anything at all
as to the soundness of the martyrs' faith or opinion is
merely one of the many cases of human folly. The
martyrdom of the Middle Ages was largely self-advertisement. In days when there were no illustrated news-

papers a martyr gained the maximum possible notoriety with the least qualification, and satisfied his or her self esteem completely. The idea of martyrdom has not died out yet ; the suffragette antics were akin to it. In all political disturbances now, each side tries to be martyrised and to prevent its opponents being martyrs, as it is realised that nothing attracts public sympathy more than anything like martyrdom. The so-called hunger-strike of felons is a method of gaining foolish sympathy. It is not a strike, but the term strike suggests a struggle of the down-trodden against capitalists, and thus excites sympathy, but the main point is that the culprit is called a martyr, though his or her action has nothing to do with martyrdom. To sympathise with the people in a movement is to adopt their opinions, however absurd they may be.

Martyrdom is relevant only in showing the great power of pride in human conduct, and its special power when in conjunction with opinions with no foundations. The same pride, especially in conjunction with religious opinions, drives people towards murder even more strongly than to merely suffering death themselves. Thus, as Lecky pointed out, once the Christians got power in the Middle Ages, their murders and other cruelties far exceeded anything they had ever suffered in earlier days. At first it seems most extraordinary that a religion pretending, that is claiming, to be that of Jesus, with Love, Charity, Long-suffering, Gentleness and Justice as its root should degrade men into savage devils; but their religion or pretended religion was not the cause at all. The qualities just mentioned have to do with conduct. If a man is kind to those about him, he does not find he is looked down upon, as being in error, and his pride is not affected. It is the pride of opinion that controls him. His religion has no direct influence on his conduct to make him gentle, kind, or just ; it is his opinion or what he calls his belief or faith that degrades him below wild beasts. Such questions as how many gods there are, or how there can be two numbers of them at the same time;

are not only nonsensical and childish, because the words used in the discussion, denoting nothing within human experience, are meaningless, but the questions are of no importance whatever, as their answer would have no bearing on conduct. But it is such matters that lead to the *odium theologicum*. Men will persecute and kill those who disagree with their opinion on what they would call much less important matters, such as the tenets of different branches of the church. Coming to more recent times, much sympathy is generally felt for the early settlers in New England. They were called the " Pilgrim Fathers," and the popular idea is that they longed for freedom of conscience, and left all they loved at home in order to establish religious liberty in a new settlement. Their quarrel at home was not about anything fundamental. It was not even a question of heathens or atheists against Christians ; it was only narrow and quite unimportant sectarianism that caused the friction. The puritans thought they were right. And their enemies thought they were wrong. And each lot felt the other lot did not appreciate them, so trouble came. The puritans may have been quite wrong, but nothing would convince people, especially of that type, that they were wrong, or that they were quarrelling and murdering wholesale about points of no consequence. When they settled in Massachusetts, did their sufferings in Europe teach them to form a gentle society where people might follow their own " consciences " in religious matters, living in kindness and good fellowship? Not a bit of it. The very intolerance that sent them over the sea made them religious murderers of the ordinary sort, and woe to anyone who did not agree with them. Of all gentle victims the quakers must have been the least offensive, but even they were murdered until Charles II had the persecution stopped. Care must be taken not to ascribe to religion the crimes due to religious opinions. Opinion is the cause, and religious opinion happens to be the most provocative, because it has least foundation on which any argument or reasoning can be based.

Though it is intimately connected with patriotism, or patch-pride, militarism is not the same thing. It depends on another kind of pride. In the early stages of social life the man who defended his tribe or was successful on their behalf in raiding other tribes was looked up to by his opponents as dangerous, and by his tribesmen as their hero, and he was especially admired by women. Personal courage, or manliness has thus come down to us as a leading merit. From this idea we get the notion that there is something grand in fighting, because it shows courage and fortitude or strength. So fond are we of this idea that we press it into all sorts of absurd places. We forget that a soldier's real business is killing his fellows. The pretext does not matter to us, and it seldom matters to him. The idea of bravery and fortitude overrides that of killing fellow men. Religious people call themselves soldiers of the Lord on every conceivable occasion, and sing about blood-red banners and all the rest of it. Nothing can be more opposed to the real spirit of Christianity than the glorification of the killing of our fellow men. One religious body boldly calls itself an army, with bogus officers of various ranks. Certainly in one hymn the elect are workmen of the Lord, but as the hymn says they know when to strike, it is felt that the notion was an irruption of militarism rather than artistic colour. When people ask a judge to decide between them on a money matter, they call it a fight. Even during the war politicians described elections as fights, and when the voting went their way, as great victories.

The soldiers and sailors in the upper ranks have handles to their names and take precedence of other and better people. This privilege is granted to royalties, peers, baronets, knights, parsons, medical men, holders of doctor's degrees and certain pedagogues ; a very odd collection. A really important person has to give precedence to his son, if he has his captaincy.

Thus do we keep militarism in the forefront. Militarism, as so far discussed, is merely admiration

for soldiering. The term is used in a much larger
sense to denote the doctrine that nations must, in the
nature of things, go to war at intervals. Some hold that
this is inevitable because it is human nature, while
others argue that war is not only inevitable, but that
it is a good thing generally, while others hold that it
is good for those who win.

Like most of the tendencies discussed, war is based
on tribal instinct handed down. There is patriotism,
which is a form of the tribal solidarity, which kept a
group together and enabled it to hold its own. There
is the love of fighting and killing men, which also
enabled a tribe to survive, and there is the hunting
instinct, which is still older. This instinct is still
strong in Western civilisation, especially in England.
It finds vent, and is encouraged in what is called sport,
an amusement which consists essentially in killing small
and inoffensive animals for the mere pleasure of hunting
them. When one sees a big strong man, got up in
special clothes for the purpose, armed with a hundred
guinea killing machine and assisted by dogs, returning
from an afternoon's sport with a few poor bleeding
little furry bunnies, against whom he has nobly and
victoriously pitted himself, sport seems too ridiculous
for serious discussion, though one cannot help being
sorry for the little murdered rabbits. When a fox
takes refuge in your garden with the terror of death on
it, panting and ready to drop with fatigue, followed by
a lot of trained dogs, and men, and even worse, women,
or ladies, who are for the time being just a lot of
depraved savages, one realises that civilisation is only
skin deep. The sportsmen no doubt say that their
victims like being killed, or that as they have to die
anyhow, perhaps painfully, they are no worse off, and
may as well have their lives given to pander to man's
love of killing. No doubt the young Greeks told off
to kill the poor when they had multiplied too much
used the same argument to justify their sport. That
argument would not appeal even to a sportsman now,
if men were the game, but we are still too uncivilised

to have sympathy with and kindness for dumb animals. The fate of the poor animals is not the important point here, though ; it is that by encouraging what is called sport, we are keeping alive a bad instinct that is one of the causes of war.

Mere cruelty to animals, apart altogether from the hunting instincts of primitive man, is still very common. We are cruel to horses. We keep all sorts of wild animals, such as birds, in cruel captivity ; and a man who thoughtlessly keeps his miserable animals tied up calls himself a lover of dogs. Small boys, especially among the poor, are extraordinarily cruel. They smash nests and eggs, and kill any wild animal they can, out of pure savagery. Whether Lytton was right in alloting killing to women, in the " Coming Race " or not, the little girl in the poorer classes is not a cruel little savage like her brother.

If it were asked why we went to war in 1914, the answer was that we were obliged to fight for Belgium, which is true; or that we were in honour bound to help France, which was also true. A further reason was given that if Germany beat France now it would attack us later, and we could not hold our own then. Or again, we were fighting for democracy. This was largely a politician's cry. We were fighting to preserve our trade. In fact we were fighting for all sorts of things.

Perhaps the immediate cause of our fighting was that we had to fight. Consider therefore the German point of view. Before they began, the feeling was that Germany wanted a place in the sun. This meant that their position somehow did not satisfy the Germans' vanity. They looked down from the exceeding high mountain of their own conceit, and saw all the kingdoms of the world and the glory of them, but very few of the patches were of their colour. There was a large American patch, there were French patches, and even small countries like Holland and Portugal had colonial patches, while England's colour was splashed and dotted about all over the map in a most irritating way. All

the patches that are thought to be of any value were
taken. Germany had one or two daubs of colour, but
her colonies were not important.

Then there was a confused and inaccurate view of
the population question. Germany found her population was increasing rapidly. It was not realised that
this did not mean in the least that population pressure
was greater in Germany than elsewhere, but that it
meant just as much that the country was enabling itself
to support more people, and therefore the people grew
to fit the opening. It was thought that Germany had
somehow developed some sort of special fecundity,
so that her population had acquired the prospects
of increasing with an irresistible force. Improved
industry enabled the country to support a larger population ; but the population would go on increasing in a
relentless way, and the increase of means of living
would not go on in the same way, so that room must
be found elsewhere for the new-comers. It is quite
true that the Germans were very well trained and very
industrious, and the whole world was open to them.
They came to England and flourished, they went to
America in large numbers and got on splendidly, and
in almost every country they could settle down and
compete easily with the natives. A German had no
disabilities anywhere. The world was his open oyster.
Not only was there room everywhere for him to make
his way for himself, but he worked in with his native
country and pushed German business everywhere.
Germany was developing an enormous foreign trade in
spite of an uneconomical policy of foreign trade
restriction.

It is difficult for anyone not versed in the opinions
of the various groups in Germany to form any accurate
idea. It is possible that the Junkers and militarists
were rather jealous of the increasing power, importance
and influence of the commercial men. Germany, like
Japan, was only half civilised in the sense that one
part of the influential people were mediæval in their
ideas, and thought that it was disgraceful to make a

living by doing anything for the community, and that
all business, trading and professional work was low.
Even in England now a man who does nothing is
described as a "gentleman." America alone is civilised
in this respect. This class may have felt that to let
Germany become the dominant nation of the world by
peaceful penetration of other nations, until the majority
of the property and influence in the more civilised
countries was German, did not glorify them in particular ; it showed that the industrial and commercial
people were superior. What they wanted, therefore, was
to conquer by war managed by them, so that all the
credit, and what they call glory, would be theirs. The
fundamental ideas are childish. The notion is that if
Germany conquers another country, that country then
belongs to Germany, and all the wealth in it becomes
hers, and all the industries become hers too. How
any individual German is any better off no one tries to
explain. After war in modern times, the conqueror
does not confiscate all private property. At most he
demands a large indemnity. But, unless the victory
comes very soon, there is no chance of a serious
indemnity, as, if the war goes on long, both countries
will be nearly exhausted, and the most thoroughly
exhausted will give in.

To put a very extreme case, suppose the Belgians
had let the Germans come through, and when they
reached France, suppose the French had hospitably
offered them coffee and rolls and asked what they
wanted. They would have said they wanted to conquer
France. They might not have said "Give us five
hundred billion francs," that would have been such
obvious brigandage. But they might have hidden the
demand for ransom under the name of indemnity.
France might say "We have not so much ready money,
but you are welcome to it if you can get it." Germany
would have said "In that case we cannot conquer you,
as you do not resist, but we will just take France.."
France would then be part of Germany, and that means
that Germany would be part of France. There would

be no sense in taking one part of the big, new country, in favour of the other. But even if they did not exact a payment, the Germans might choose to govern France, or to try to govern it. The German desire to do so and the French objection to their governing it would depend on pride on both sides. Imagine this part of the case to be between Germany and England instead of France. Before the war many Englishmen went to Germany for business and other purposes and lived there very happily. The German Government did not make them unhappy. They may have thought ours better, but if they compared their freedom in Germany ten years ago with that of an Englishman after the war, with all the restrictions under the Defence of the Realm Act, and all the government control and pernicious interference with industry, there was more freedom in Germany. Then there is the increasing truckling of the British Government to the labour leaders, and its fear of the ignorant voter, encouraging strikes and all sorts of kindred troubles. Considered apart altogether from national pride it may be said that one would suffer much less under the German Government before the war than under the British after it. But the government of a civilised country plays very little real part in the happiness of its inhabitants at all. Suppose, therefore, that the British Government, in the hands of British politicians, were like the German Government ten years ago, and the result of a war was to change it into the British Government as it now is ; it would certainly not have been worth while for us to have gone through our four years' war with its aftermath to secure the present conditions including as a crowning attraction the after-war government. In discussing government in a later chapter it will be urged not only that each country has the government it deserves, or that the government is as foolish as the people, but that the government in all countries is as bad as its people will stand. Our real objection to a German government of England is not any question of the nature of the government. Our pride would make it hateful to us to

be governed by Germans. Our objection to being
conquered by them is not that they would impoverish
us. If the Germans had come into England in 1914
unopposed and demanded a ransom it would not have
cost us anything like what the war has cost, apart
altogether from the actual miseries of war.

There are really at least three or four ostensible
reasons for war, which may be considered more fully
one by one.

The first and most popular is the idea that each
country is necessarily put to great expense in keeping
a good defence in order, and that if war breaks out
it is entitled to an indemnity if it wins. The popular
idea is that a country can any time, even at the end of
a war, hand over millions of pounds' worth of gold.
The next idea is that the conquered country can be
taxed, and that money, which is generally confused with
currency, and especially with gold, will be collected and
paid. Those who know anything of economics of course
realise that the conquered really pays its indenmity in
commodities. After a war it has no commodities to
send, so there must be delay. Instead of a fixed payment, in commodities, the country therefore pays tribute
for a fixed number of years, or permanently. But what
probably happens in due course is that the ownership
of the wealth changes. The wealth of a conquered
country is mainly factories, railways and transport and
rentable land. These are wealth only if the conquerors
allow them to be used productively. If the victors
prevent their use there is no wealth. Thus suppose the
Allies insisted on getting the maximum reparation out
of Germany, they would put Germany in such a position
that all the population were working at the production
of commodities which would first provide them with the
necessaries of life, and would, beyond this, provide the
maximum of exports. The works would soon all be
owned by various allied or neutral capitalists, the
Germans who were formerly rich men would be poor
and would have to find salaried work, or to earn wages,
and all the workers at the production of luxuries of all

sorts for German consumption would change over and produce goods for export, and the necessaries for home use. The whole German population would then be hewers of wood and drawers of water.

This is assuming the purchasers of the works in Germany did not move in and live there. If they did, Germany would be the same as before except that the individual rich Germans would have become poor, and would be replaced by foreigners who would, or might live in exactly the same luxury as the Germans they replaced. The result of the war to Germany might therefore be that she paid her indemnity by passing all her wealth into the hands of immigrant owners, so that the country consisted entirely of alien upper classes and German workmen. It would not take long for perfect fusion to take place, and in a generation or two the only difference would be that the rich men of the country had foreign grandfathers.

Taking the case then of two countries which go to war ; they fight until both are poor, then an indemnity has to be paid by the loser. This may be paid by men from the victorious coming into the conquered country and settling down as proprietors. In a few generations the net result will be merely the few effects that may still remain of a change of individuals that own the wealth.

Otherwise the countries are both poorer than before, and population will have decreased, other things being equal. But in fact the wealthy men that come and settle down in the conquered country will largely be neutrals, will be richer, and life will be easier for them, as they will not be so unpopular as men from the victorious enemy country. A country can thus pay either by exporting goods or by importing property owners.

It is conceivable that a conquered country might have its factories owned by foreigners, and controlled by native managers employed by the foreigners. This would differ little from the case in which the original owners kept the factories, but were so heavily taxed that the factories made nothing but home necessaries and goods for export, while the owners remained poor. Neither the poor, heavily taxed owner, nor the paid manager arrangement could compete with the immigrant owner, so that the tendency is for a conquered country to pay its indemnity by submitting to its property passing into the hands of immigrants, who may be few in number. Though they may have great commercial power, it may be coupled with very little political influence.

The net result of war so far is loss of life and loss of wealth. In ancient times the loss of life was so great in proportion to the loss of wealth, that war made the survivors richer for the time, and was thus a simple and obvious way of easing population pressure. The reduction of pressure was due directly to the soldiers killed, and of course to the civilians killed too, in cases of massacre and starvation. But it must also be remembered that the soldiers who were killed were mostly young men, and their deaths also meant a great reduction of births.

In modern war there has been a tendency to limit the death-roll to soldiers, and to convert war into a sort of sport, governed by sporting rules. According to these rules certain ways of killing enemies were dishonourable ; for instance, it was against the rules to use dumdum or similar bullets, shells under a pound, poisoned projectiles, and so on. It was not the game to kill men who surrendered, even if they had been working machine-guns under cover up to the moment of capture. Poisoning wells was quite improper. Chlorine and other poison gases had been proposed by Lord Dundonald, but were not according to the rules of the game. The consistent end of such a system is to settle international disputes by a fight between a few picked champions on each side, or a single knight, and they might contend without killing either. The Germans held a different and much more logical view. They realised that the object of war is to injure your enemy as much as possible in every conceivable way. They therefore eliminated all traces of anything like chivalry, honour or generosity from war. They introduced poison gases, they bombarded defenceless sea-coast towns, they organised air raids to murder civilians, some tortured and ill treated prisoners, or were bestial to women in their power ; they murdered civilians and they organised their submarines specially for murdering more civilians, and they made certain prisoners work as slaves. In short, they realised that war is a beastly business, so they made themselves into hypobeasts with outstanding success. But did the Allies wage war so as to press on soldiers only? On the contrary, we starved Germany and Austria, and the sufferers were first the poor children and poor women, then the poor men, and after them the children and women of the next higher grades and so on. The soldiers were the only class not affected, because they were always fed well to make them good fighters. It is easier to write about the German atrocities, because they are picturesque in their abomination. Gradual starvation of a country like Austria inflicts infinitely greater misery on non-combatants than all the German atrocities.; but the misery is of a kind that is already so familiar to human beings who ignore the principle of population that it does not appeal to the imagination, though the suffering caused not only during the war, but after it, when the intensity and the duration of the misery and the number of sufferers is considered, must dwarf the results of the German atrocities altogether. It is said that reducing a besieged town by starving it is according to the best practice, or the rules of the game, in war, and there-fore reducing a couple of nations in the same way is according to the Queensberry rules. But that is not really to the point.

Ten years hence a young Austrian coming of age may remember how his father was killed in a war made against his will by his government. He will remember his mother toiling for scraps of food for his sisters, and how they all starved in pain and spun out misery. He will remember his own robust constitution and how it let him pull through, though now feeble and deformed. He may not think of the English gentleman as a very noble being. Our blockade after the armistice, when our enemies were at our mercy, will send the name of England stinking down the ages.

It is difficult to realise the indirect effects of a war like the last on population or on wealth. The loss of wealth or rather the effect of the loss of wealth in war is apt to be over-estimated, because we forget the continual consumption and waste of capital in peace, and do not deduct that from the waste in war to find the real loss due to it.

On the other hand, we are apt to consider only the soldiers killed in action. Those lost by disease, especially in hot places, is very large. Though great care is taken now, the loss by disease is very serious. There is indirect loss by disease too. Syphilis was more serious in this than any other war, for example. The loss of life in the poorer parts of the middle East of Europe by starvation and misery, including the losses by massacres of Armenians, must have been very large. An ideal war, if such an expression can be used, would merely kill off a good percentage of inhabitants in the least unpleasant way. Which side won would not matter much. Then people would set to work again at once, and produce practically as much as before, with fewer mouths to feed, so that population pressure would be eased for a time.

The last war has developed a state of what people who like malformed words call "unrest." This is due partly to the strong one-sided hostility of the hand-working classes towards those who are, or are supposed to be better off, which causes a fissure which goes right across the international enmities. The politicians in the various countries pander to this hostility, and the result, partly due to this feeling and partly no doubt to the strain people have been through, is that even in neutral countries which have not been at war, and such distant countries as Japan, people have not settled down to make the best of things, but are still laying up debts of further trouble, which must certainly be paid some day soon. Directly war broke out there was a shortage of hand-workers, as many men were wanted as soldiers, and munitions were needed. The demand sent wages up, and though a wave of patriotism swept through the country, it was not enough, or did not last long enough to prevent the demand for high wages. The politicians were not bold enough to put munitions makers on the same basis as soldiers, as they feared they would lose votes and go out of power ; so they bowed themselves to the hand-workers, flattered them in every way, promised them a glorious lotusland after the war, encouraged strikes and paid ridiculous wages. Their officials and other fanatics led the hand-workers to believe that the high wages were their just reward, or at least part of it, and that the difference between their old and new wages was the whole, or perhaps only part, of what the capitalist stole from them in pre-war days. Then the demand was so great that women were trained to do unskilled men's production work, also at ridiculous wages, and were also employed in the old and the numerous new government offices. At the end of the war it might seem that we were in a first-rate position to recover lost time ; we had in addition to the original hand-workers a large number of newly-trained workers and a host of trained women. Besides, we had developed works organisation on mass production lines so that a better output could be secured. In other countries the conditions were more or less the same. But instead of settling down to reproduce the wealth that had been lost, the world seemed to run riot in idleness and extravagance. It may be asked how countries which were impoverished in a war could indulge in idleness and extravagance directly it was over. Extravagance is impossible unless there is something to spend.

The conditions are complicated by the debasement of the currency. In war the government wants money. Money can be raised properly by taxation or by loans. Taxation is unpopular and a government, whether

14

democratic or not, is especially anxious not to be unpopular while waging war. In a democratic country
this may be because the individuals feel that if they
are unpopular they will go out of power, but a higher
motive is also present, and is alone present in the case
of non-democratic governments, and that is that it is
bad for the country if its government is unpopular
during war. Raising money by issuing loans, or
borrowing from banks is more popular, especially as
many people imagine it puts the burden of war on
posterity instead of on the living, and as posterity is
supposed to benefit by the war, it is supposed to be
sound finance. Of course it is nonsense. The money
is spent at once, and the burden is not on posterity. If
a man has a thousand pounds and the government takes
it by taxation and spends it on shells, it is spent and
gone, and the man is poorer by a thousand pounds, and
so is the country. If the government borrows the money
at 6 per cent., the money is spent, and the man gets
£60 a year ; but if he is taxed to enable the government
to pay the interest, he is taxed either £60 or considerably more to pay the expenses of collection and administration. He is thus in exactly the same position as if
he had lost the thousand pounds, or in a worse position.
In practice people do not pay taxes in exact proportion
to their loans, but that merely alters the distribution of
the losses ; it does not take the burden off the present
and put it on posterity. If the money is borrowed
from abroad, it puts the burden on posterity as far as
the country, but not as far as the world is concerned.
It is merely from the patch point of view that the
posterity comes in. There is a difficulty about borrowing money to an unlimited extent. Each war loan
is at a higher interest than before, and interferes with
previous loans on the same security. The way most
obvious to a government is to put out paper currency.
The idea that you can make wealth by printing is that
of a child ; the idea that you can make yourself rich
at the expense of the community by printing is that of
the forger. The crime of the forger of a five pound

note is not that he makes himself five pounds richer, but that he makes the rest of the community five pounds poorer. By issuing paper money a government makes itself a little richer temporarily, and it makes the rest of the world so much poorer ; but that is not the real injury it does ; it impoverishes some classes and enriches others to the same extent, and disorganises industry. The first result of a war is to depreciate gold, chiefly by the various countries issuing convertible paper. This brought gold down to about 70 per cent. of its pre-war value. The British Government then went on issuing unconvertible paper until £100 in paper was worth about £70 in gold. As gold had fallen 30 per cent., this meant that the paper pound was worth almost exactly half the pre-war sovereign. The usual result of gradually rising prices is that wages do not rise quickly enough, so that the hand-workers suffer. This is partly because people do not understand falling money and think prices rise. If we suddenly altered the standard yard to half its present length and re-made our foot rules and re-dimensioned our maps, people would easily grasp the notion of America being six thousand miles away, and men being from ten to twelve feet high. They would realise at once that the units of length and not the rest of the universe had altered. But few people can realise the alteration in the unit of currency. The results of the debasement of currency are far-reaching. To begin with, a large and important class lives on salaries and professional fees. It is much more difficult to raise these. Take the case of a man who earned fifteen hundred sovereigns before the war. He is paid fifteen hundred paper pounds, worth seven hundred and fifty sovereigns. A large portion is taken as income-tax, leaving him with much less than half his pre-war income. If he succeeded in doubling his nominal income, so as to get three thousand paper pounds, his taxes would go up from, say, a quarter to a third, leaving him two thousand paper pounds, or one thousand pre-war sovereigns. As salaries and professional fees have hardly gone up at all we have what are broadly called the middle classes producing as much as before the war for one-third of their pre-war income.

There is also a large class, partly overlapping the salaried and professional, who live on the interests on investments, such as government loans, debentures and other stocks which pay a fixed percentage. Their interest is all reduced to half its proper value. If they hold government securities the government takes the other half. The debasement of the sovereign to half its value thus wipes out half the pre-war national debt. In the case of industrial concerns, debenture holders, and those who hold shares paying fixed dividends lose half their property. This is partly given to the ordinary shareholders, and partly taken by government. Thus suppose a pre-war company has £100,000 in ordinary shares and £100,000 in 5 per cent. debentures, and the ordinary shares also pay 5 per cent. regularly. The company pays £5,000 in debenture interest and £5,000 to the shareholders. After the war, the same company doing the same business has its cost and selling prices nominally doubled. If a new company started in competition, it would need 400,000 paper pounds for plant and working capital, and it would pay 20,000 paper pounds to its share and debenture holders. The old company thus pays 5,000 paper pounds, really 2,500 pre-war sovereigns to its debenture holders, who find they have really had half their property taken, while there is 15,000 paper pounds or 7,500 sovereigns available for dividends. But if the company declares 15 per cent. dividend the workmen who are already receiving nominally doubled, or really the original wages, say that the capitalists are robbing them, and go on strike, and the government claims that most of the profits are excess and belong to the State. The ordinary shareholders are thus deprived of their property too.

There are many more cases. A man who has insured his life, for example, finds that half his prospective property is gone. The insurance companies may get some of it, but it is difficult to trace it. If the insurance companies pay large dividends as a result, they may be mulcted for excess profits, and of course, much of their dividends themselves are taken as income-tax.

It is not altogether irrelevant to point out that the additional sufferings of the middle classes, through the absence of domestic servants, owing to the government overpaying girls of the servant class with money taken from the middle classes, even paying them doles if they prefer not to go back to work, means that middle-class women are doing more work and the lower less. The main point to be put forward here, however, is the injury done by the debasement of the currency.

Not only does a government halve its national debt by debasing the currency to half its value, but it gets into very serious trouble as to the post-war future. Thus if it increases the national debt to an almost fabulous amount by issuing loans after it has debased the currency, the loans are taken up in paper pounds, and as long as the currency remains debased the high interest is paid in paper pounds. This makes it very difficult to get back to normal currency, because that involves putting the old national debt back to its original value, which is only fair, but it also involves paying the subscribers to the later loans, who subscribed paper pounds, in reinstated sovereigns. That is to say, it is doubling the value of the recent portion of the national debt.

How a government which has debased the currency of a commercial country is going to put things right, is a great question. The debt may be repudiated in some indirect way. It is very foolish of any country to give a government power to issue paper money ; it gives an ignorant and irresponsible set of people facility for ruining the commerce of the country. The debasement of currency in England is bad enough, and the possible eventual repudiation of debts is a threatening disaster, but some other countries have carried that form of folly farther. Russia and Germany are a good example. The governments there turned out so many paper notes that their value sank to nothing, and the countries were without currency.

The debasement of the currency has, as one effect, the impoverishment of the middle classes. This enables the hand-workers to go on for a longer time consuming more than they produce. But it is not possible to impoverish one class in favour of another as a permanent state ; so it means that when the bad times for hand-workers come, those times will be so much the harder.

If the currency necessary for the commerce of a country is x million pounds, it might be supposed that a government could make only something less than x million pounds by debasing, but if the inflation is conducted slowly and the real value of the total currency remains constant the government raises a value equal to the logarithm of the ratio of the new to the old currency. This may be increased without limit, but as the currency has to increase much faster, the disastrous state of Russia or Germany is soon reached. The harm done to the public is, of course, out of all proportion to the money raised by the government.

It is not generally realised that their control of the issue of currency puts the whole of the fabric of commerce at the mercy of irresponsible and ignorant governments. A whole class of investors may find their property confiscated, or given to others who waste it ; or the value of currency may be made to vary so that no commerce is stable, just because we allow a set of ignorant politicians to donkey with a die-press.

In discussing depreciation of currency, nothing has been said about the government borrowing from the banks, especially from the Bank of England. That is a text-book source of high prices, but as I do not see how the effect can be more than temporary, it is left out, though I may be wrong there. The influence of shortage of capital on the effect of plentiful currency is also left on one side.

A modern war might have the result of lessening the population pressure for a short time, if people came to their senses directly it was over. Even then it would be a fearfully cruel as well as a very inefficient way of producing this result. But in practice people are so unsettled after the war, and the return to common sense is so strongly opposed by politicians, " labour " leaders and their like, that it does not produce even this slight temporary benefit. It is not impossible that war will end not because people become wiser, or more civilised, or because we slowly get more cosmopolitan. A universal belief that everyone is as good as the best, and therefore much better than most is incompatible with discipline. It is doubtful whether a war could be waged successfully without discipline. Democracy is at present a mere veneer, and the large majority of a nominally and politically democratic people may be quite capable of forming a disciplined and efficient army, but it is not easy to see whether democracy will ever become real.

The evils of war do not end with it by any means. It might be expected that after a war people would settle down and work with double vigour to get straight again. This does not happen. To begin with, the politicians have to settle and agree on the terms of peace. They wrangle for months over details which sound serious but are of no real importance, and they keep matters unsettled for so long that their discussions and delays are almost as damaging to all the nations concerned, including the victors, that it would be simpler and better if all the points were settled by tossing coins. It may sound odd that delay should hurt the victors, but as all countries are interdependent on industry, what is bad for one country hurts all the others. Then there is the question of indemnity. Obviously the conquered countries cannot pay hundreds of millions in gold, and if they did, the victors would have to change it for goods. We can imagine negotiations carried on, of course, with no end of circumlocution and formality, between the representative politicians. Germany would say she has no gold, but she will pay willingly. She will set to, and work hard, and her people will sell us a million pounds' worth of goods. This will be paid for in cash, and the cash, as it comes into Germany, will be collected by taxation and returned to us. We thus get our indemnity paid in kind, million after million. But the Allies' politicians object. They say that every million pounds' worth of goods deprives the Allies' hand-workers of a million in wages, so that they are put out of work. Moreover, the Germans want to give a great deal of goods for a million pounds, perhaps two million pounds' worth, depriving the Allies' hand-workers of two million in wages. Germany must not send any goods at all, or if she does they must be taxed, and every obstacle must be put in the way of her paying the indemnity. But they must pay the indemnity at once without any more shuffling or duplicity ; and if they do not, the papers shout that the Allies should march to Berlin and take the indemnity. This is not a humorous book ; these imaginary negotiations are hardly a travesty of the actual foolery about the indemnity. The war was a very big human affair, and the bigger a human affair is, the greater the folly in working it. It is only carrying the foolishness a little further for the Allies to say that as Germany's payment in goods does the Allies harm and the Germans good, we should enforce the indemnity the other way. We should pour goods into Germany, thus throwing their workmen out and starving them, while we have plenty of employment, and plenty of high wages. It is perhaps only because we are too war-worn that the politicians do not bring on another great All Fools' War, the victors to trample their vanquished enemies in the dust by sending them all the remaining wealth still left. Such a war is not really necessary ; the Allies can now set to work and dump every bit of our movable property and can employ all our hand-workers fully in producing a colossal river of free goods flowing into Germany, till that country is ruined and annihilated.

CHAPTER XIV

THE PREVENTION OF WAR

MANY causes will arise to prevent war as we get more civilised and less ignorant ; some of these have to do with Population Pressure, and some have not. The first necessity is that people should understand that war does not pay even the victor. This has been pressed home so ably and so thoroughly by Mr. Angell that there is no need to deal with it, less ably, here.

As we get more civilised we will eventually have enough sympathy to dislike murder. If a man insures the life of a victim and then poisons him, he is hanged when found out. If he wants to be king or president of some unsettled people and spurs discontented and ignorant men to revolution and bloodshed on a large scale, he is called a patriot, a leader of men, or a hero, if he is successful ; whereas he is only a bloody-minded murderer, who excites others on to slay to gratify his vanity. Whatever the legal definition of murder may be, by murder I mean taking the life of a human being to benefit by it oneself. If he works on a large enough scale, like Napoleon, or " Alexander the great Murderer," his name is blazed down history. If he fails nothing much is done to him, because he was engaged in a political movement. We punish a retail murderer because we want to discourage other people who might murder you or me if they did not see that it might get them punished. This reason does not hold in the case of killing foreigners, and as killing foreigners and killing wholesale in wars has come down from old times, we do not realise how vile it is. Having the idea that killing foreigners is no crime, because we do not see how stopping it will make our own lives safer, we let the opinion that killing is no crime spread into cases of civil war, rebellion, class riots and strikes. A great deal of the trouble of smaller disturbances is due to want of discipline. The boy, and now even the flapper, are very dangerous. Democracy involves absence of discipline. During the war, again, the German small boy had no discipline. Photographs of rows in the Ruhr and elsewhere showed that the fighters were boys. It was the same in Ireland. The murderers were mostly ignorant and irresponsible boys, and sometimes young girls. We have the same thing in strike riots. The trade unions are controlled by boys so far as they are controlled by the members at all. The responsible older and saner men generally do not vote ; that is left to the more ignorant and inexperienced.

As we get more developed, and gentler, and learn to love our fellow-beings a little, the idea of murder will grow hateful, and the glamour will wear off the soldier or fighting sailor, and the popinjay uniforms and titles will go ; and before the professional fighter disappears he will in an intermediate state be merely an unavoidable evil like the public hangman. This change will be all the easier because modern war is getting meaner. It was possible to weave romance over battles where there was something of personal conflict and prowess ; but there is nothing inspiriting about a lot of chemists experimenting, or looking up books to find poison gases, nor about killing a people by a system of spies organised in an enemy country in advance. Starving an enemy by blockading him may be heroic only if he can retaliate. Burning down a few big towns and scorching the inhabitants without declaring war, before a country has had time to organise its air defences, or dropping a new and very virulent poison that wipes out men, women and children, may at least be considered low and vile. The more war developes along modern lines, and the sooner it becomes wholly repulsive to high-minded and generous people the sooner it will stop.

Disarmament is often proposed, with a League of Nations or some equally ridiculous body to settle disputes between countries. In the first place there are no real sensible disputes between nations, as nations have no real interests as such. This does not mean that there would be no disputes, but that they would not be such that any tribunal could settle unless it had independent power to enforce its judgments. It must be remembered we have not yet developed any sense of national morality. We think we are moral nationally, but we have only to ask impartial outsiders their opinions of the Opium or South African War. A picture was drawn last chapter of France welcoming the Germans with rolls and coffee ; such a course would knock all the honour and glory out of war, but it is not in the least practical, as long as ordinary ideas live. If we had no navy or army, other countries would invent grievances and demand indemnities.

We are not yet arrived at disarmament, but we are very moderate in our ideas. All we want is to have a navy as strong as any two other navies. This idiotic notion, appealing to all nations, leads to the race in armament. The common idea is that the race in armaments impoverishes the countries competing. The population principle shows that, taking the long view, it merely means that fewer people can live in those countries, not that the men and women are poorer.

It is possible that Mr. Angell's clear logic may persuade even the fallowest mind that war does not pay ; and it is also possible that the Great War has made people realise that even the victors, whoever they really are, are not enriched. In that case it will not be necessary for each nation to strive to be able to fight any two others ; all that will be necessary is that each nation should be able to put up such a resistance if attacked, that though it fails to protect itself, it causes the victor to lose, so that war is not worth while.

The problem of nations and war has never been tackled from the population point of view. It is quite true that a nation is not a commercial, but a war unit, and that it is composed of elements which form various international, or rather non-national trading units. But when a nation goes to war you can think of it as a unit, all the more because the war isolates it. Suppose Germany had not been ignorant of the effect of 42 cm. howitzers, and had gone straight into France, destroying the frontier forts before they were altered, and had taken Paris in 1914, without delay in Belgium or British opposition, and extorted a big indemnity. This indemnity would, of course, really be paid in imports, and the argument that Germany would object to imports, as they are trade restrainers, is unsound, because the question whether they think an indemnity good or bad is not to the point. They would be better off, as wealth would be pouring into the country ; and all the Germans might be richer in proportion, living in a perceptibly higher degree of comfort. But this would be temporary only, as population would grow until the people got back to the normal condition. If the indemnity consisted of a flow of goods which lasted twenty years and then suddenly stopped, the Germans would find they were plunged into trouble, as the population would be adapted to a district getting goods gratis, and would have to give way to population pressure and sink in numbers suddenly when the inflow stopped.

Consider, on the other hand, France in the imaginary circumstances. After the war she has lost a lot by damage and war costs, and she has to send out a lot of goods for twenty years. As explained already, a people meets the loss of war by the well-to-do going on doing the same work as before, and living economically, so that the production is great in proportion to the consumption ; and it was explained that that can only be a temporary state. The real adjustment is made by a reduction of population. After a little, Germany has a larger and France a smaller population, and the men and women in each are just as well or badly off as before the war. When the indemnity stops, Germany is in trouble, and France is relieved, and the men and women there have a good time until their population comes up to normal.

Another method of stopping war, which has appealed

to people strongly in old days, is for the victor to go on
kicking his enemy when he is down, until he is so
broken that he can never fight again.   We can imagine
a politician putting the words of Satan into his enemies'
mouth : " Henceforth their might we know, and know
our own, so as not either to provoke, or dread new war,
provoked ; our better part remains to work in close
design, by fraud or guile, what force effected not ; that
they no less at length from us may find, who overcomes
by force, hath overcome but half his foe." The politician's idea is that if the enemy is allowed to trade
outside his country he is hurting all the countries that
trade with him ; and that if he is allowed to trade or
even to live unmolested with his external trade repressed,
he will get strong enough to fight again. Any idea that
France can make herself safe against Middle Europe
by grinding it down into a pulp is absurd, and unless
she can grind all Europe, not to speak of America, into
a pulp, she can never make herself safe—as long as we
hold the mediæval idea that war can be good for the
victors.

There is more chance of stopping war by removing
some causes which depend on questions of population
and food as understood, and as misunderstood.

There may easily be war with our own colonies if
England arrives at a state of understanding of international trade before them. Imagine all our colonies
combined into Colonia, for simplicity. In the past England annexed Colonia, which was then unoccupied by
civilised men. She sent out a few colonists, and they
increased until they were a small but not negligible
portion of the population. They were in new country,
which was naturally rich farm and agricultural land.
It was clear that if Colonia supplied food and wool, and
England supplied manufactures, and if a steady flow of
emigrants went to Colonia as it developed, both England
and Colonia would " flourish." But the Colonials argue
that though Colonia originally belonged to England,
and they went out merely as a first batch of colonists,
the whole place now belongs to them, and in no way to

England. They will keep it to themselves, shouting " Colonia for the Colonials," and will stop any immigration. They know no economics, and think that if they prevent English manufactures coming in they can manufacture for themselves locally, employing more people, and can still send out as much food and wool as ever. Suppose, what after all is a big supposition, that after two centuries of teaching work by economists, the English have at least understood just the simple fact that any change of imports of a district involves an equal change of exports. The English will then realise that the Colonials are not only " injuring " Colonia, by setting people on to manufacture badly, instead of to grow food and wool well, but are starving England by refusing to let them have food, though England originally started Colonia to get that food. They may then argue that the Colonial government is responsible not only to Colonia, but to England, because any action of any government in restraining her own trade restrains outsiders' trade to the same extent, so that on the matter of restraining trade a government is responsible not only to its own people, but to the whole civilised world. If countries which have the food supplies of the world play the fool with their external trade for what they think is their own benefit, it is possible manufacturing countries which depend on them for food, and are as much affected by their restrictions as they are themselves, may be foolish enough to take forcible measures to prevent their welfare being interfered with by ignorance.

It is quite true that the effect of the ignorance of the Colonial government is, in the long run, merely to lessen the population of England, and that in the long run the individuals in England will not be poorer, there will merely be fewer of them. But it will take very many centuries before a people will think it does not really matter if they are reduced to a smaller population by outside governments, which they can easily control if they like.

Restraint of its own trade by any government may thus soon be recognised not only as a foolish act towards its own people, but as a hostile act to all the other peoples. If the manufacturing country restrains its external trade artificially it inflicts a similar injury, as it compels the food-producing colony to manufacture for itself, growing less, and thus becoming inefficient, and therefore eventually smaller in population.

An elementary understanding of international trade may thus remove one cause of war.

At present a locality in which there is extra population pressure eases its pressure by some of the people moving out. If a country has extra pressure it is not so easy to lessen the pressure in this way. The number of people moved would have to be very large, and it is a much more serious matter for people to change countries. As explained earlier, emigration is no use as a relief for normal population pressure. But as population questions are not understood, countries are often anxious to send out emigrants. The emigrants may be men from the lower strata who are no good at home, or such men with their families, or they may be the best and most enterprising men, either with or without families.

A nation is not likely to declare war on a country because it refuses to let in riff-raff, as the nation does not generally worry about its riff-raff. It might be a benefit to the nation to get rid of some of its worst and lowest grades, but these people multiply up again so quickly that the nation gets no good, and the country that receives the incompetent and probably rebellious emigrants suffers. If the nation sends out its energetic and enterprising men it loses some of its best people, and suffers still more if only the men go. In spite of this, the nation is much more likely to go to war, to get room for its energetic men, because these men are most likely to make a fuss. A nation, while present opinions hold, is thus more apt to go to war with the idea of getting rid of its best men, rather than its worst.

CHAPTER XV

POLITICAL ECONOMISTS AND POPULATION

IT might be expected that the whole theory of population would be discussed freely in every text-book of economics. If political economy is to be of any value it must deal with conditions of a community ; and if conditions depend on the population on the one hand and the population depends on the conditions on the other, the principles of population must be fundamental in economics.

Though the political economist has no influence on public opinion, and an avenue for some knowledge of the principle of population is thus closed, it does not follow that the economist would have helped, in any case, as he has never appreciated this fundamental principle of sociology.

Broadly, the anomaly has risen through the development of political economy.

In the first place the economist is largely concerned with such questions as Value, Theory of Rent, Wages, External Trade, Money, Supply and Demand, and so on. He sometimes considers the whole of a country and discusses measures which will affect its total wealth. This discussion may be sound enough in itself, and it is simpler to assume that the population is constant, so that it is good for the country to increase its wealth. The wealth may be distributed in this way or that, and assuming the good of the greater wealth is not counterbalanced by bad distribution, the people are individually richer as a general rule. But as the people alter in number, increasing more or less, or even diminishing in case of loss of wealth the whole point of the discussion is turned.

Generally the attitude of the Economist is that the principle of population is a fallacy ; that there is perhaps some tendency to increase, but it is so small that it is completely controlled by other more powerful influences, that the tendency to multiply either' exists only among the very poor, or strictly proletariat, or that though the principle of population is sound and unassailable, it has nothing to do with Economics.

This last curious view was held by Jevons. His idea was that Economics is the science dealing with the wealth of a constant number of people. That the number varies, in fact, does not matter to Economics ; its only result is that Economics does not fit the facts, and if it were reconstructed to fit the facts it would not be Economics, but something different. So it would, no doubt. Jevons called taking account of the principle of population, altering the independent variable. He practically naïvely admits that Economics is a branch of what was known in Erewhon as Hypothetics. It not only does not fit the facts, but it is not intended to fit the facts, and would not be Economics if it did. It would save much time if writers on Economics, who hold this humorous view of their subject, began any book or article by saying so at once. Jevons playfully puts his explanation at the end.

It is not that writers on political economy deny the truth of the principle of population, or even try to refute it. As a rule they do not discuss it at all, and when they do, they do so with no understanding. The idea of population pressure crops out occasionally in rather vague form in the *Wealth of Nations*, though it was written before Malthus' essay. In fact there have been indefinite ill-digested notions on the subject for centuries. Mill seems to regard irresponsible multiplication as something apt to occur among the hand-working, and especially the lower classes, and realises for an occasional page or two that nothing can be done for them in the circumstances ; but the basis of his work is fixed population. Apparently economists either do not read Malthus, or misunderstand him, and think his point is

15

that there will be trouble in the future if populations go
on growing. One will point out that emigration is the
solution. Another will urge that if the grain used for
alcohol were sold as food there would be plenty.

Another view is that Malthus was a crank who said
that food increased in arithmetical and population in
geometrical progression, so that at some date, when the
curves cross, there will be universal poverty, as we will
all get below the limit. They think that if they prove
that food does not follow a straight line law, and that
population does not increase at a constant logarithmic
rate, they have disposed of the whole question. The
reasoning of Malthus was elementary, and his examples
are very simple, because he wanted to make ordinary
people understand what he meant. He pointed out that,
if not checked, population would increase logarithmi-
cally, or as he put it, in geometrical progression, which
is quite accurate. A population in a new country may
increase at a perfectly definite rate of 5 per cent. per
annum, doubling every fourteen years or so. Malthus
assumed, as a simple case, that the food would tend to
increase more slowly, and as an example he took simple
arithmetical progression. A series increasing in arithmetical is always overtaken sooner or later by one in
geometrical progression. But the explanation or example does not break down if the percentage rate of
increase varies from time to time, or year to year. It is
quite obvious the population might increase 4 per cent.
one year, 6 per cent. another, and so on, while the food
increase might be similar percentages of the original
yearly supply of food. As long as the food increases
are finite percentages of the original supply the population must eventually overtake it. Another argument
sometimes used is that the population principle is discredited because the population of France is decreasing
and has been decreasing for some years, apart of course
from the war.

This is a confusion between pressure and quantity.
Plagues and famines reduce population, but the results
of the Black Death do not disprove the principle. If a

cubic foot of air is compressed in a cylinder to half a cubic foot, that does not prove that there is no pressure in the air ; on the contrary, the compression of the gas is a proof that there is pressure on it. Similarly, during a famine the population pressure is temporarily, very excessive, and it reduces the quantity ; that is, reduces the number of people. The gradual reduction of the population of France may be due to increase of population pressure. The limitation of offspring, which is, or has been more common in France than in other countries, is a special question.

One argument that is sometimes put forward by political economists is that the Malthus principle is disproved by the fact that capital has recently increased faster than population. It is a little difficult to deal with this, as it seems to be a mere irrelevant statement. Malthus did not say that population tended to increase faster than capital, but faster than food. The statement about capital is put forward by able men, so it must be a good argument from some quite sensible point of view. Probably it is argued that if a community with a given population increased its capital, it must be, on the average, richer, and therefore more able to buy food and live well, so that if population had the tendency to increase, as Malthus thought, it would at once increase.

It has been pointed out in Chapter VII that as a people becomes civilised a smaller proportion of the population is engaged on runcitic production, and a larger on gratular. This change is one of the results of civilisation, and is a necessary result. When people consider a community in which only a few produce necessaries, and the majority devote their energies to supplying the wants of the very rich, the rich, the professional classes, and the lower middle classes, and even the better hand-workers, they find it a little difficult to realise that population pressure is the same as in the case of a community of poor agriculturists ; and they think that population pressure would make those who were not feeling the pinch of poverty multiply rapidly, until they were all as poor as possible. This is not the case, however. People in the upper classes marry later and have smaller families. This does not mean that there is no population pressure among them, but that they resist it to this extent. There is also the tendency for the less successful to fall into the stratum below, and so on. If the community were not made up of grades of well being there would be no civilisation, because there would be no brain-workers, and no industrial enterprise. As a community gets more civilised the strata of the middle classes increase in two directions ; they become more numerous, and the people of them get richer. The result of the increase of the wealth of the middle classes is that there is a larger proportion of saving people, and each of them has more to save ; this spells increase of capital, and in stable times a somewhat lower rate of interest. Large capital per head of population is thus a result or part of civilisation, not of any absence of population pressure. If all the people in France, for example, were suddenly to live the simple life, and spend the whole of their time growing food and producing the bare necessaries of life, or runcitic goods, of course the population would increase enormously. But in a generation or so, if not interfered with from outside, they would be a nation of ignorant peasants. They would soon forget what their experts know about agriculture, and as their machinery wore out they could not replace it, and would have to go back to primitive tools. They would soon be an uncivilised collection of human beings, some thousand of years behind the times.

More than this, when they had become quite primitive again, and cultivated their ground in the way of their forefathers of, say, two thousand years ago, the population would have dwindled down to that supported by the same ground then. Thus the absence of capital, and the civilisation for which it is necessary, means a much smaller population. For the population of a given area to increase therefore, it is broadly necessary not only that the capital increases, but that it increases faster

than the population, so that the capital per head increases. By capital per head is not meant the capital
of each person, but the total capital of the community
divided by the number of people. The property will
not be evenly distributed, or it would not produce the
result of large population, as a community consisting of
people who were all uniformly rich or poor would not
produce men capable of developing industry. We thus
get the result that not only a more rapid increase of
capital than population is necessary to go with an increase of population, but that the wealth must be unevenly, perhaps very unevenly, distributed.

The curious point about economists' treatment of the
population principle is that they never seriously discuss
it or try to refute it. They never deny that the race is
continued by having children, but they give no explanation how a race of men or any other animal can be
carried on without population pressure. They never try
to think how it is that the populations of various countries are what they are, instead of totally different
numbers. To an economist the population of Great
Britain is forty million or so, and that is all about it.
Why it is not seventeen million or seventy million does
not concern him or interest him in the least. As a sort
of independent happening it is forty million, and that
settles the matter. A walk through the East End back
streets, swarming with miserable children, never suggests
to him that various forms of saving in industry, or the
understanding of the " wages fund " theory will not
enable all these children to earn their bread.

As political economists in particular ought to have
popularised the population principle or disproved it, it
seems that they are very much to blame. In fact this
chapter seems largely to be an accusation of incompetence made against a whole class of specialists.

The position of economics is anomalous. Such sciences
as chemistry and physics have industries behind them.
Chemistry is the basis of the heavy chemical industries,
and of the making of dyes and drugs and finer chemicals,
and is also concerned with agriculture, manures, dyeing,

inks, photography, paints, gas, carbide, metallurgy and other matters. Physics is of still wider importance, as it is the basis of mechanics and engineering, electrical engineering of all kinds, flying, railways, steamships and smaller industries. It is thus essential that a large number of able men should be well versed in these sciences, as their living depends on them.

A knowledge of Political Economy is of no direct use to anyone in industry. It does not help him to manage any business. An exporter of British manufacture generally feels no concern about restriction of imports, because he does not realise that the restriction of imports affects his business in any way. If he knew some elementary economics he might agitate against the throttling of foreign trade. But this would be political. The knowledge would not help him directly in his own business.

Constraint of foreign trade, under the name of protection, is known as the policy of the ignorant. They took a religious census in New Zealand not long ago. There was a very large and varied assortment of tenets and creeds, from Episcopal, Presbyterian, Roman Catholic downwards, with decreasing numbers ending with a religion which had only one adherent. He believed in Free Trade. Apparently he was the only free trader in New Zealand, and to him it was only a pious belief.

There is a general idea that financial magnates in the city, and especially bankers, have a profound knowledge of the branch of economics that is concerned with money, exchange, finance, and so on. But there is no reason why they should. A banker knows all the intricacies of the practical part of his work, and knows the exact effect of " Not Negotiable " on a cheque crossed on a particular bank ; but he may be quite uncertain as to whether his business creates credit, or is largely pecuniary pawnbroking. If a stock-broker is asked to advise he will say " So-and-so are generally considered good, and are generally expected to go up ;

buy them." The public opinion of a well known stock settles the price of it, so the advice is idiotic ; yet it is very common.

The great majority of people are entirely ignorant of economics, and care nothing about the subject.

Economics differs from such sciences as chemistry and physics in being a study of tendencies. There is no exact measurement. It may be said that what has no exact measurement is not a science. From the nature of the study, and the general ignorance of it, arise the curious condition that people do not realise that there is any such study, and everybody is quite ready to express opinions and convictions on economical subjects without any knowledge whatever. One has only to read a politician's speech, or a leading article in a daily newspaper to realise this. If anyone opens a discussion on, say, capital and labour in a train, the most ludicrous statements are made with violent seriousness, in an atmosphere of circumambient balderdash. A man who knew no chemistry would never dream of airing ignorant and absurd opinions in the presence of people who might have studied that science, but everyone is quite ready to lay down the law on any economical point whatever.

There is thus no proper opening for economists, and no adequate inducement for men of first-rate ability to devote themselves to the study. The highest pinnacle an economist can reach is a professorship at some university or college. He may also write a text-book or two, and there his career ends. A first-rate text-book on economics must need a very clear and logical head, and an enormous amount of reading and mental work, but it would not bring the author anything like the return of the works of Marx, George, or even Ruskin. But his prospects are not even as bright as they might be, because he may never get an appointment. Who is to know he is a sound economist? The bodies who appoint professors of chemistry or physics may know little or nothing of either science, but they have no difficulty in electing good professors. It is true that out of two very able men they might not select the best, but they would never go far wrong. In the case of an economist there is great difficulty ; so that his career as a profession is precarious. It is conceivable that there might be a college of economics controlled by a committee containing people notorious for a negative knowledge of the subject ; and their appointments might average out well, or they might appoint men alternately under the impression that free traders and protectionists are two great schools of economists ; just as people used to think that homœopathy and allopathy were the main divisions of modern medical thought.

Economics is supposed to be taught at the universities, but the teaching is not alive and produces no perceptible results. It has been suggested that one reason is that it is taught to the wrong type of men.

Not to mention those living, economics has attracted the attention of some first-rate men, such as Adam Smith and the younger Mill ; but generally speaking, an able man who can do anything else well has a strong temptation to leave political economy alone.

Political economy, not so much as it is now, but as it would be if it were treated seriously by the well informed, is the most important science there is, and everyone ought to study it to become a good citizen.

It is needless to point out that as long as governments interfere with, control, or have anything to do with industrial matters, all members of Parliament should be especially well versed in economics so as to have some idea of the real effects of their measures.

There is little chance that economics will flourish unless there is good soil for it. In such a case as music, geniuses as, say, Schubert, Mozart, or Wolf, or even Beethoven may get very little encouragement ; but even in such a special case as music a suitable public seems necessary. None of the men mentioned could have made much of a living at anything else, but that is true of most musical geniuses. In England and America, where men take no serious interest in the art, and leave it largely in the hostile hands of women, musical geniuses do not flourish as they did in the old days, when

Englishmen were musical. Women seem to be taking up economics now ; it is to be hoped they will not reduce British Economics to the level of British Music.

Take the case of science in America. For a new country with enormous internal resources, industry grew rapidly and easily, and could and did flourish with little or no technical knowledge. The result was that not so long ago there were practically no great scientific technologists or academically scientific men there. Now competition demands good technology in American industries, so there is soil for science and both technology and academic science are now flourishing.

The case is much stronger in the case of economics, because a man who might be a first-rate economist can do nearly as well in many other directions that give more return, and naturally he does so.

CHAPTER XVI

GOVERNMENT

MAN has been defined in all sorts of ways. He might be defined as the animal which is quite unable to govern or to be governed. He has tried since prehistoric times, and he is always trying, and he has always failed, and he goes on failing. In comparison with his other development he is no better than he was when we first hear of him.

In most cases of social imperfection an ideal can be thought out, and then a comparison can be made to see how far the real falls short, and to show what changes for the better can be made. But in the case of government there is not even an ideal. No good scheme of government has ever been imagined, except for perfect, or, at any rate, ideal people, who would not need it. The problem is to contrive a system of government, which could work well, suitable for real people.

The main difficulty lies in the general ignorance of members of a community, and in the absence of any active sense of real citizenship.

The government of a perfect people would have universal support in every detail, as every detail would be good. There would therefore be no place for it, as a perfect people would behave so perfectly in every way, that nothing in the shape of external control or even of indication as to conduct would be wanted. This assumes not only that what is good is known to be good, but that every individual knows it on his own account.

In fact, there is uncertainty and very widely different views as to what is good, and men will not always do what each considers right for himself, still less will they do what others think right for each of them.

A real community is made up of people who are not all well informed, and who are not all wise, and who are not all interested in questions of government. How ought it to be governed? If all the people discuss a measure, some are for it and some against it. There may be no half way courses; for instance, the question might be whether the community should go to war ; a half measure by which those who liked could go to war, and those who preferred peace would remain at peace, is impossible. Such a case might be decided by the majority, and the minority ought to act loyally according to the vote of the majority, though it is a little difficult to know what " ought " means in this case. This loyalty is not due to a feeling among the minority that the others are right, or more likely to be right, it may be due to a spirit of fair play, but that is the result of a habit of thought, the root principle being that the majority is stronger, and can enforce its wishes. This is a fundamental difficulty in the less virile communities where women have, and in the future children may have, voting power. If a majority voting for war were made up of women, and the men voted against it, there would be no war. The men would not consider the women wiser than they, and the majority would have no power to force the others to adopt their policy. A community in which women vote has thus the germ of anarchy, a point which is really weak, especially as an argument against female franchise. To the extent that the idea of loyalty to the majority, which has become a habit, is founded on the power of the majority, it will gradually yield when it is realised that the power is no longer there. Leaving out the question of women voting, the power being with the majority does not mean that the majority is more sensible, merely that the will of the majority is stronger, and must prevail if put to the touch. The will of the majority thus becomes the foundation of all government, but it does not follow that government, in fact, rests on this basis, it may rest entirely on false foundations, and still be settled and very durable.

In the case of a very small group, questions might be discussed by all the members, and they might act upon the will of the majority ; but no exhibition of force would be necessary ; the notion of the will of the majority being paramount is soon accepted as axiomatic. After a little it will seem best for the little community to choose one or two by the vote of the majority, and to leave them to settle questions that affect the whole group, while the members attend to their own work. The difficulty now begins. Is each of the men chosen to do what he himself thinks best for himself, for the community, or for the particular group that elected him, or is he to do what he thinks the majority that chose him would like, or what he thinks would give him the greatest majority at the next election, though it may be made up largely of a different set of people? The temptation to do what is best for himself, while pretending it is best for the voters, is strong, but his inborn wish to do right will come into play. The little community will not choose their ablest men, partly because their ablest men will have other things to do, but mainly because real ability does not appeal to them.

Take the case of a larger community. It is not homogeneous. It can be divided up into sets of units having prejudices and special kinds of ignorance of their own, and having, or thinking they have, special interests. As all people cannot vote as to each of the candidates, the public will be divided up into sections, and each section will then choose one or two. The simplest device is to divide the country into districts. If the people have to vote personally, this may be convenient, but now that there is postal service, there is no sense in it. One district has no special interest compared with another, and can hardly have special knowledge. The more ignorant may be thicker in one place than another, but that is a different point.

In developing the examination of the conditions of absolute democracy we may pass to a nation of many millions. On the principle that one man is as big a fool as another, they all have full and therefore equal

voting power, including the women, if they have accepted
the principle of the majority so completely as to over-
look its basis of force. Districts again will vary as to
the proportions of various kinds of ignorance and prejudice, and as to what the local people consider their
interests. Thus one constituency may consist mainly
of agricultural people with a numerical minority of land-
owners and residents, another may be full of engineering
works and cotton mills, where the majority of voters are
hand-workers of a different type. Is the man elected
by this constituency to do what he thinks best for the
whole country, or what he thinks best for the hand-
workers, or the cotton-spinning operatives who voted for
him, which may be quite a different thing ; or is he to
do what he believes the hand-workers or operatives
think best for the country, or what he thinks the
operatives imagine is best for themselves? This last
is the only practical course, as otherwise he will lose his
seat at the next election. In an ideal community the
electors might carefully select the best and wisest man,
and leave everything to him. But this would come back
to the same thing, because they would judge of his
wisdom in future elections, according to their notions as
to his actions. But it is infinitely worse than this in
practice. Most of the voters take no real interest in
the matter at all. Bodies of people never vote or act
sensibly. For example, take a village meeting about a
local matter. There will be a desultory discussion, and
the chairman, who is practically self-elected, controls it.
Then he suggests that a committee be formed. Someone proposes a friend of his, who is quite unsuitable.
No one will oppose him. Then somebody who wants
to be in evidence proposes someone else, without any
reference to his fitness. A woman then says she thinks
ladies would be specially useful, and proposes a friend,
and so on till the chairman says the committee is large
enough. This is only a small model of the working
of larger bodies, the only difference is that the larger
the body the more inefficient the work. Moreover, the
large body is swayed by party or class interest, or both.

Party spirit depends on vanity, not on reason, and it warps, or rather suspends, people's judgments. Class interest, in its simplest form, would be the interest of a number of individuals added together. But in practice it developes into a type of party spirit, and is also dependent on vanity, as in the larger case of patriotism, and on crowd sentiment.

Class and party are quite different, though they are always confused. Thus, a red party may be made up of all classes, and be in opposition to a blue party, which is also made up of all classes. The red party may advocate, say, free travelling, and the blue party may oppose it. This is actually because free travelling has become a party question, but the members of the red party all profess to believe free travelling is good for the whole community, and not especially for themselves, while the blues are equally sure it is bad for the country. Whether the members of the parties really know anything about the question is not the point, it is that each party professes and tries to work for the good of the whole community, and not specially for its own good. The case of an interest, as opposed to a party, is quite different. Thus the middle classes might organise themselves and return representatives, they would most likely be known as the middle-class party. Their object would be, not to do good to the community as a whole, but to legislate for the benefit of the middle classes, or to bring about legislation they thought would benefit the middle classes, which is a different thing. They might argue that a happy and contented middle class would leaven the community, and make everybody happy in the long run ; but that is, at most, quite a secondary point. We are more familiar with a Labour Party now, the same thing has come up under different names. The Labour " Party " is really not a party at all, as it is not working for the good of the country, but in what its members consider, or pretend to consider, the interests of the hand-workers, as opposed to the community at large. Its members may think that if their schemes were carried out it would be good for the whole community, including their supposed enemies, the capitalists, or they may think that the hand-workers and their families are so important numerically that their interests are practically those of the community. That the labour parties, even in places like Australia and New Zealand, do not succeed in hurrying on what they think would be the millennium, is due to their ignorance as to the power of government, and of the real effect of their measures. The woman's party, again, is not a party at all. The object is to benefit women generally at the expense of men. They may argue that they want to improve women's position without injuring men's, and that their goal is the improvement of society in general, but that is clearly not their real object, as will be explained later, the real primary object of the leaders of all political and other movements is their own personal advancement. The cause they take up is merely a convenient horse to ride, and to make it a useful horse it must be popular among a number of people. The women's cause, in fact, mainly appeals to women's vanity as it asserts their mental equality with men, but what is put forward is obtaining a number of rights or privileges for women at the expense of men, so the movement is of the nature of class tyranny, like the labour movement, and there is no women's party. Though the strength of the vote of the majority may be based on physical force, people develope a sort of crude political morality. According to this the will of the majority, as expressed by vote, is respected because it is assumed that it ought to be. As long as this principle is recognised, and provided no real strain arises, the objection to women's franchise on the ground of her inferior physical power is now hardly valid. This principle is generally extended so that the wish or vote of a majority is respected even after the majority has dwindled away out of power. For instance, when there is a change of parties in power, a parliament does not set to work to repeal all the laws made by the party just gone out. The decisions are left standing, though the majority is nominally against them. This is mainly an anomaly due to party government.

There is another direction in which there is some development of political morality. It is sometimes considered wrong that a majority should coerce or tyrannise over a minority. Thus a body may have to settle some point in which the whole community is interested, and in which all the members of the community are interested in the same way. The majority is then assumed to be wiser, and their collective voice is willingly obeyed. But there are two other cases to be considered. Suppose a section, perhaps a small section, has a real or imagined interest which is to be considered to be against that of the whole. The majority can then override this section. They may override it in what they consider the interest of the majority only, or in what they really think is the interest of the whole. It is then considered immoral politically for the majority to tyrannise over the minority for what they think is their own benefit, or even for the general benefit of the community, if that involves apparent injustice, and the most common case of this type of political immorality is when there are race or class interests. Thus, in old Hungary the country was controlled by the Magyars, and other races complained that they were not treated fairly. In this case the Magyars were not really in numerical majority in the country. In the United States there is the curious, but very difficult, problem of the coloured people. These are cases of race division apart from race sentiment. The coloured citizens have no interests of their own, and need no more special treatment than, say, people with red hair. We need not go outside our own Empire to find examples of the race anomaly. If it is right that everybody, or, at any rate, everybody who is of age should have a vote, and that all should have equal political power apart from questions of mental ability, training, or knowledge, the people of India should have votes, and if India is kept separate from England, it should not only govern itself to the same extent as England does, but it should have

just as much control over England as England has over
India. It is not suggested that such a change in
Indian Government is advisable in any way, the point
is that if absolute democracy does not fit India as well
as it is supposed to fit England, there is something
wrong with the principle. It may be said that India
is not ready for democratic government, but what does
that really mean, unless it is an admission that the
principle is fundamentally wrong, because it gives power
to the ignorant majority, or, at any rate, because it
gives too much power to the ignorant? But this is not
the point we are on at the moment; it is that democracy
gives the majority the power of oppressing the minority,
and that this abuse is checked by a form of political
morality. But the effect of this check is really slight.
If we pass from race to class we come upon what
appears at first glance to be one of the greatest dangers
of the times; government controlled by the hand-working classes.

If the people who had hair of any other colour voted
that red-haired people should pay double taxes, it would
be so clearly a case of tyranny that the discussion of it
is quite fanciful. The majority in such a case would
not be a party at all, as it would not be acting, or rather
voting, in the interests of the community. It would
be a tyrannous majority of politically immoral people.
What is called the labour party in this, and other
countries is not a party at all. It does not even profess
to consider the good of the country as a whole. It
wants to re-arrange the world so that the hand-workers
have happier lives, and the re-arrangement is to involve
higher wages, shorter working hours, State employment, State insurance, employers' liability and so on.
All this is to be brought about at the expense of the
numerical minority, and especially at the expense of the
small numerical minority who are employers, capitalists,
land-owners, or, in fact, rich. The point is not whether
the hand-workers' policy would produce the result they
expect, or whether the principle of population, not to
speak of ordinary economics, shews that it would be

16

awful failure, but that the principle is wrong and immoral. Yet, in spite of this, labour is called a party, not a class, and hand-workers are advised not to strike or riot, but to get their wants satisfied by constitutional methods, the constitutional methods being majority class tyranny of the worst kind.

It is clear that political morality is not high enough to prevent class majority voting of the most venal type. So powerless is it, that not only the hand-workers, but the ordinary educated man, looks upon labour as a political party, not a class, and contemplates a Labour Government as being a normal alternative to Liberals or Conservatives being in power.

Returning to our elementary case, we have a community selecting members of a governing body to legislate. Unless the community is very small indeed, the individuals are not known to one another. The public will then vote only for those who have put themselves forward as candidates. These will not be people who are likely to be good representatives. They will be pushing self-advertising men who love notoriety and prominence, or men who can use their success to advance them in their professions. As already pointed out, there are no clear-cut ideas as to what the representative is to do when elected. There is at most a vague notion that he is to act in the interest of his constituency when it clashes with the interests of other constituencies, as the interests or supposed interests—a very different matter—of various place constituencies seldom clash, or are supposed to clash. This notion is unimportant. Another vague notion is that he is to judge for himself in the interest of his constituents, or perhaps in the interests of his country. The man is chosen because his mind is supposed to be such that he will probably arrive at conclusions on different points which agree with the conclusions the voters would arrive at if they thought each matter out, or because his mind is supposed to be such that he will arrive at a sensible conclusion on each subject, the voters assuming rashly that a sensible conclusion is the kind they would arrive at if they thought the various matters out. They might conceivably choose such a man, and let him represent them for quite a long time, without examining his record, or rather without judging it, as they would never be competent to examine it, even if they tried. He thus might become a sort of permanent representative without really representing his constituents at all.

So far we have assumed that the voters are not very sensible, and not very well informed, but that they vote with the idea of doing the best they can. Let us come a little nearer real conditions. In the first place the voters are not only ignorant, they are full of negative knowledge on all political matters. They either never think about political questions, or, at most, they allow their fallow minds to browse on the subject in a sleepy and ineffective way. They do not choose their candidates. They are hypnotised by any name they know. If a student of public matters somehow came to be put forward, and a popular actor was a counter-attraction, the actor would be elected. But such a student would not be put forward in practice. If some people who knew him personally, or knew of him, put him forward as a candidate, he would have no chance against the nominees of the party associations. The nomination of the candidate is in the hands of the political machine. At an election each party puts forward one candidate. There will most likely be a red and blue candidate if red and blue are the parties of the day, and a yellow candidate representing a class as opposed to a party. Except in special cases, there will not be two candidates of any colour, as that would split votes, and spoil the chance of both. In due course the candidates open their sluice gates and let forth a mississippi of mendacity. This pours out at all the political meetings, and through the newspapers. A red political meeting is full of reds, as the speeches are not intended to convert the blues. The blues are not there, and do not want to be there, except occasionally to disturb the meeting. If possible, they are kept out. The speeches are lies and exaggerations delivered to unthinking people. Not only do they listen with the fallow mind, but what is infinitely worse, with the crowd mind. The candidates and their supporters set to work to inflame their passions, and to work on their prejudice and ignorance by every kind of clap-trap, misrepresentation and exaggeration. They promise that if their man gets in, he or his party will give them all sorts of benefits, and will work all sorts of miracles that are quite outside the power of any government.

No bitter experience, no study of the past, or no thought of real conditions seems able ever to disabuse the public of its belief in politicians and governments. Government thus becomes a close organisation worked by, and for the benefit of, its own members. The representative finally has not necessarily to please his own constituents, but what he has to do is to please his own party leaders. If this involves displeasing his constituents, he is, by arrangement, put up for a safer constituency next election. Every individual who thinks will realise that he has no appreciable political power at all in virtue of his vote. An Adam Smith or a Mill has the chance of voting for a red candidate, for whose qualifications he has unbounded but deserved contempt, or for a blue, whose ignorance and dishonesty are in his opinion equally great. He has one or two political tenets which are nominally held by each of the candidates, but he is entirely out of sympathy with the general policy of both. When he does vote, his choice is wiped out by his gardener's assistant, or eventually by his scullery-maid. His only chance of exercising any influence is by writing, and if he succeeds in producing any perceptible result by that laborious and unsatisfactory method, it does not come about until long after he is dead.

But government is not really in the hands of his gardener's assistant or his scullery-maid either, nor in the hands represented by them. The voters have practically no power and no control. They can put one party in and keep another out of power, and that is all. There is thus a continual competition among the parties to keep in power, and new parties are formed from time to time, or old parties gradually change what they call their policies, to suit the popular ideas and secure votes. The representative body thus consists of men who have no special knowledge or ability. The qualifications are facility in speaking, especially in speaking at the intellectual plane of the masses, leisure or money or position. No man with a balanced mind can get elected as an active politician unless he is dishonest. It may be argued that political lying is so fully recognised and so customary that it is expected, and it is no disgrace for a man who is straight in business, and upright in all his private dealings, to lie like a Cabinet Minister, if his ambition prompts him to get into Parliament. That may be so. Probably the average member of Parliament is honestly under the impression that he is there for the good of the country. He may be interested in party politics to begin with, and he is under the hallucination that if his party gets into or stays in power the public gets some great benefit. He also thinks that as he is very keen about his party, his help in Parliament must be worth more than that of other people.

It must also be borne in mind that there is a number of respectable gentlemen of good local position in Parliament. It is not suggested that they get elected solely by mendacity. This body forms a good solid block of common sense and moderation resting on a solid and extensive foundation of concrete ignorance.

Government is thus an organisation working really for its own members, and not for the country. It is made up of men who have no real qualifications for their position. It is sometimes urged that the ignorance of politicians does not matter, because they get expert advice. This would be Solon's principle of having wise men to advise and fools to decide, if the politicians chose wise men. They are more likely to choose well-known people, whose views suit, just as a foolish invalid chooses a doctor who prescribes what the patient likes. Politics is just a business in which people become proficient by experience and special aptitude. To get into Parliament and to become, say, Chancellor of the Exchequer, needs very great ability, but it is the ability of the politician who has to compete with other politicians, not ability that makes a Chancellor of the Exchequer, who is of any use to the country as such. Anyone with the right kind of brain, who studies the theory of finance, would make a much better Chancellor of the Exchequer than the politicians who hold that office, but even if such a student were put into Parliament, or got in by being a peer, that sort of knowledge and ability would not help him to the position he would fit. He would have to compete as a politician, and the competition would be just as difficult as the competition for any other big prize that many people want. The public thinks the people who are always in print in all the newspapers are a kind of intellectual giant. They talk of statesmen, and school history books are full of long accounts of the policies of so-called statesmen, as if their policies were dictated by some sort of wisdom. The politician has, as a rule, no knowledge of sociology, economics, history, science or anything else that fits him for his position. If he is a barrister, he takes up politics largely because it advances him in his profession. His training at the Bar enables him to talk. Most barristers spend their time as vocal advocates. It is their business to put one side of a case only, and to see the other just enough to obscure it, and to present everything from a peculiar artificial point of view. A barrister's training makes him specially useful as a party man. In law it is understood that the advocates put the strongest cases they can, and the question whether they believe in their own cases does not come in. It is a well-understood method of arriving at something like justice. But in a Parliament what members say is supposed to be what they honestly think, and the introduction of methods, which may be quite admirable at the Bar, is pernicious. In addition to this, as barristers get promotion to the bench, or to the position of law officers by political influence, they are tempted to be strong party men for their own professional advancement,

If a member is a successful business man, being a legislator gives him a special standing. If he is a man of leisure he finds the same thing.

The demagogue is a very powerful factor, which needs separate study. It is not government alone that developes into an organisation which works entirely for itself. The phenomenon is universal. Take the case of a large railway company, the directors are nominally elected by the votes of the shareholders, but the directorate is always in the hands of a clique, and though they are formally elected by the shareholders, the shareholders have practically no power. If they wanted to put on a director who knew something about railway management, they would first have to find him. This would mean that the shareholders must meet and discuss all the competent men they know, and choose one or more of them. But they do not know who is competent and who is not, and they cannot meet in this way, and few of them take enough interest in their company to trouble, so the directorate gets into the hands of a clique, a family or a group, and nothing happens unless the company is so badly managed that there is a stormy shareholders' meeting. The directorships then fall into the hands of a new group or clique, and the company settles down into a different type of inefficiency. In the case of scientific, technical, and other societies there is always the complaint that the council or committee is not representative, is out of touch with the body of members, and mismanages the affairs of the society ; being, in fact, in the hands of a clique. The rules are such that the council of to-day nominates that of to-morrow, and the body of members is powerless. No way of electing a committee or council of a scientific or technical society has been devised, such that the best men are chosen by the body of the members. If a society met to appoint a new committee for the year, and election was quite open, the pushing, self-advertising men would get themselves proposed by their friends, while the abler and more modest would be left out. Next year the members of the council would propose and back one another up, and though apparently freely elected, the council would very soon be a self-nominated, and practically a self-elected clique again.

The existence of ratepayers' associations throws a curious light on municipal representation.

In the case of a trade union the body of men have practically no power. A young and ignorant man who is generally not a workman at all, but who has a glib tongue and a peculiar kind of mental quickness, finds that he can get the ear of the majority of the men in the union, especially of the younger men, by working on their vanity, prejudice and ignorance, and flattering their passions. He is, in a fashion, sincere. He probably believes what he says in a way, and he gets carried along by his own flow of words, and especially by the support of his audience. Man's vanity is such, that a talker who finds an admiring audience can never believe that he knows nothing and is wrong. Such a man develops into a demagogue, and in due course becomes one of the controllers of a trade union. The body of the union is made up mainly of men who may be quite out of sympathy with what are called the leaders. The leaders have the support of the younger men, who have not lived and worked long enough to know that the schemes do not come out right in practice, and the majority have no control. The voting is not really free, and those who vote against the policy of the leaders get into difficulties. In this way it is possible that a trade union may, for example, vote for a strike, when the great majority are against it, because no one likes to break the ice by voting as he thinks. The control of trade unions thus becomes an organisation working for its own advancement, and not for the good of the trade union. What a bait there is for a trade union official ! A man with no knowledge of the real problems of sociology finds that he has a ready tongue, and that he can flatter the hand-workers by stirring up class feeling, and misrepresenting facts, perhaps unwittingly ; and he can get himself into such a position that he has interviews with Prime Ministers,

who have to kow-tow to him ; and he holds the power in
his ignorant hands of crippling the industry of the
country, unless some concessions are granted, which
increase his position with the hand-workers, and give
him more power and more prominence.

We have, so far, discussed government in a democracy, with the view of showing that it is really an
organisation working in its own interest. It is practically self-appointed and self-appointing, and the voters,
as such, have no real control over it. What power there
is, is in the hands of the multitudinous ignorant who are
controlled by prejudice, envy, and what they believe are
their class interests, and are guided by newspapers,
demagogues, and appeals to their crowd-minds.

Such a government always glorifies its own office. It
therefore claims infinitely greater power than it has,
and pretends that it can control wages, that it can make
industry prosperous, that it can educate the people so
that they can all earn more in the day, and enjoy
elegant leisure in the evening, that it can make a nation
thrifty by compulsory subsidised insurance, that it can
prevent poverty by feeding people who do not earn their
living, and that it can carry on certain industries, such
as letter carrying and telegraphy, better than private
concerns; which last may be or may not be true. It is
therefore to the interest of the organisation in its self-
aggrandisement to have not only the largest possible
Navy and Army and Air Service, departments which
have to be considered in connection with war, but an
enormous civil service. If the government ever gets a
chance, it increases these departments, because that
increases its patronage and its importance. The war
gave the government the excuse for creating all sorts
of new departments, and nothing but the universal
opposition of the country can get these stopped long
after the war is over. It might be thought that the
country would object to the expense and the waste, and
object so strongly that the exaggerated bureaucracy
would stop ; but the money is raised at first out of the
rich and the middle classes, and the hand-workers have

the tune of their wages set by the government, so that the voters do not realise that they will eventually pay their share. .When their time for payment comes they will be told that they are being ground down by the capitalists, and will believe it.

A democracy is supposed to be government by the people. It is, of course, nothing of the kind, it is government by a self-interested organisation, over which the people have no real control. Other forms of government, such as unlimited Monarchies, Oligarchies and Aristocracies, or, as the Greeks put it, government by the rich, tyrannies and conqueror governments are, if that can be, still more self-interested organisations. The difference between the most extreme form of one man tyranny and the most thorough democracy is really minute. In both cases there is an organisation. In both cases it depends to some extent finally on the people. The more the government is organised the less power the people have. A tyrannical one-man government is so only in name. The Prince has to balance the power among his subordinates in such a way as to have the casting vote in his own hand. The whole machinery of King, Barons, Chiefs, and perhaps Tribunes, or their equivalents, has to be organised so as to work in equilibrium, though all its members are really working for themselves. And the organisation has to cultivate popularity enough to prevent popular outbreaks. Such a government is always in a kind of unstable equilibrium, but it may be very permanent, because it can be opposed and overthrown only by a rival organisation, and it is very difficult for any rival organisation to start. It is generally nipped in the bud, and its initial leaders run great risks. The overthrow is generally the result of a comparatively small local disturbance of equilibrium, due to some little demagogue, who has at first nothing more in his mind than a little local celebrity. He finds he produces much greater effects than he expected, and he gets carried like the froth on a wave. Like it, he is soon left behind, and bigger waves with more inflated froth come along.

It is questionable whether a democracy is more stable than a real monarchy. In a monarchy the governors may be no more sensible than in a democracy, but they are not to the same extent obliged to do foolish things because they are popular. Again, it is more difficult to start any sort of organisation under a strong monarchy. In a democracy there is anarchy going on almost continually. Democracy itself has a strong tendency towards anarchy. It teaches that the opinion of a fool is as important as the conclusion of a wise man, so that all sorts of people are apt to form opinions on political subjects and think they have a right to get them put in force.

There are so many things for man to settle that wise people find it economical to consider a matter, settle it, and leave it, and go on to other work without continually reconsidering their decision.

Thus, when a country decides on, say, a limited monarchy, and establishes a monarchy, that monarchy is permanent. It is above its ministers and its advising Parliament. It is so permanent that any attack on it is High Treason, punishable with death. Recently there has been a discussion in the *Trail*, a boy scout journal. The Second Scout Law enjoins loyalty, but a number of correspondents argue that loyalty is a matter of personal opinion, and as a great many scouts are opposed to monarchy, that is to say, happen to be traitors, the scout law should be altered to include traitors without hurting their tender consciences.

The boy scout paper discussion is merely a ridiculous example of ignorant popular treason, but as the boy scout movement, which, by the way, is not militarist, is important and serious, this sort of dry-rot in it might do a good deal of harm. We have the same thing on a larger and more serious scale. If a trade union leader thinks he can enhance his importance, he will try to coerce the government to do something which is not the will of the country, as expressed legitimately by democracy, by a strike of those who can inconvenience the community by stopping work. The strike, as coercing the government, is pure anarchy. The basis of such policy is that everyone has a right to act according to his opinions, even when in a small minority. The recent case of Ulster is another example. The Ulster men, incited by a Cabinet Minister, took up the position that if the government of the country did what they desired, so that they were in the majority, they would agree ; but if they were in the minority they would refuse to accept the decision of the majority of the government, in which they are fairly represented, and would take up arms and start a civil war. I have no opinion of any value as to whether a decision against Ulster would be unjust ; that is not the point ; however unjust people may consider any particular legislation, rebellion is anarchy.

On the other hand, the heads of a nominal one-man government are apt to get more inflated by conceit than a human being can stand. An Emperor is fed up like a Strasburg goose, and his vanity and conceit are pampered through his whole life till he becomes very foolish and pernicious. God in His infinite humour never made a funnier forked radish than an Emperor of Germany ; an American President is not nearly so funny. This conceit and its effects run through a governing organisation, and the result is that the organisation always exaggerates its power and influence, and people believe in it. In all countries, and all times of which we have any record, all men have believed that their welfare depends on the government. They have never been well off, in fact, the only difference is that they are sometimes badly off, and sometimes more miserable still, and they always blame their governments. When a country, or rather, when those few people in a country who are articulate, are less miserable than others, that country gets the credit of being well governed. Thus, an ancient community which had any of the types of government fashionable in Greece may have had slaves, under the thumb of a small number of privileged people. The privileged may have lived on the work of the slaves, killing large numbers for sport when they bred too rapidly for convenience, and may thus have been well off. Historians would say little or nothing about the real mass of inhabitants, and such a state would be handed down as a specimen of a happy community, happy because so well governed.

In old days governments, and the ruling classes outside governments, used to tyrannise over the masses, and inflict all sorts of injustice and commit all sorts of crimes. Modern governments of civilised countries do not do these things now, probably because civilised countries are too democratic to stand it. It is true that though there is not one law for the rich and another for the poor, there is a totally different administration of the same law. If a lot of East End roughs after a football match broke loose as hooligans in the evening, they would get into serious trouble, but if they come from Oxford or Cambridge nothing is done.

The real trouble with modern governments is that the people in power are ignorant of their business, and they waste money by employing huge civil services doing unnecessary or harmful work, and that they always like to glorify their office by extending their power and interfering with industry. It is natural that governments should be as bad as people deserve, because no way of getting a good government has been invented. We go on century after century increasing our idiotic faith in governments with nothing but a perpetual object lesson in their folly. After the Great War we still have all the smaller countries quarrelling as to whether they are to be preyed upon by King Stork or King Log, and we have had the same sort of thing in Ireland. It never seems to occur to people that it would be better to go on with their work and cut their governments down, confining their attention to maintaining order, and the few other duties that must be left to governments.

It is very difficult to realise that through all historical times people have believed that their welfare depends on their government. The effect of population pressure is felt in waves or irregular cycles ; whenever it pinches most there is an outcry against the government. This may lead to revolution or small changes, and very often it leads to war. Even to-day we have wars between various patches of the globe, and civil wars within patches all carried on about governments, because the people think that governments control their welfare and happiness. This delusion is important for two reasons. It causes untold unhappiness because it makes all the unfortunate feel that they are unjustly treated by the government, so that they are always smouldering under a sense of wrong, and it prevents people realising that there are causes of unhappiness other than bad government. This is true not only of the uninformed, but universally. Practically all Utopias are really so many different schemes of government, and are thus waste of imagination.

CHAPTER XVII

WOMEN

WOMEN have never had fair play. Among early races, among savages, and in the humbler classes of existing peoples they have had, and still have, an infinitely worse time than men. Man never has developed the chivalry of many of the dumb animals.

In the Middle Ages there was a sort of superficial chivalry which is quite beautiful as represented in romances; but in fact it appears to have been a sham, covering a state of low licentiousness and little else among the powerful, and little or no advance on ordinary savagery among the poors; the poor women being the victims not only of their own class, but of the priests, and of all those in power.

In modern times the lower we go down the worse women are off in comparison with men. In backward countries this inequality reaches farther up the social scale. We, by which is meant those who are born into a pleasant walk through life, are far too apt to consider our own class as if it were the world ; it is only a very small bit of it. In this chapter we have to take a much larger view. Take the case of the daughter or wife of a hand-worker in humble circumstances. Chivalry did not prevent her being fed badly, put to walk too soon, and coming up by chance, because chivalry did not give her mother time to attend to her or her little brothers; the mother was in a mill. Later the child spent her whole time looking after her little brothers, and doing all sorts of work which her mother should have been able to do. In the nineteenth century and earlier, and up to the present in other countries, children were worked long drab days and part of the weary night to earn a shilling or two extra. This is at last stopped in many countries. The board school steps in now. This may be a haven of delight to boys and girls alike, but as the association is entirely, or now almost entirely for work and uninteresting and non-competitive work, without the zest and esprit de corps of games, perhaps it is not. After school hours she is at work at home, practically straight on. When she marries she ties herself down to dreary drudgery for the rest of her natural life. She has no holidays. When the trade union leaders order a strike, it is she who suffers, but she has even less say in the matter than her husband. When people in the district get up anything, it is a treat for the children or for the husband. There is a subscription-supported football and cricket club for him; he has also an evening club, and an instrument is bought for him to blow in a brass band. The free library and the mechanics' institute are for him, she has no time. Her good looks are gone in her twenties, and she is old at thirty-five. She suffers from bad teeth. She may be driven to work in a mill. She has a long series of children against her will. She is told they are blessings sent by God and she ought to be delighted. She is not. Sometimes she rolls herself downstairs to avoid having more gifts of God to feed and look after. It is difficult to know how the other half, or rather nine-tenths, of the world live; but a little sympathetic thought for others will make anyone realise that the lot of humble women is not as we would like it. One can get some idea of what it is from books like Miss Loane's.

The first thing that strikes one is that poor women have too much work. They are competing with men under great disadvantages, and for reasons to be explained directly, competition in her class can be on much more even lines than in the strata above.

What is clearly needed is that women should have much less work, and that they should be provided for by their husbands or fathers, so as to make all hard work unnecessary; and a man who allowed any of his women-kind to work for money should feel it a disgrace.

It does no harm to repeat that the misery of the poor and the general discontent and consequent unhappiness of the hand-worker generally is our fault, because we do not bother to teach ourselves, much less to teach them anything about the cause of poverty. The drunkenness, when it exists, of the poorer classes is largely the result of the example set by our grandfathers, and recently, especially since the war, it is not an unknown thing for a young " gentleman " to take more than he ought. It is the same in other directions ; the improvement in the morals of the rich during the last part of the nineteenth century percolates down, and the slackness of morals since the war, not to speak of the general badness of manners, are copied downwards.

Recently we had an outbreak of feminism. This craze comes up periodically under different names, but it has been more acute than ever before. It is a very serious step backwards for women, not only because it means unsuccessful competition of women with men in the upper and middle classes, with a decline of chivalry and a lowering of women's position, but it will set a further bad example, and make poor women's lot harder than ever, if such a case is possible. This is the grave aspect of it.

All the trouble arises from the modern pretended discovery that women have intellects exactly like, or, at any rate, equal to men's. It is difficult to discuss this question quite frankly, as one is apt to give great offence. If one says anything generally about men, a particular man to whom it does not apply realises that, and then considers whether it applies generally or not. But if you say women as a rule are behind in some particular line, say, the deciphering of Runic inscriptions, some highly intelligent woman, who is an expert in Runic inscriptions, knowing more than most men in her line, and infinitely more than a poor writer on rabbits, is highly indignant because it is said that women are not good at Runic inscriptions, and she is a woman.

17

It is commonly thought that during the last decade or so, and especially during the war, women have demonstrated that the orthodox estimate of their ability, as old as the hills, and based broadly on the experience of mankind, is entirely false. They are supposed to have shown all sorts of new abilities in unexpected directions, and to have made it quite clear that they can do everything men can just as well, or better, except such work as demands great physical strength or exertion.

This change in public opinion has been brought about largely by the New Woman movement, which has directed attention to the questions of the positions and relations of the sexes.; and like all questions of public opinion, it has been discussed very superficially. Novels and newspapers have done a great deal to bring the change about. Probably the majority of novels are read by women and written by women, who take themselves and their sex very seriously. There is, therefore, a tendency to endow the heroine with all sorts of attractive merits. She may, at the age of twenty-four, write a book, probably a novel, which sets the world ablaze, or she does all sorts of marvellous things with perfect ease. The newspapers are, if possible, more absurd. Whenever a woman does the most ordinary work that has not been done by women generally, there is a portrait of, say, a lady ticket collector, and an article to show that the old idea that women could not collect tickets is wrong, and that women can collect tickets quite as well as men.

Many women and a few men suppose that women and men are mentally alike, or equal, but that man is physically stronger than woman, and has used his strength to keep her down; and has then raised an unfounded prejudice as to her mental qualities, so that in spite of the obvious fact that they are mentally equal, people have gone for thousands of years under a sort of hallucination, seeing differences that do not exist.

At the present stage of civilisation people take pride in mental ability rather than muscular strength, and to be thought clever is much pleasanter than to be considered strong. Feminists are therefore quite ready to admit physical weakness in women if, by doing so, they can get them credit for mental power. If we had been in a stage of civilisation in which physical strength was valued most, a similar argument could have been used which would not even be quite so weak. It would have been said that women are really just as strong as men, and that the popular notion that they are weaker is a prejudice raised by the superior cunning of man. Man has already got the best of it by mere brute brain power. Civilised man has dominated the infinitely more muscular and superior savage by brain power; and throughout the ages this low and mean qualification, if it is worthy of such a name, has not only enabled men to conquer the enormously more powerful and noble world of so-called lower animals, but has led the weak to triumph over the strong in every direction. Women are really just as strong as men. That their muscles measure less is no proof to the contrary, because women are smaller. The muscles are just as strong, or stronger in proportion to the size, and strength is a matter of proportion. Then men have cunningly raised a prejudice against women developing their muscles, and women have fallen into the trap, and unknowingly have imagined they were weaker, and unable to compete on equal terms in all exercises of physical strength.

Apparently the mysteries of the brain have not been solved far enough for difference of mental power to be estimated by dissection. At least it is known definitely that women have smaller brains, with a smaller supply of poorer blood. On the other hand, women's bodies are smaller. It is often argued, first, that size of brain is no test, as quality is more important than quantity; second, that women's brains, though smaller actually, are larger in proportion, so that this test is in favour of women's mental superiority over men. Whether quality is more important than quantity in the case of the brain or not, there seems to be clear proof that quantity is one factor. Man has a larger brain than apes, and the more highly developed man has a larger brain than the lower savage, and so on. The complexity of the convolutions and the area of the surface seems to be another factor.

The brain does a great many kinds of work. It governs all the really unconscious movements of the body, such as the working of the heart, stomach and intestines. These are almost wholly outside the control of the will, and automatic. It governs such movements as breathing, blinking, blushing, sighing, yawning ; which are almost automatic, but can be modified by the will. It governs all such movements as walking, eating, drinking, directing eyes, listening and smelling ; which are mainly automatic, but are much more under the modifying control of the will. And still of this class, it governs speaking, writing, playing games of skill, singing, playing musical instruments, typing, dancing and the thousands of movements of the body, and especially of the hand, that go to make up skill in workmanship. But the brain has another function, and that is to think in the sense of reasoning, remembering and imagining ; which are interdependent, and it is the seat of all the passions.

It seems quite possible that the parts of the brain that are occupied with the control of the various parts of the body may be smaller in a small body with equal efficiency. They may even be as small in proportion as the body they control. But in the case of the part of the brain that produces the work of a genius, it is difficult to see what the size of the body has to do with it. The idea is that if this part of an ordinary brain were to find itself in a large body, with long arms and legs, it would be handicapped ; while, if it found itself in the head of a woman with small body and limbs, it might produce the works of Newton, Shakespeare, Plato, not to speak of Mrs. Somerville, one after the other. It seems much more likely that intellectual power depends on the size and quality of the cerebrum or whatever parts of it are involved, without any reference to the size or weight of the body. If this view is just, we would expect women to have about as much control of the body as men, but to be behind in intellectual attainment. If the body controlling brain for a given efficiency has to be exactly proportional to the weight of the body controlled ; and if women's brains are, on the average, slightly heavier in proportion to their bodies than men's, women ought to be better in all matters of skill.

The extreme cases are body-controlling brain efficient in proportion to its weight, independently of the size of the body it works ; and efficient in proportion to the ratio of its size to that of the body. Most likely the truth lies between these extremes, and a woman with the body-working part of her brain in strict proportion to her weight is behind in her control, and she is equal only when that part of her brain is out of proportion to her body in some unknown ratio.

When it is pointed out that women have throughout the ages done little or no first-rate work, the answer always is that they have never had the chance, and their education has always been repressive ; yet neither education nor convention has ever repressed genius in man. But there are many subjects in which women have not been kept back, but have had special advantages, yet the result has been poor or negative.

The difference between the mental capacities of men and women is not only in degree, but in kind ; woman is unscientific and unmechanical. Some men are unscientific and unmechanical. There are men, who are not fools, who are quite unable to understand elementary mathematics, and to whom a machine is a complicated and wholly uninteresting mystery. When a leading barrister had been coached for months, and the great telephone and telegraph case was just coming on, he is reported to have said, " Now I understand, you speak into this thing you call a receiver, and it comes out in Morse at the other end. But why did you not tell me that at first, instead of muddling me up with your complicated and irrelevant technicalities ! " This man was a very able lawyer, but one faculty was almost wholly absent. No quantity or quality of education could have made him scientific or technical. Many men are like this, but nearly all women are devoid of any sort of scientific or mechanical faculty whatever. This is not a matter of training. Like most other faculties, this can be trained and developed, but it must be there to begin with. Most men can understand a machine without any training. A certain small proportion of men who have this faculty are trained and become scientific men or engineers of various kinds, but the great majority go into various trades and professions in which neither science nor mechanics helps them. Many of them are amateur mechanics. The woman amateur mechanic hardly exists,; a girl may do a little as a pose, but, in the whole of England, how many women over thirty are there who have a workshop with a lathe and necessary tools, and who make small engines or do other mechanical work for the pure love of it? The male amateur mechanic is not the result of any special training, he trains himself, as far as he is trained, but he knows his work largely in virtue of an innate mechanical or scientific faculty, and he picks up miscellaneous technical knowledge by experience, observation and reading.

Take again the case of a motor-car. A man whose profession has nothing to do with mechanics, buys a motor-car. He not only drives it, but he pulls it more or less to pieces, and studies its working and all its tricks. He takes in two or three car papers, and follows all the newest developments, and spends money on all sorts of tools and recent " gadgets " for his car. He converts his motor shed into a workshop, where he can do many small repairs. Women drive motor-cars, too, but they do not tackle the matter at all in the way men do.

Looking more broadly at the matter, women are not engineers. No one who thinks of women, constituted as they are, can picture to himself a dreadnought in which the ship, the engines, the armament, the electrical equipment, and the various scientific instruments have all been invented by women, designed by women and made by women, while the ship is worked by women and officered by women. It is not true that we are unaccustomed to such things, only owing to universal prejudice; the fact is that women cannot invent or design, make, work or control complicated and elaborate machinery because their brains are not like men's. It is not a matter of training, because many inventors and many engineers have had no special training. A lad goes into a drawing office and picks up tracing by practice, he gradually gets to drawing, and developes into a draughtsman, and rises from that to a high position. Women have been employed as tracers for at least forty-five years, but they get no farther.

Passing to electrical engineering ; again the man who has had no scientific training, and who has no opening for science in his work, has a private aerial of his own, and makes his wireless gear himself. In earlier days he made induction coils, reflecting galvanometers, bridges and telephones, or did electro-plating. The boy who is going into his father's business in the city enjoys such work, and will convert any room in the house, or any outhouse, into a workshop. There may be some girls who do such things, but it is imitation of brothers or pose, and in that case they will stop when they get older or marry.

The man or boy amateur photographer again differs from the girl or woman. He understands his camera, knows something about the properties and relative merits of different kinds of lenses, developes his own negatives and makes his own prints, lantern slides and enlargements. Women sometimes do their own developing and printing, and every now and then produce good work, but that is by patient and blind following of instructions. The man tries half the plates in the market, experiments with all the various developers, and prints on all sorts of papers to get new effects. His sister in nine cases out of ten uses a film camera, exposes at random, and sends the films to the druggist to be developed and printed.

Becoming more domestic, a woman generally uses a sewing machine. She threads it, and arranges tensions and winds, and replaces the shuttle bobbin according to instructions ; but has anyone ever yet met a woman who could take her sewing machine to pieces and clean all the mechanism, or suggest an improved mechanical movement to the makers? There are many women cyclists. How many could even describe, much less invent, the mechanism of a three-speed hub? There are many men who neither know nor care how such a hub works, and who could not understand one if they tried, but very many have the innate mechanical sense which enables them to grasp such things without any training or special experience.

These homely instances are mentioned to show that the fundamental difference between the male and female mind is not hidden away from ordinary observers, it is patent to all who will take the trouble to look.

That women are not amateur mechanics is very obvious, but it is only a special result of the absence of a faculty.

Taking a broader base, mathematics are taught at girls' schools, and women have had the same chances as men for many years. But after all, in the case of a girl with high mathematical ability, school teaching is necessary only to introduce her to the subject. The study of mathematics by a competent person requires nothing but a few books, and pen and paper. It can be carried on at any time and any place. A teacher may help in the early stages, and a coach may be useful if the object is to pass examinations. But passing examinations is only the apprentice stage, the student is merely learning a little of what other men have produced already. To be a great mathematician it is not enough just to go over portions, even large portions, of work that others have done. What woman has ever invented, or rather developed, a new calculus?

There are two comparisons to be made; the one between the best men and the best women, the other between all the men and all the women. In mathematics the best woman is further up the scale than in most scientific subjects, this is apart from the question of passing examinations. Mathematics is a very special subject, requiring careful deductive thinking and concentrated attention, as if the mind were a microscope focussed on one little spot, seeing it more or less from all sides at once, and seeing nothing else, with all extraneous light cut off. It requires also a special kind of imagination, enabling the mathematician to picture in his mind a collection of lengths and directions in three dimensions, to take a single case. This kind of imagination is akin to that of the skilled chess player, who can imagine the board as it would be if a number of moves were made, or who can play several games at once. Good mathematicians are often good chess players. Women, on the other hand, have never shone at chess, and there is no question of prejudice, early training or opportunity there. The mathematician's imagination also resembles a little that of the composer who, at least in many cases, works out a complete composition with every detail in his head, and then writes it out mechanically, as Mozart did, with his wife talking to him to keep him amused during the drudgery. Those who think a competent composer fumbles out stuff at the piano will hardly be able to realise the curious type of imagination of, say, a Macfarren who, when blind, would dictate a full score by humming the parts one after the other to an amanuensis. Many mathematicians, however, seem to lack this curious type of imagination. They take great care in getting a problem stated correctly in an equation, but once that is done they work their mathematical mill, and grind out answers which are logical deductions from the statement, without having any sort of physical conception of the intermediate steps. It seems possible that women fall short mainly in this point of imagination. Their deficiency in chess and in musical composition point that way. But care must be taken not to make assumptions just because they appear to explain differences in a consistent way. This backwardness in chess may arise, not from any want of ability, but from the absence of love of games.

That women do not play chess with one another, join chess clubs, or publish problems to any extent, is another instance of mental sex difference. The play of animals, by the way, is said to be an instructive training for their life's work. Thus, the play of kittens is training in catching small animals, and so on. The games of boys are training in fighting, and in beating one another. They are competitive, and they are instructive so as to be useful in adult life. The play of little girls with dolls' houses, and so on, is training for motherhood, and is also instructive. That is why girls games are so feeble. There is no educative basis for them, and their brains are different from birth upwards. Girls' modern games are a mere imitation of boys', and have no vigour in them. With the exception of such social games as lawn-tennis and golf, they do not survive school.

In natural science, again, women are nowhere. For many years there has been taught at girl-schools something that might have been science if it had not been taught by women; but women now attend university and college classes, and have the same chances as men. The best scientific women have done some good work, but none has done anything that would put a man in the front rank if he had done it. Any good work done by a woman has always been under the direction or influence of, or in conjunction with, a man, and infinitely more notice has been taken of it, just because it was done by a woman. This treatment of women's work by the public and the press makes it difficult to estimate it at its real value. Women have also a great advantage in another way. A lady starts on terms of equality with all the leading scientific men she meets, because she is a lady, whereas her brother, of the same age, and let us say the same ability, is, in comparison, nobody. Then men like women, and take interest in everything they do, so that if a woman does anything, or even pretends to do anything, it is known at once. She thus has not to fight to get known as a man has, she gets known at once because she is a woman. In the scientific journals and abstracts a lady's name is always in full, or it has " Miss " inserted to show that she is a lady, and this attracts attention to her.

The branch of science in which women are doing most is chemistry. This is to be expected, because chemistry is still a science which depends largely on memory. The various elements and compounds have properties which have to be remembered, like the habits and character- istics of animals in Natural History; and conventional chemistry might be called the Natural History of the elements and their compounds. It is not a systematic science yet, and the nomenclature even is much less logical than it sounds. Duhem points out that the directions for preparing a substance are of the same order as a recipe in a cookery book. Chemistry is undergoing great changes now, as it is developing on the basis of the principle of degradation of energy in all change; and it is probable this aspect of the subject will make the study more difficult for women.

Though a few women have done good work, especially in chemistry, women as a whole are very much less scientific than men. They show no curiosity about things, though people interest them keenly. They will absorb the biography of a man without having the least knowledge of his work.

Many women are now qualifying as physicians and surgeons. The fact that they pass the difficult exami- nations as well as men, or nearly as well, is generally taken as proof that women are as good doctors. There are two or three fallacies in this argument. In the first place women develope more quickly than men. A girl of 15 is mentally about as old as a boy of 18, and a girl of 21 is not only much more developed in proportion as to brain than a man of the same age, but she has already had some extra years of maturity. A man and a girl sitting for an examination at 21 are thus not at all on equal terms, the girl has several years to the good. There is no certainty that the examiners do not unintentionally favour girls. It is practically impossible for men not to be biassed in favour of women, especially young women ; and the examinations cannot be conducted wholly without the examiners being able to identify the sex of the candidates. Another factor is that girls take themselves much more seriously than boys. A boy reading for an examination is apt to treat his work as a " bore," which commands unwilling attention, and interferes with his mere engrossing pursuits, while a girl takes herself and her work very differently, and thinks the world revolves about her examination. This may be a feather in the feminine cap. The result is that the fact that a man and a woman have passed a given examination at the same age is not the least guarantee that they will remain level. In any profession a man who has finished his examinations is just ready to begin serious study. His brain goes on developing, and he goes on learning all his life ; there is no reason to suppose the woman will do the same. Women seem to have less faculty for self-teaching than men, a self-taught woman being rare in any branch of acquirement ; moreover, she is physically weaker, and she has very probably more or less permanently injured her health as a student by working far too hard and taking her career too seriously. Brain work such as vain mothers now inflict upon their girls is a serious injury to their health. It is not unusual to meet pale, undeveloped girls who have broken down through trying to do boys' work at school.; and at Girton and Newnham it is said that the pressure suppresses natural functions in most cases of hard work.

The fact that girls' brains develope more quickly than boys', and then stop at about 18 or 20, while men's go on to 30 or so, misleads a great many people. The American experimental work in psychology is largely marred because the comparisons are made of college students, and the men and girls are approximately of the same age, and not at the corresponding degree of brain development. Joint education of boys and girls is apt to give them both a wholly false idea of the relative abilities of men and women for the same reason. During the whole of the course of the joint education the girls of the same age as the boys are comparatively older in brain development, and in brain experience, but as they are the same age, it is assumed by both that the women in proportion to men are much abler than they really are.

This is particularly hard on many women. A girl working in competition with boys of her own age is pleasantly surprised to find she beats them. She embraces a career, she orders every detail of her life to fit, and subordinates every other consideration to success in some examination or other. To her a University degree is a distinction that lifts her above common mortals, and she finally gets it. Then she finds, to her astonishment, that she gets no farther. The stupid men have a way of going on past her, in the real work of life, in a manner that is quite incomprehensible to her, and she finally puts it down to gross prejudice against her sex, and becomes a bitter and disappointed woman with a grievance against mankind.

Pictorial art and music are two subjects in which women have had plenty of educational opportunities for many years. Take the case of music. What is woman's record? It is usual to quote a list of women composers who are mostly unknown except as items on such lists. There never has been any woman composer that could compare with even the third-rate man.

It is often heard that though women have done comparatively nothing as composers, they can compete with men as performers. They are probably best able to rank with men in singing, but singing involves very little musical knowledge or ability, it is mainly a question of a good voice and command over it. The public is apt to look upon a popular singer as a leading musician, but the trained musician generally regards the singer as an unavoidable evil, that is really outside the circle of music proper. The public also regards music and playing the piano and violin as synonymous. Women certainly show great skill in connection with both instruments. If what has been said about the brain is true, this is to be expected, as women's brains are as large or larger than men's in proportion to their bodies. It might be supposed, therefore, that they would have as good, or nearly as good control over their muscles. But it is doubtful whether women have as good technique as men, or whether any woman of those times was as good as Paganini, or was equal to Liszt as an executant. The violin, as a solo instrument, appeals to the public like the solo singer ; but to the musician the violinist is a person with great skill, and he ought to play with feeling and intelligence too, but after all he plays only one line of music, and his instrument is incomplete in itself. The piano is complete in itself, and gives much more scope for musicianship. Here is where the woman pianist falls short. In comparison with her skill, her musicianship is far behind, and though she plays all the notes accurately, and apparently perfectly from the purely mechanical point of view, the result is poor. A small schoolboy may pronounce every word correctly, articulating each sound beautifully, and yet his reading of a great poem is ludicrous. It is as one writer puts it, a popular delusion that women can play the piano. But even if they did, music does not consist entirely of composing and of playing an instrument. There has been no woman musical critic of any note. No woman has devised any of the numerous systems of harmony. Some may think this is to their credit. No woman has written a first-class text-book on any branch of musical education. No woman has invented a new musical instrument, nor made any improvement in the piano, the organ, or any of the instruments of the orchestra.

Music seems to have nothing to do with science, the point mainly under discussion at the moment, but there is a curious connection. A great many men who have devoted themselves to music have either shown early love for mathematics, science, law, or engineering, and many were and are amateur mechanics, or are keen on science. Many are interested in organ building. On the other hand, a very large proportion of amateur musicians are scientific men, engineers or lawyers. Poets and

" literary " men are unmusical as a rule, while the musical mistakes of novelists are a byword. The clergy are notoriously unmusical.

It has often been pointed out that there is nothing women can do that men cannot do better. Even in cooking and dressmaking men take the front places. In all the arts women are so much behind that art has been considered a secondary male characteristic.

But women are not equally far behind in all directions. Many people rank Jane Austen, Charlotte Brontë and George Eliot as but little behind English novelists of the first rank. Then women can learn languages nearly as well as men. They can master an enormous number of small details, and do a great deal of brainwork in managing a household, and making everything work smoothly. It does not follow that they can organise large affairs, because they have little sense of proportion, and they spend a great deal of brain work on details that are not worth it. This absence of sense of proportion is most evident in the general want of sense of humour in women ; humour being based largely on sense of proportion. This want of sense of proportion comes out in most women's work. A woman who does anything, or thinks she does anything, is apt to regard it as the only matter of real importance in the world. Women seem to be much less conceited than men, and this is not exactly conceit. An eminent geologist, for example, is quite aware that he knows more about geology even than most specialists, but to him it is a mere fact and little more, and of no general importance. Most likely he takes little pride in the matter, though he may be very conceited about his golf, what he calls singing, or his imagined ability as a playwright. A woman, on the other hand, who studied geology, would believe she was one of the first geologists in the world, and that the community were depending on the result of her researches. Her household, her dress, her time, her social intercourse, and everything about her would be arranged to promote her study of geology. This is hardly conceit, it is more nearly a form of hallucination, and it has little relation to her real knowledge of her subject.   Probably it is just the result of her want of sense of proportion or humour.

Broadly speaking, there are two types of mind for which it is difficult to find good descriptive names. They might be called the rational and the absorptive. The rational includes the scientific in its broadest sense, and the legal.   Anyone with an absorptive mind may be good at languages, history, the more descriptive aspects of botany and natural history, and has a great respect for precedent and authority.   For simplicity, the rational may be called the masculine mind, as it is found almost exclusively in man; and the absorptive the feminine, because it is characteristically the feminine type of mind.   But it must not be forgotten that a large proportion of men have almost purely feminine minds; while many women, especially women who are able in certain directions, have minds largely of the masculine type.   The feminine mind may go with a kind of creative power in poets, dramatists, novelists, and in those that produce the endless series of books about other books commonly called literature.   The feminine mind is at its highest development in the clergyman, minister or priest.

The idea that if women have scope now, they will acquire new qualities in a generation or two, means not only that acquired characteristics are inherited, but that they are inherited down one side.   In other words, it assumes that educated women would have clever daughters, but ordinary sons.

The relative position of man and woman is profoundly affected by sex influences, of which chivalry is one outcome.   To begin with, sex influence alters men's opinions about women.   Men like women, and idealise them, ascribing all sorts of qualities to them that they would like them to have; but man does not let his idealism control his judgment completely, he only idealises women while of an age to be sexually attractive.   The thoughtless, that is the ordinary man's opinion of woman, apart from the sex bias, is embodied in the old woman, old lady, or the dear old lady of comic papers. When men think of women in Parliament, or at the Bar, or in various professions, they picture them as young and charming. A movement for getting old women into Parliament, on to the Bench, into the Church, or even to give them the vote would have little chance of success. Then the feminists, also, believe in man's superiority. To imitate men in dress, manners, especially bad manners, or conduct, is to proclaim their superiority.

While there is the sex bias which makes men endow young women with all sorts of good qualities, and perhaps makes many women think too well of men, especially young men, there is also what is often called sex hatred. This is very common in men. Most men, even those who claim that women and men are intellectually the same, strongly dislike being beaten by women in their own lines. The spirited boy objects to being at a dame's school or to being under the control of any woman except, perhaps, his mother. The admission of women to university degrees, or to their examinations, has already lowered the prestige of these distinctions. Giving women titles as rewards for merit will tend to reduce the value of all such titles; and the husband of a lady who is given one would seldom care to have a handle to his name because he is her husband.

On the other hand, many modern women show a sort of hatred of men in all sorts of fantastic forms. Many school teachers have this feeling very strongly. They have often taken degrees, and find they do not bring the consideration expected, and they pass their views on to their pupils.

These last are all cases of what may be called sex prejudice, using the word in its colloquial sense ; but on more careful examination they may be found to be examples of class applied to the sexes.

Chivalry is not a fantastic and out of date survival of the supposed ideas of the Middle Ages; it is an instinct which we inherit from the dumb animals. In fact, chivalry of a purer type than the human is widespread among animals that we choose to look down upon, though the dumb animals are much better than we are in many ways. It supports women in an artificial position, putting them on a sort of pedestal, which is effective enough, though it is realised that it is artificial. This puts men and women generally on the same level, at least in the upper and middle classes. As explained already, most men devote the whole of their active mind to their work, and in all the ordinary intercourse of the day they use only the fallow mind. The result is that among educated people, outside professional work or business, women and men are on equal terms. In the humble classes the women are generally more intelligent than the men. In few trades does the hand-worker need enough brain-work to keep his mind keen; so that it is apt to be fallow through most of his life. His sister, as a child, looked after him as a little mother, and took life seriously from the beginning. All through as girl, as wife, and as mother, she has been managing affairs and puzzling out details. Her brain is more active. If you stop at a cottage and ask a man any question, his wife will answer first, and will often be able to answer when he cannot.

There is much more opening in the way of competition with men the lower we go down. Men's work is getting more and more monotonous and simple every day, and the hand-worker, who is normally a man who uses his hands as well as his brain, is becoming less and less dependent on brain or skill. Purely hard physical work, such as that of the navvy, is getting replaced by machinery, and if it were not, women can do a good deal, and in other countries—worse luck—they do it. The result is that the male hand-worker will soon have nothing but the fallow mind; and women, who in that class have to do more thinking from childhood, will compete on nearly equal terms. This means that a couple, where the man used to earn thirty shillings and the wife ran the house, will earn thirty shillings, not more, between them, the husband working normal hours, and the wife working normal hours at the factory, and the rest of the twenty-four, less a few for short sleep broken by children, at work at home. There is no six, eight, nine, ten, or any other hour working day for women.

It has just been said that the existing pedestal of chivalry is artificial. But the fundamental question is : Why should the pedestal be artificial? If one puts it that the pedestal cannot be intellectual attainment of the money-making kinds, that men use in their daily work, because such a pedestal is obviously hollow, he is told he is insulting womankind. All the same, it is pretty clear that women in general never have had, and have not now, intellectual ability, not merely to do some of the work of men, but to excel them generally. Unless the majority of women cannot only equal men, but can generally excel them, it is quite clear they cannot be on a sound pedestal of intellectualism. But is this any loss? We all take it for granted without any thought that intellect is the criterion of merit. This seems to be a purely modern, and perhaps local, idea. That women should hold it so strongly is particularly unfortunate, and this is not a very recent phase. Chesterfield shows that women had this weakness fully developed in his time. It is probably a particular case of the general rule that people are vainest over their weak points.

If one urges that there is a solid pedestal of character; that women are infinitely less immoral than men ; that they are much more modest, by which is meant less conceited; that they are more sympathetic and kinder; and that they are beyond all comparison more unselfish and self-sacrificing; he is told this is all nineteenth-century nonsense; and that no modern woman will be grateful for any such tributes.

And yet there has always been an ideal, according to which woman is the influence that is to raise mankind, and men would yield her this position, and help her to hold it, if she would only take it. The position of the mother in France is the nearest approach to it.

The modern feminine movement has been due almost

entirely to middle-class women. It has been really based entirely on chivalry. Even the wildest suffragettes were never punished as men would be punished for the same offences. In the beginning women can have the advantages of equality and none of the drawbacks. It is probably not generally realised by women how completely most men look at them through sex spectacles. To a virile man a woman is first and last a woman. If she paints pictures, to him she is a woman who paints pictures. The pictures are interesting merely because they are done by a woman. Whatever work she does, if it is generally thought of as man's work, is looked at from this point of view. It is not taken seriously on its own basis as work. This attitude may be a survival of some primitive instinct. It is often said that the ablest men think most of women; but that view, even if unconscious, is very general. Not long ago some American women got up a great procession to prove that women could do something or other, and it was headed by a girl as Joan of Arc or Boadicea or somebody. The leaders of the movement expressed sorrow when a paper said it did not matter what the girl was intended for, she was a " peach, anyhow."

This view of women's doings disappears when the doings are common and recognised as women's work. The work of a housemaid, for instance, stands on its own base as work. Again, there are so many women writers that their novels are treated almost, if not quite, on their own merits. While the movement is new, women who do work formerly done almost entirely by men are in an artificial position. They get the advertisement of sex, and use it to the utmost. For example, a medical man is known by his surname only, Smith or Jones, but a woman doctor calls herself Dr. Flossie Robinson, so as to show she is a woman, and to call attention to the wonderful fact that a woman has a degree or other proper qualifications.

Many women singers have advanced far enough to be known by their surnames; but it is not possible to compare men and women singers. Only one woman musician has reached the eminence of being known by her surname, with nothing to show she is a woman. As the novelty wears off, women will find that their abilities, compared with those of men, are just the same as they have been for millions of years. Even now they are finding it necessary to get work belonging to much lower social grades. They get over the difficulty temporarily by putting " lady " in front of their occupations. If a gentleman's son has to drive a cab, he is a cab-driver, not a gentleman cab-driver, and he sinks to the general level of a cab-driver. If a gentleman's daughter becomes a chauffeur, a gardener, a cook, or joins the police, she can prefix " lady " to her calling, and wear a comic opera uniform; but in a short time she will be a chauffeur, a gardener, a cook, or one of the police, and nothing more. Those who get into professions will find they can only do the low grade work. Thus, the first few women barristers or solicitors will have their portraits in all the papers, and may be notorious and may start well ; but after a little, women lawyers and women doctors and so on will take the positions women now take in these professions in countries where they have been open to women for some time. Chivalry will tend to die out in an atmosphere of competition of the sexes, and the result seems inevitable, a general lowering of the status of women.

Among the hand-working classes this sort of competition has, unfortunately, been going on for a long time. At intervals various Acts of Parliament have had to be passed to prevent this competition pushing women too far down, but the general result has been that, as Booker Washington put it in " The Man Farthest Down." In Europe, at least, " the man farthest down is Woman."

There is a common impression that women do not get fair wages because they are women. It is supposed that a factory that employs men at, say, two pounds a week, to do certain work, should also employ women to do the same work, and should give them two pounds a week. If women did the same work equally well they would, of course, earn as much as men ; they might earn more, because they are generally keener, more conscientious and patient, as well as more regular, so that they are easier to manage. They do not mind monotony as men do, either. But the fact is that they do not do the same work as men. If one factory making, say, boxes, employed men at two pounds a week, and a rival factory got women to do exactly the same work at thirty shillings a week, the second factory would undersell the other, and the result would be not that the women would get two pounds, but that both factories would employ women at thirty shillings. This is merely a case of men having been employed at work that women can do better, or better in proportion to their wages. In most factories now there are women doing some of the work, and this has been so for centuries. As mass production and repetition methods come in there is more unskilled work that can be done by women. But that men and women are doing the same work at widely different wage-rates in industry is a myth. No manager would be such a fool as to pay highly where he need not.

There were cases during the war where men were replaced by women, and the women produced a much larger output. But the small output of the men was artificially produced by trade union interference. The only other case that comes to mind where men get much higher pay for approximately the same work is practically controlled by women themselves. Probably not a single one of all the women who go about talking about their underpaid sex has ever dreamed of giving her maid-servants men-servants' wages. No woman who does not give all her maid-servants men's wages ought to have the face to accuse others of injustice.

There is much misconception as to women's work and pay in industry. Women's factory work is quite unlike men's. What they do best is monotonous repetition work, which does not vary. They will look after automatic machines of all sorts, but they do it like trained animals. If the machine goes wrong in any way, a man has to put it right. In making electric incandescent lamps in early days, when the industry was young, and one had to make frequent changes in the manufacture, I found that once girls had learned one process one way, it was almost impossible to get them to do it differently. The only course was to wait until two processes had to be altered, and then change the whole of two batches of girls over, so that each had to learn quite a new method. Recently I asked a lamp-maker if he found the same difficulty, and found he had hit upon exactly the same solution.

Women operatives do their own work well and keenly enough, but they take no interest in anything outside their own little bit. There are many thousands of girls in electric lamp factories now, but probably there are not half a dozen among them who know or care in the least how a lamp is made. Generally they are much more easy to manage than men. They do not drink, or stop off, and they seem to work straight on whether watched or not. But they are at a great physiological disadvantage. As one manager exaggerated it, they are impossible or crazy for four or five days every month, and four or five years every lifetime.

There are many cases where men and women are apparently doing the same work for different wages, and doing so permanently, not merely during a change. In the case of a box factory, a man at two pounds a week may put, say, 200 boxes an hour through a process, and a woman may put 180. It may be thought that in that case the woman is worth thirty-six shillings a week, instead of thirty. This is not the case, because her wage is only a part of the cost of the process. She may have an expensive machine doing less than its full output and the costs are generally otherwise higher in proportion.

The result of women working and earning wages is not that the families in their class are richer. Population pressure comes into play, and the result is that the family is as a whole in the degree of comfort or the reverse corresponding to the value of their work. If women had never taken up wage-earning work the country would have been less productiver; but this does not mean that the people would have been poorer, but that there would have been fewer of them.

There are two possible positions for women. They may be treated as the privileged sex, that is, partly as man's equal and partly as his superior, and this last not altogether as a convention. Chivalry to women is natural, and it may be a very good instinct. On these lines women would not be expected to work for their living, and it would be a disgrace for a man to leave his wife or daughters poor. This is one extreme position in which wife or mother is a queen and the daughter a little princess. The other extreme is that women and men are to compete for their bread, and that the struggle is to be to the bitter end, with women handicapped all the time by inferior brain power, inferior muscular strength and physiological disqualifications. The feminist movement is thus heading for the degradation of women.

Little has been said as to women and politics. Women seem to think that they got the vote because they showed that they deserved it. Politicians will always debase the franchise, just as they will debase the currency, if they think it will keep them in power. Before the war the politicians were against female franchise. But during the war women were wanted to make munitions and do other things. A campaign of over-payment and over-praise was most successful, and it was obvious that the politicians in power had pleased women, so that if they gave them the franchise they would probably secure a majority of the new votes. Whether the franchise will have any perceptible effect is another question. Wage-earning women think that the vote will increase their pay in some way or other. This is just a case of the ordinary superstition as to the powers of government. Where women have had the vote for some time there is no particular result to be seen. It might have been expected they would introduce prohibition of alcohol at once.

In the middle classes, and to some extent in the

upper, their political incursion has excited a set of
women a great deal. One of the results of population
pressure is that in the middle and upper classes women
marry later in life, and many do not marry at all. There
is thus a gap of about ten years, say from eighteen to
twenty-eight, when women have nothing to do and
nothing to aim at. Some take up Art, Literature, Music,
and so on with a big capital, only to drop it on marriage,
others do bits of work belonging to other social levels.
There is now a new outlet in sex advertisement societies,
with the word " Woman " prominently in the title.
We have Women's Leagues and Associations for interfering with everything. There is also an idea that
woman is a newly discovered kind of animal with
women's views of all subjects, which places them in a
new and unsuspected light. This all tends towards the
development of the platform woman, and the woman who
is always in evidence in the papers. There is thus a
small but very noisy set of middle-class women, who may
have much influence, entirely out of proportion to their
ability or number. They cannot affect woman's pay
or final position, but they may procure some alteration in
the law. The law generally is already notoriously unfair in its favouritism of women, and when it is not
glaringly unfair, it is seldom enforced, as, for instance,
in criminal cases.

Women's present demands are often quite illogical
and inconsistent. For example, if a married man com-
mits adultery, it is in a way outside the circle of his
family. But if a woman does so, and introduces an
interloping child into her husband's family, the matter
is obviously much more serious.; it is quite different
owing to the physiology of the matter. Yet women say
in this respect men and women should be on absolutely
equal footing. On the other hand, women want the age
of consent raised to eighteen. A girl who is nearly
eighteen is in proportion as old as a man of twenty-one,
and sexually she is quite mature. But if she induces a
boy to be immoral with her, she is to be regarded as a
poor, weak, half-witted sort of creature, and the boy

is to be subjected to a savage punishment that will ruin the rest of his life. If the sexes are equal, she has suffered no more damage than he has.

Except that they may get a few absurd laws passed in their favour, the political women may do no direct or not much harm. No one can seriously suppose a woman member of Parliament can add to the wisdom of that august assembly. This is not because a really able woman may not have ability above the average of the House of Commons. The main difficulty is that apart from women who merely replace a husband, or who are popular public pets, and do not count ; the wrong type of woman alone has any chance of being elected ; that is the empty-headed, self-advertising, platform woman. She has probably never earned her own living, and has not the ability to do so, yet she will as often as not pose as a " labour " candidate, and rail at those parasites who take the good things of life without having worked for them. The harm this type of person does is much the same as that of all demagogues. She stirs up misdirected discontent and class hatred merely to gratify her own vanity.

The admission of women to the House of Lords is illogical on the face of it. The whole theory of the peerage depends on obsolete ideas as to heredity. The theory was that the mysterious essence of goodness which produced the best, and entitled them to rule, went down the male line only, and especially through the eldest son. The female side did not count. If the lines are traced upwards along the female side they are generally side tracked to the ballet or the chorus in a generation or two—a very good thing, no doubt, for the older aristocracy. But though we go on thinking of the peerage as made up of " old families," it is largely made up of or descended from politicians, news-paper men, rich men who bought titles, and people of that sort, steadied by successful brewers, distillers and other able business men. But to have women born into the House of Lords is quite illogical.

The general tendency of the Feminist movement, from

the population point of view, is to put women into competition with men. At first they will be helped by chivalry, but competition will tend to strangle chivalry. The result will be that a people will become more productive, and therefore the population of a feminist country will increase, while the people reach no higher degree of comfort. But this competition is a step backward in civilisation ; it involves women having, if possible, more to suffer than they have at present, while they are sunk to lower relative levels than men. It cannot have the effect of rendering women independent of men and better off pecuniarily. The tendency will be not to value women as an equal but different sex, but to estimate them by their money-earning capacity. The relation of woman to man as a sex, when man and women are complements making a complete whole, is not really dependence at all. But the relation of a much less competent half of the world to the other half, when both are struggling for life, and are working along the same lines, is a very different matter. And all this is really to flatter the vanity of a small number of noisy and self-assertive middle-class women. It is not possible to know what will happen. One of the most likely solutions is that someone will discover a means of predetermining sex ; and after that there will be fewer women produced, so that they become scarcer than they are now ; and they may then regain the position from which a few of the noisier and more conceited women are now trying to push them down.

This chapter may appear to the superficial to be an attack on women. It is nothing of the sort. It is an attack on the evil that women are bringing on themselves by trying to compete in intellectual and hand-work. Intellect is not a test of merit at all. A clever man does no particular good to the world at large, or to those around him. At most he makes more for his family. What is really admirable is character, kindness, unselfishness, modesty and goodness generally. Women have no need of any sort of advertisement movement to put them really in front. How often, for one example only, do we see the male counterpart of the daughter, who gives up her whole young life to looking after an invalid or a selfish father, knowing that it means she will lose most of the sweets of life herself? But this is " Early Victorian."

CHAPTER XVIII

DOLES

THE question of doles has been touched upon in a recent chapter, but it is so large, and comes up in so many places, that we may look into it more thoroughly. We ought to consider such things as poor relief,; hospitals ; charity, organised and general.; old age pensions ; compulsory subsidised insurance.; State education ; free libraries ; and subsidised art. Doles to those out of work is the only form so far discussed.

The case of what is ordinarily called charity may be taken first. Suppose anyone who is not poor meets someone in the street who is in difficulties, either starving or very poor. The only question people ask generally is whether giving money does good or harm to the man who gets it. He is in the field of view, and they never think of the effect on those who are outside it. Suppose Dives gives Lazarus a shilling,; people will say Dives can well afford the shilling, and will never feel the loss,; so it is right that he should give the shilling. As to Lazarus, it will be said that it is a great thing for him to get the shilling,; it does Dives no harm, and it does Lazarus a great deal of good. The only point is that getting shillings without working may tend to demoralise Lazarus, and make him lazy. But if Dives had not given the shilling to Lazarus, what would he have done with it? He would either have invested it in some concern which employs men usefully and wanted capital, or he would have spent it on his own enjoyment. It sounds odd to talk of investing a shilling, but that does not matter. Dives may give large sums away in charity. If he stopped doing so he would, other things being the same, either have more to spend on his own or his family's comforts and amusements, or save more and invest it. He might devote some to gratular expenditure and some to investment. The shilling may be considered as belonging to either lot.

If the shilling would have been invested if it had not been given to Lazarus, the result is that Dives had the choice of putting some money into a business which would then have employed more men ; and he preferred that the men should to that extent not be employed, in order to benefit Lazarus. Otherwise the shilling might have gone towards the wages of a gardener. In that case Dives decides that there shall be less employment in his garden to the extent of a shilling. The gardeners may be taken to be deprived of the chance of earning a shilling by doing a shilling's worth of work, in order that Lazarus shall have the shilling in return for doing nothing. A rich man's wealth from this point of view is merely the power, not of giving money with a corresponding effect on himself only, but of saying who shall eat and who shall not. When he says to Lazarus, " You shall eat," he says to someone else, " You shall not eat, though you are willing to work ! " The man who loses is never thought of at all ; he is not in sight, and he must suffer undeservedly without anybody realising anything about it. Lazarus is taken as a typical case of a man who does not work, whatever his reason for idleness may be ; and has neither worked in the past and put by for well-earned leisure, nor inherited leisure from somebody else's work. He thus lives entirely on charity, that is to say, on the rest of the public. It is clearly an injustice to other deserving people that the community should support Lazarus. He really thrives on our sentimentalism. If he did not get odd shillings he would not starve. He would work for his living and be a Lazarus no longer. One or two such people in a community does not matters; but in a sentimental country like this we have not a few, but of the order of millions of lazari. Under this form of plural are included all those who live wholly without working, or partly so. This includes all those who get poor-relief, all those who live wholly or partly on charity, in or in connection with benevolent institutions,; those who get old age pensions and government insurance benefits ; and the class extends into the realms of respectability, as it includes people whose children are educated free or at specially low rates. But we may consider first a large mass of low grade lazari, namely those living on charity, poor-relief, out-of-work doles and so on. England being a country that suffers from great sentimentality, keeps up a large number of lazari.

Suppose there is a country which supports forty million people, of whom a million are thorough-going lazari, it may be regarded as a community of thirty-nine million, saddled with a dead weight of a million loafing consumers. The popular idea is that the burden of supporting the lazari all falls on the rich, or on the capitalists, so that there are only two results, the presence of a million lazari and less wealth among the rich. This cannot be so. Take, for instance, the case of the capitalist,; if he has to pay for the upkeep of lazari out of his profits, other things being the same, he will make less profit. If the average profit in the community falls below the normal, say 3 per cent., people will not be induced to save, so the profits on capital will rise until it is worth while to save in spite of having to support the lazari. The load therefore does not come primarily on the capitalist. Take the hand-worker next. He lives in a certain degree of comfort, and gets wages to suit. If the wages fall short of what are needed for that degree of comfort hand-workers, with the corresponding skill, get scarcer. We are dealing for the moment with a permanent state, not a rather sudden change. The hand-worker apparently gets the same wages, and the capitalists the same profit after paying for the idlers. The consumer consisting mainly of the hand-worker, buys as cheaply as before,; the presence of a population of idlers does not enable him to buy the same goods in the same quantity at higher prices on the same wages. It looks as if the idlers were supported on nothing, and it might therefore be suggested that they are kept by the State. The solution is quite simple. The community is smaller. Then suppose it is a self-contained community, growing its own food and necessaries•; if thirty-nine million people can live in a certain state of comfort, that is to say, with each stratum in the degree of comfort normal to it, an addition of a million lazari means first that the food producers will have to produce $2\frac{1}{2}$ per cent. more food, and the clothiers more clothes and so on. The extra food can be produced with the same work only by reducing the total produce, so that the better land alone is culti-vated. To get $2\frac{1}{2}$ per cent. more per man employed may involve a large reduction in the land in use. There are thus fewer food producers, the reduction being more than in proportion to the idle mouths. The rents fall.; so the number of landlords will decrease so that they live in the same degree of comfort as before. The result on the whole is that if a percentage of a population is idle, the population, including the idlers, is smaller.

The effect on the idlers themselves may be considered, and then put aside, as it is quite easy to follow. The idlers are rather the result of the doles than the other way round. If the doles, after being in force for a generation or two, were suddenly stopped, a large pro-portion of the idlers would be forced to work, but a good many would starve. No one would propose to stop old standing doles quite suddenly. There are lots of sudden changes in communities, and many of them cause great undeserved distress, though they enable more people to live. One of the commonest is the invention of a machine to do the work of many men who are highly skilled in one special way. In a short time matters straighten themselves out, but at first these men may suffer. Almost any kind of sudden progress has this sort of effect locally. At the lowest strata of society popu-lation pressure is always causing starvation and misery, and there is irresponsible multiplication of ill-developed, ill-nourished, feeble-minded and generally incompetent human beings. There is a practically unlimited supply of these people. If a country decides to support a million of them by doles, broadly there will be that million extra ; but the supply over and above the million will be substantially the same as the original supply before the doles. The poverty and starvation and general misery will be that due to the stress in a community of about forty million people living in ignorance of the principle of population. Putting a million of the lowest aside and feeding them does not stop the further supply from the rest of the community. It does, encourage the lazari who are supported to multiply on their own account, and to produce more lazari than ever, and those of the very worst type. The result of doles is thus to increase the very evil they are intended to cure, and to do so very seriously.

The result of a community of forty million keeping a colony of a million lazari is, first, that the community is considerably smaller than it would be if it did not keep lazari, which may not be a matter of importance ; and that the society is more like a triangle or a pyramid resting on its base than it might be ; the base representing the lowest strata, composed of the starving, the underfed, the half-witted, the criminal and the miserable submerged. This layer of human beings that ought never to exist is also a hot-bed of all sorts of crimes against society ; and a mass of inflammatory matter which may augment any disturbance at any time, and cause a conflagration.

Any community can keep as large a proportion of lazari as it likes. There is no limit to the proportion, until the corresponding shrinkage of the community as a whole finally makes community and its lazari disappear with it. This never happens in practice. Before Rome fell one of the signs of decay was the prevalence of doles. It might be said that Rome fell because it ran to seed in the matter of doles. It is easy to select some weak point such as dole giving, and to put all the blame on it ; but it might be just as sound to point out that the Romans indulged in actor-worship, and an actor left a fortune of, say, £20,000 ; and that this country is also in a rotten state, as is shown by the

19

way the thoughtless treat contemporary mummers. Such a thing is the result of mere frivolity, and may be of no importance at all.

The chief offender in keeping the social sore open and as large as possible is the church. The church and stage both live largely by advertisement; it is the breath of life to them. There is this difference, though, actors and actresses advertise themselves personally. Parsons do this, too, but they also advertise their churches as a whole. For instance, parsons wear special clothes, and many of them adopt a special affectation in speaking. Church bell ringing is entirely advertisement. No one needs bells to catch a train, to go out to dinner, or to attend a concert. Almost every marriage notice needlessly advertises a parson or two. Parsons of all kinds are always ready and anxious to take the chair, or speak at every sort of local public meeting, and to put themselves in evidence on every occasion. One of their main channels for advertisement is what is called charity; that is subscription of money nominally and intentionally to reduce the poverty of existing poor people. Its effect is, as already explained, to take money away from workers and give it to idlers, so that it increases poverty, and is, in fact, the primary cause of a great deal of the poverty among us. Every charity list has a collection of ecclesiastical and other advertisers at the top as being a council, a committee, or as patrons. Similarly every charitable institution gives a gratuitous advertisement to people of the same type. The clergy therefore support the vice of what is called charity as a matter of business. They have collections in churches, and they go round to one another's pulpits to preach special charity sermons, their sermons being duly advertised.

It may sound extreme to call charity a vice ; and like many other vices, it shades off gradually into a virtue; in fact, kindness to and sympathy with our fellow men is a very high virtue. To see if charity is a virtue or a vice the motives and the effects have to be taken into account ; and it is difficult not to allow a good motive to obscure the real effects. One's heart naturally warms to Pope's *Man of Ross*, for instance. The clergy, no doubt, think that they are doing good in getting people to subscribe money for the poor. But the advertisement factor is there, too. By putting themselves forward as the advocates and instruments of charity they get a sort of patronage which increases their reputation and importance. Then there are many rich people who like to be known as charitable. They often give a good deal themselves ; but they also like to be on all sorts of councils and committees. Many people are charitable through a kind of good-natured indolence or incompetence. A man feels that he is very well off, while others are not, and he hears a good deal of the common talk that the poor are poor because the rich have taken their money from them, and he feels that if he subscribes to some charities he is putting himself right. In many country districts it is very difficult to avoid subscribing to many kinds of schemes that are clearly hurtful, as refusal would cause all sorts of unpleasantness and ill-feeling. Vanity is here some of the motive. Vanity is at the bottom of a great deal of charity, as of other vices. For example, a number of untrained people will combine to give a theatrical or musical performance. The theatrical performances may often be amusing ; the musical may not. In order to persuade themselves that their work is as good as that of select, trained performers, they charge full prices for the seats, and give the proceeds to any charity, it does not matter what. The audience go because they want to see members of their families distinguish themselves ; and they tolerate the prices because the performance is " for a charity," and the performers then boast that they have made so many pounds. It is not easy to say how much money is paid by audiences at such performances ; it probably is only a very minute percentage. The case is cited to show how vanity comes in as the mainspring of vice, even on that small scale.

By far the most serious form of the evil is relief under

the Poor Law. Here the politicians gain popularity with the hand-workers, as the ordinary voter thinks the money comes out of the rich. The injury and folly of the Poor Law have been known for a century. All that happens is that it is tinkered occasionally. The Poor Law is a badly devised and expensively administered method of ensuring that there shall be at least a certain number of artificially produced paupers in the country, in addition to the large numbers produced and maintained by voluntary contributions, and to the small number that always come down through normal pressure of population.

It is a curious thing that the active spirits in charity are the politicians, the clergy, and rich philanthropists, who generally remain rich. They work for their own credit, but other people subscribe and other people still pay indirectly.

The politician is not content with the mischief he causes by the Poor Law ; he has further bids for popularity with the crowd in the way of old age pensions, compulsory insurance, and so on. These are all welcomed by the masses as ways of taking money back from the rich man, and giving it to them. Of course it does not come from the rich in particular. The chief harm done in the case of compulsory insurance and old age pensions is that they demoralise the people. If a man does work for which he is fully paid all his life up to a certain age, he has received all his dues. There is some idea that because he is a hand-worker, he really deserves something more, and that not from the people who have employed him, but from the public at large. The tendency is for the employers to give, or the man to take (very slightly) lower wages because he need not save against his old age. The result is that his wages are slightly lower; but what is more important is that he is demoralised to some extent, and he is taught to believe that because he is a hand-worker the public owes him some reparation when he is old.

It may be said that the military or civil servant gets

a pension; this is true, but it is not demoralising in the same way, because the government servant realises that he gets less pay, and that the pension is deferred pay only. It comes from the same employer. The arrangement may be slightly demoralising. The main reason for its existence is most likely that the government comes off the best. A man estimating his salary assumes he will live to enjoy his pension, whereas if he dies before it is due, he loses it. Generally, if a man insures for an annuity at sixty, he has options of taking his accumulated premiums at any time, and they go to his heirs if he dies before the annuity begins. Some societies have two rates, one for returnable premiums, and one on government lines. Probably very few government servants look into such matters closely ; no doubt the government actuaries do.

When we come to hospitals it is difficult to know whether the system is good. Certainly it seems absurd that they should be supported directly by the well-to-do, and not by the people who use them. The principle of population throws little light on the economical side of the question ; and there is thus no reason to discuss along old lines what others have often discussed with fuller knowledge. It is clearly a crime against society to look after the feeble-minded and consumptives and others who will hand down bad constitutions ; and then to let them marry and produce children whose existence is a curse to themselves and to everybody else. The tendency of the time is to do everything that tends to produce a maximum number of useless and miserable people at the lowest level.

It may be asked when charity ceases to be a vice, or shows any sign of becoming a virtue. In many cases the dumb animals instinctively kill, or leave their inefficient to starve ; and from the simple preservation of the race point of view they are, of course, right. The prolongation of the existence of the incompetent is preventing that of the fit and useful. Though man is morally below many of the dumb animals, in that he is generally more or less immoral and inherently bad,

he can certainly rise above them in enlightened kindness and sympathy. No one can say that it is wrong
to help anyone who has met with an accident. If a
perfectly healthy man breaks his leg, his friends, or
any strangers will, of course, take him home, and have
incompetent. There are many cases, now too common,
just as much accidents as breaking a leg. A man
may lose his position or lose his invested capital in
some way that does not in the least show that he is
incompetent. There are many cases, now too common,
of men who have lost their positions, or spoiled their
careers through going to fight for their country. Then,
coming to family casesı; people can hardly leave their
brothers and sisters, or other close relations stranded,
owing to some misfortune. There is clearly plenty of
room for real charity and kindness which does not
involve the multiplication of the idle, the incompetent
or the unfit.

The giving of doles has grown in an appalling way
since the war. The government overpaid men during
the war, and told them they would never have to go
back to pre-war standards. The trade unions insist on
high wages, and the inevitable result is unemployment,
high wages and high prices at the same time. The
politicians then pander for votes by giving doles, or out-
of-work pay, raised by taxation of those whose votes
are less numerous. The politicians will naturally go
on doing this until the hand-workers, or rather their
demagogues, find that the hand-workers are very badly
off, and therefore are not so keen on voting for
" labour " policy. The politicians can then say, " We
are not a labour party. We cannot recommend a
labour policy," and they will then leave their dupes in
the lurch, and have an election, in which they seek the
taxpayers' and the sensible hand-workers' vote. If
they do not adopt this trick, it will be because they
have found another. But in the meantime we have a
country very much impoverished by the war, in which
most of the hand-workers are doing little work and
are not earning their wages, and a large number are

out of work receiving doles. It is quite obvious that having part of the population idle means that production is below normal, and we are gradually getting nearer famine. If there is not employment at a high rate of wages, the obvious course is to let wages fall until all are employed. Paying high wages and doles means unstable equilibrium. The doles of the unemployed must be considered as added to the high wages of those in work ; so that wages are really rising higher and higher and production is getting less and less.

A community which reduces its production all round is unable to support the same population. If it makes a change suddenly, as we have done, the reduction of population will be sudden, too; that is to say, we are running grave risks.

CHAPTER XIX

THE RIGHTS OF MAN

To say, " I do not see the necessity," to a poor devil, who urges " I must live," shows almost inconceivable brutality. This is because the answer was given to an individual ; and a true answer to an individual may have a cruelty that is absent when a class or a number of people is discussed in the abstract. " I must live " is not the cry we hear now; it is " I have a right to live," " I have a right to work," " I have a right to a minimum wage." It is very difficult to grasp the popular idea of a right. Why should a man, who does not earn what he consumes, have a right to consume the results of other men's work? The root mistake is probably some vague notion that, as all wages are far too low for the work done, the hand-worker has a right at least to enough to live upon, and will be under-paid still. This absurd idea has been discussed rather fully already.

The true position is clouded up by the complications of civilisation. To get the matter clear we may consider an island with one man cast on it, and imagine that he finds he does not get enough to eat. This may be because he is lazy, the fact being that he could get enough if he worked hard and provided for the winter; or he may be more or less incompetent, whether owing to his own fault or not does not matter; or there may be too little food available, however competent and hard-working he is. In such a case it is clearly nonsense to talk of the right to live, or the right to do anything else. If the man does not get enough food, whatever the reason, he will go down, and nothing can help him. Suppose instead of one, two men are cast on the island; one works hard and finds enough to eat, the other for some reason does not, what is the position? Has the starving man then a " right " to live upon the other, and if so, why? The active man might say, " You are weak in health, and I am sorry for you, so I will work very hard and feed you too." That would be mere kindness on his part. He might say, " You are lazy, and do not try to get food, though you could do so if you stirred yourself. But I cannot see you starve, so I will work for you as well as for myself." This would be very kind of him. There would be no question of rights in the case.

To get nearer reality, suppose two couples cast on the island. The active couple work enough to feed themselves, and they have a family, say, a small family, which they can feed while young, and bring up to feed themselves by work in due course. The other two not only do not work hard, but they have a large family of incompetent children, who are not brought up to work for their food. Have they a " right " to other people's work, or the results of it? Have the parents any " right " to produce any number of children, without any intention of working for them, knowing they will have to live on the work of other people? It may be said that we must look at it from the point of view of one of these children. He will say, " I am brought into the world without my consent, and I am therefore not responsible for my existence. I was brought into this community without being asked, so the community is responsible. It is mere luck that I happened to be the son of the incompetent father ; I might just as well have been the son of the able man." Nothing need be said about the idea of a man having an identity beforehand, and then coming into the world by a channel chosen by chance, as it is childish. Our friend may say that he is entitled to be brought up properly by his father. This is merely a result of evolution. Peoples, tribes, or what-not, in which the parents do not bring up their children, die out, so that bringing up their children has become the normal conduct for parents.

Perhaps, therefore, a son has a " right " to be brought up ; but this " right " is against his parents, not against any larger group, such as the tribe, or the inhabitants of a particular town, or of a county, or a country or an empire, or of the whole world. When this son is grown up he has no longer any claim on his father. His argument that he has been brought into the community without his consent, which is, of course, nonsense, is answered by, " Your parents gave you your choice of living or not living, for which you should be very thankful. If you like to live you can work for your food; we are not going to work for it, we have enough to do to get our own. If you do not like life as you find it, you can remove yourself painlessly. Your relations and friends would be sorry to lose you; but the community will be better off."

The idea of a " right " to work or the right to a minimum wage does not come into the primitive example taken, because each is working for himself or his family. After some time we may imagine the island as containing, say, a hundred people. Most of them have a very hard time, and infant mortality is high, and starvation and insufficient food are common. One man, after working hard all day, instead of resting in the evening, makes some sort of crude machine, some kind of plough, let us say. It takes two to work this, but the two do the work of three men easily. He offers a man, who can just make enough to eat, a chance. He says, " If you care to come and work this plough with me, I will give you rather more food than you can get as you are now ; so you will be better off; and I will, of course, get a good deal more than I did. But you need not come unless you like." The man comes, and is a wage-earner, though paid in food. This does not give him any " right " to work, nor any right to a living wage. The man who made the plough is a capitalist employer. He can get two men to work his plough for him, and they produce enough food for three, that is to say, for themselves and for him, while he does not work. He is now the type of the idle rich. He has done a service to the two men he employs. This extra work in making the plough has given two men a chance of getting their living more easily, and they are better off, or they would not have made the bargain with him. He is better off, too. The others envy him, of course, and say that he ought to get nothing out of the plough. He ought to let the two men who work it get all they produce with it. If the rest of the people stole the plough, so that he got no advantage from it, no more ploughs would be made, as it would not be worth any-one's while to toil at night, after a hard day's work, to make ploughs for the benefit of the public. A man must expect some return for his special work, or he will not do it.

Let us suppose the islanders are sensible enough to see that the maker of a plough enables them to get more food, and should therefore be allowed to own the plough he makes. As soon as it is seen how good it is to own a plough, others will work at night and make ploughs, and this will go on until all the food is raised with their help. There will soon be so many ploughs that much more food is obtained. The population will then increase, and very soon two men with a plough will not get enough food to feed three easily. The margin of profit for the plough owner will gradually go down until the inducement to make ploughs is so small that only the far-seeing and thrifty people trouble to turn them out.

In order to escape from hand-work, the plough owner will have to own many ploughs. He may either let them out in return for a small part of what they make, or he may keep them and pay hand-workers to use them, making a small profit, which is just enough to make it worth while to be thrifty and make ploughs. By this time all the hand-workers will work with ploughs, or other machines, of which the plough is merely an example ; and as they are not of frugal mind, they will not be able to hire machines and work them with a distant harvest in stores; so they will be wage-earners. They are now in a position in which they cannot get their food without being dependent on the capitalist*;* and if they are so numerous that there is not employment for all, they will not realise that their improvident multiplication is the cause of their troubles. They may then claim they have a right to work, or a right to a minimum wage, or a living wage. But who is to give them food when out of work, or to give them a living wage, when the work they do does not produce enough to feed them? In such a small community it is quite easy to see that as the population increases it soon gets to a point at which, with whatever civilisation there is, starvation, or rather infant mortality, appears. Any arrangement by which people are fed who do not work means that the inhabitants are not all working, and a smaller proportion are working for food, so there is less food, and the population must decrease. It is clear, therefore, that in a simple society like this, doles, charity, or out-of-work support, means that fewer can live on the area. Thus, if the population of adults capable of working is twelve, and two own so many ploughs that they need not work, the population is such that ten men grow the food for twelve adults and their dependents. Suppose two of the ten can hardly do their share of work ; they might do just a little less ; but if they had trade union notions, they would not be allowed to work a little less and get paid in proportion ; they would be thrown out into complete idleness, and fed by the remaining eight workers. Eight workers would produce a little more than eight-tenths of the food, but for simplicity we can take it that they produce four-fifths. The result is that there is now only four-fifths of the food, and in due course the population will decrease by starvation, and its attendants to, say, ten ; to allow for the extra produce of the eight men in proportion. Giving doles to the two adults and their families does not prevent two people starving because two people do not work ; the evil is that it takes the burden off those that do not work, where it ought to fall, and puts it on those that do. One has sympathy for the two adults who are just unable to earn their food, and think the rest ought to provide for them ; and we picture the two, and give them all our sympathy, while the rest are a mere vague mass. But that is no reason why the vague mass, made up of more deserving human beings, should have some of its members starve, to keep the less efficient, who happen to be in the field of view. Sympathy for those in the field of view, and forgetfulness about the rest, often gives rise to all sorts of injustice. If a popular Gordon gets himself into danger, we think nothing of sending a number of unknown soldiers to anonymous death to try and save him.

In this example we have assumed that the two adults, who could not do quite enough to support themselves, did no work at all. This is, of course, assuming trade union interference. If they did three-quarters of the work necessary to live upon, the dole would be only a quarter to each, and there would then be a reduction of food in the proportion of ten to nine and a half, instead of ten to eight. Trade union practice reduces the number of people that can live on a given area, other things being equal.

It might be said that the proper cure is for the two plough owners to turn to and do some work. Suppose the two bad workers were supported by doles, and the two plough owners worked as hard as the others, there would be ten workers again, and the conditions would be as before, at first*e*; but there would soon be two changes. More workers would get lazy, so as to live on doles in the first place*x*; and in the second no one would make any more ploughs, because he would get nothing. The plough is here the symbol of agricultural knowledge and machinery. The ploughs would wear out, and the knowledge of agriculture and everything else would die out, and the people would work in a more primitive way, and get less food, so that they would have to starve down to a much smaller, more ignorant and more miserable community.

The dole has been taken as raised by voluntary subscription. This is not the idea of the advocates of the right to live, the right to work, or the living wage.

The dole is to be paid by the State, and so far we have not discussed a State in our little island community. Suppose they elected the man they thought wisest, and asked him to be the government. If they were democratic, all the men, women and children might vote, and they would choose an empty-headed talker; but for the present case that does not matter. The man chosen would, in practice, probably be somewhat below the average in ability, and he would have to consider his constituents, and would do what he thought would please the majority ; as they have many more votes than the plough owners.

When the two men failed to do their share of work, and the rest, on trade union principles, objected to their doing three-quarter work and getting three-quarter wages, there would be doles for two wanted. The Government or State, embodied in the man who was elected, would consider the matter in the evening, after work. He would probably settle on making the two plough owners find the doles, and the rest would say what a splendid thing it is to reduce the rich to their level. But one of two things must happen. If the plough owners have to give up all they get for making ploughs, there will be no temptation to make any more ploughs, and as already explained, the little community will go back into barbarism, with a smaller population of more ignorant and primitive people. On the other hand, the demand for ploughs may remain such that the plough makers still get enough to make it worth their while. That means that it will pay the community to give them such returns, that they can pay the tax levied for the doles, and have their reward, that is to say, the reward that makes it worth while to make ploughs, in addition. In that case, the plough makers will not pay the doles at all, they will be paid by the eight adult workers. This means that we have eight workers instead of ten producing the food for twelve, and the population has to starve down till each worker can produce half as much food again as he consumes himself.

The result will naturally be a compromise. The

burden will be partly on the food workers and partly on the plough owners. It will not come entirely on the plough owners, because as soon as they stop making ploughs the demand for ploughs will increase, and some inducement will therefore begin to show itself; and this will gradually increase; and a balance will be reached when the increased demand for ploughs just makes it worth while for the plough makers to supply it, for the sake of what now remains over after paying the tax for doles. As the cost of ploughs is higher, of course fewer will be used; so the plough makers suffer, and so will the food workers. It is easy to say the cost of the doles falls on the rest of the community, and leave the matter vague; but the matter is pretty clear, and ought not to be left vague, because it is very important. It might be said that the cost of the doles comes out of the community; and they will all be so much poorer, say, worse off in the proportion of twelve to ten. This is inaccurate. The only thing we are taking as of value in this little elementary community is food; and as the food supply goes down in the proportion not of twelve to ten, but ten to eight to begin with, this will not feed the community. It must shrink until, on the principle of increasing returns from the cultivation of the good ground only, each food worker can produce 50 per cent. more than he consumes. But if the two plough makers turn to, and do some food work, as they must in the circumstances, the reduction of the population is not so great. But the distribution of the load is not uniform. The food workers, when equilibrium is first reached, are merely reduced in number; but they still earn just enough to live upon. The condition of each is as before. The plough makers are worse off, however, and in the long run this tends to stop the advance of civilisation, and if carried too far, to cause relapse into barbarism.

The result of doles, charity, out-of-work relief, or anything of the sort, is that it is not paid by the rich, except to a small extent. It comes largely out of the poor, and the result of it is that fewer can live on a given area, or in a particular community.

The right to work, or to a living wage, is by no means the only " right " claimed by demagogues. There is, among others, the right to equal opportunity, based on the natural equality of men. That people are naturally all equal is fairly obviously all nonsense. A man cannot reasonably complain that he is a man, whereas he had the full right to have been born a woman, and would have preferred to have been a woman. Nor can a woman complain of the community because she would like to have been a man. Again, people are not equally strong physically, or equally robust in health, and no sort of democracy, however extreme, can make them so. Men and women, speaking quite broadly, have not the same intellectual powers, and no amount of newspaper articles can alter this. The difference, again, between a Newton and an idiot cannot be bridged by democracy ; all democracy could do might be to drown idiots young, like kittens ; but that would be very undemocratic conduct if the idiots have the rights to living wages, equal work, and equality generally as regards what they receive, coupled with great inequality as to what they give to the community in return. A simpler way of getting nearer equality, which has a stronger appeal to democrats, is to drown the Newtons.

" Liberté, Egalité, Fraternité," is a cry that appealed to the masses as nothing but nonsense can appeal. Liberty in such a connection is meaningless. Most people's ideas of liberty is that each person does just as he likes, and they forget that he cannot do so without annoying or even injuring others. Even when a man's actions are not limited by law, they are confined by custom and convention. America is the land of freedom, but woe betide anyone who does anything unconventional there. One of the most striking points about the Americans is their aggressive equality. Directly you get on a New York liner you notice Americans in the public cabins talking and laughing loudly to show they are not concerned about the other occupants ; and if the " band " plays anything they know, the Americans join in whistling, to show they are not in the least worried as to how much they annoy others. These are merely minute examples of ill-breeding, and ill-breeding generally is universal, and more common here than in America. Except in this one point of aggressive equality in public, the Americans are the best-mannered people in the world. All ill-breeding is a variety of what the ignorant call liberty. Liberty that allows people to annoy others is not desirable. Still less desirable is liberty that allows people to injure others ; and it is to restrict this type of liberty that the whole edifice of law exists. In old days, when a conqueror oppressed those he had beaten, making slaves of some or all of them, freedom and liberty had a real meaning ; in modern civilisation they have little. There are still some cases of want of freedom or oppression. As Mill pointed out, there is Sabbatarian oppression, due to people who, making it a duty to observe Sunday themselves, according to a modern puritan code, and finding it irksome, are much hurt at others who do not think that type of observance right, and give the puritans no credit. This arouses their vanity, and they insist that Sunday observance really consists, not in any observance of our own, but in interfering with other people's ways of spending Sunday. This form of oppression is dying down; but it still has a stronghold in Scotland. A more serious form of oppression is that of trade unions, which prevent men earning their bread when they are willing to work, and employers have work to give them. But tyranny of this sort is not common, and as we get more sensible it will probably be put down by law. The first element of the triple cry is really mere fustian.

Equality is obviously impossible, as men are not born equal in mind or body ; and so they are not, and cannot be, all equally well off. An attempt might be made to raise the inferior up to a higher level ; but the most popular scheme is to reduce everybody who is not

20

on the lowest level, so as to get a community of incompetents. But human nature is so strong that the advocates of this policy never want to reduce themselves. They want to reduce all those above them. Has anyone ever heard of any sort of demagogue who felt it was his duty to stop pushing himself, cease talking, and do honest hand-labourer's work? It may be urged that Tolstoy took to wearing a workman's clothes, working at some easy hand-work, and living plainly. But this was mere pose. He went on publishing under his own name, and photographs of him appeared in all sorts of papers. A popular actress, who takes the part of Poor Joe, might just as well claim that she was living the life of that unfortunate. The imaginary equality of imaginary socialism may be discussed separately. If anybody is absurd enough to imagine people are really equal in France, or really freer there or elsewhere than in England, he can easily test the matter for himself.

The right to equal opportunity is often put forward. The idea is generally in connection with education ; and it is urged that we should have State education for all, so that all boys have equal chance of rising to the highest positions in society. This is an absurdity on the face of it ; because if we are all to be equal, there will be no high positions. The real motive of the demagogue who puts this forward is to curry favour by telling the poor that they and their sons are ill-treated, because the rich are well educated and the poor are not, so that the rich are kept rich and the poor are kept down. In short, the poor are ill-used, and if they will support the demagogue, he will help to put things right.

But equality in education, or equality of opportunity, is a special case of the broad statement that people should not have any wealth, position, or other advantages which they have not themselves earned ; that is to say, they should not inherit advantages or privileges. Take as a simple case, that of education. Suppose the man who invented the plough in the earlier part of this chapter, and got two men to work it, so that they were

a little better off than before, and he himself was provided for, has a son, and also has a good deal of leisure ;
the fair reward for the service he did in inventing the
plough.   He is a wiser man in some ways than the
others, or he would not have invented the plough.
Perhaps he is wiser in many ways.   He devotes some
of his spare time to the education of his son.   This does
not mean that he makes his boy learn pages of *Hamlet*
by rote, and calls it literature ; or forces him to scamper
through the doings of kings of one country from
Ethelred the Unwashed to the so-called Commonwealth,
once a year, without getting further, and calling it
history.   He might tell his son, in the first place, all
he knew of the principles of mechanics, so as to enable
him to produce further inventions, for which he will
deserve remuneration.   He might tell him what he knew
and had observed as to the best way of keeping strong
and healthy, and able to do work.   He would, perhaps,
discuss all matters of citizenship with his boy, and would
get him to understand the population principle, and,
though he would not call it by any such name, the basis
of sociology and polity.   The son, unless much below
the average, would then be able to compete later on,
even if he were not allowed to inherit anything more
than his knowledge, his manners, and his character.
Perhaps he would compete all the better, and do more
if he did not inherit any material wealth at all.

Here is a man who is privileged.   He is qualified
to take a top place in the world merely as an accident
of birth ; how is this to be stopped?   There are two
obvious ways : either the father must not be allowed
to teach his son anything, or to feed him well, or to
look after him in any way; or he must be made to
spread his teaching over all the youth of the community,
and to share his food and means with them.   But this
is robbing the father of the results of his work for the
community.   He worked at night to make the plough
in order to get some advantages for himself.   The chief
advantage was time to himself in which he could teach
his son.   If he is not to be rewarded for making the

plough, neither he nor anyone else will make any more ploughs. That parents, especially mothers, prefer their own children to those of other people is the result of evolution. It is part of human nature, and it cannot be crushed out by any shouting of " egalité," or by any scheme of equality devised by anyone to put himself on the top.

It may be argued that making a plough, which has been taken as a typical simple case, does not really benefit the community, it only allows more people to live on a given area ; therefore there should be no reward. The reward is in return for an immediate good. If the good is only for the time, and not permanent, that is the fault of the public, who do not understand the population question. But though the main clear result of the invention of the plough is merely that a larger population can exist on a given area ; the really important point is that it gives the inventor time to think, and finally produces a class with time to think. Some of the class do think, and it is these that produce civilisation ; and it is to these, and these only, that we can look for all advance in the future.

The right to equality in natural endowments, such as physique, health, brains, and, especially in the case of women, appearance is obviously nonsense. The right to equality of opportunity is also nonsense. It has no foundation, and equality of opportunity involves crushing parental instincts. Equality as a means of general happiness will be discussed under socialism. If a community decides that the best sort of constitution of society is that all are to be equal; then people have a right to be equal, because it is the law that they shall be equal. This is a legal right, and it would depend on the law of the land, not on any fancied natural right.

We hear a great deal now about the right to strike. If such a silly and mischievous conspiracy as striking is legal, of course people have the right to strike. As long as hand-workers believe that strikes injure capitalists much more than hand-workers ; or as long as the matter is in the hands of demagogues who live by agitation and cow politicians, who fear their influence on votes, hand-workers will retain the right to strike. At present a batch of hand-workers, who combine into a union, have also the right to prevent other people working. Of course, a strike prevents others working in kindred trades. For example, a colliers' strike takes away the steel-workers' right to work. This is a curious kind of liberty. The steel-workers and other hand-workers, whose right to work is taken from them, do not generally mind, because they think the strikers are really getting something out of the common enemy, the capitalist. A trade union also has the right to prevent non-union men working, because the law does not prevent this tyranny. Thus, after the war, the hand-workers who stayed at home, getting ridiculously high wages, prevented their comrades from getting a living—comrades who had been risking their lives, and suffering the greatest hardships, receiving less pay than untrained women. This sort of ingratitude makes the very name of trade union smell to heaven. One feels that the ordinary hand-worker is not such a mean and low thing as to act thus, and that the trade union leaders are the real evil.

Fraternity is a very attractive idea ; and when we all love one another as brothers, and all do to others what we would like them to do to us, if we can manage that feat logically ; then human nature will be entirely changed for the better, and the millennium will be at hand. Unfortunately, man is " the Bad Animal," and we have to undo the work of many thousand years of evolution before we are up even to the mainly negative morality of many of the dumb animals.

CHAPTER XX

SOCIALISM

THIS vague subject deserves a chapter to itself. It is difficult to discuss because no one knows exactly what it is.

The socialist always begins by pointing out the evils of existing society ; this is very easy, and most of us know them very well without his help. But to the socialist there are two main types of society, capitalist and socialist. All the evils of existing society are paraded, and the conclusion is that as they all exist in society, they are all due to capital, because capitalism exists, and would all disappear under socialism. Of course this is absurd ; it would be just as sensible to say that society can be divided into any other pair of classes, one real and the other imaginary, and to put down all the evils of the world to the particular characteristic chosen. Thus, we might have a school of barterists. They would hold that money or currency is the root of all evil, and they would advocate revolution into a state of society without money. Or they might say that the two classes of society are religious and rational. All society is religious, and no purely rational community exists. The rationalists would then ascribe all the evils of existing society to superstition, and so on. This point is dwelt upon because we have heard so much socialist talk that people have come to think there are two rival states of society, one with privately owned capital, and another without it. Privately owned capital is only one out of all the many characteristics of civilised society.

Socialist propaganda consists almost entirely of girding at the evils of society, and asserting that they will

disappear under socialism ; but there is no definite statement as to how socialism is to work, or what it is.
The main idea is that productive capital is to belong
to the community, or to the State, which is to be much
the same thing. The State is to employ hand-workers
and to remunerate them properly. The hand-workers
are then going to be much better off than they are now ;
that is to say, they are going to consume more than they
do now, while they produce less. The difference is
going to be made up, partly or wholly, by saving the
interest on capital. As shown in chapter on " Capital
and Labour," the average rate of interest is really under
3 per cent., so, of course, there is no such saving
possible ; that is a mere dream. This error is due to
socialists not appreciating the arithmetic of the case.

But suppose somehow in a socialistic State the present
poor found themselves fairly well off, with plenty to eat,
and warmly clothed and housed. The infant mortality
among them would fall, and population would increase
quite rapidly, until they were all as poor as ever, in
spite of capital getting no interest. Unless socialism
provides for a population rapidly increasing without
any limit, it is clearly no cure for present evils. Infants
die now among the poor because they are ill-cared for
and ill-fed. The birth-rate now is so high that if it
were not for infant mortality population would increase
rapidly ; and if the parents were better off it would
increase still faster. It may be urged that poor people
are more prolific than those better off, and that the birth-
rate goes up in bad times. This is so to some extent ;
but it means only that nature makes the race struggle
harder for existence when its existence is threatened,;
it does not mean that as a general rule man is less productive when fairly well fed. If it were so, man would
be in unstable equilibrium, and would perhaps have
disappeared long ago. Suppose married couples had
the same number of children as at present, instead of
more, the increase of population under socialism would
be very much quicker than one might expect. Then
suppose the present birth-rate is 3 per cent., and suppose

under perfect socialistic rule we were all equally healthy and all equally well off, and all men were provided with equally attractive wives, and all women with equally glorious husbands, and we all lived to 70, and then died peaceably of plethora of contentment : if the population remained stationary the death-rate is 1·43 per cent. If the population is increasing it is slightly less, but we may take it as 1·43. Now, as infant mortality, or more broadly, pre-parental mortality is done away with, and everybody marries, and has only the same number of children as married people do now ; or if only twice the proportion marry, the birth-rate will go up to, say, 6 per cent. There are a number of minor considerations which may be omitted ; we may put it broadly, that owing to disappearance of infant mortality, and owing to more numerous and younger marriages, even if each marriage is not more productive, the birth-rate would rise to 6 per cent., while the death-rate went up to 1·7, leaving a rate of increase of 4·3 per cent. Let us give the socialists the benefit and call it 4 per cent., so that logarithms are not necessary to make a calculation, and even a socialist can see from an interest table that the population would more than double in eighteen years, so that England would have two hundred million socialists in forty-two years, and the country would be peopled with a thousand million happy, smug and plethoric socialists at the end of this century. The more the better, if they are happy.

It cannot be said that this little calculation depends on any assumption of the truth of any unaccepted or unproved theory. The birth-rate is such as we know it, and the only change made is that it is assumed that the infant mortality is wisely prevented, and that the people are normal and happy and practically all marry. The assumption of seventy as average age is of no real moment in the calculation.

The advocate of socialism has to meet this difficulty ; but he ignores it entirely. He might say that Nature has a very nice way with her, so that when people are comfortable and the struggle is less keen, the fecundity of the race falls, and adjusts itself to the new conditions. This would mean that the race is in unstable equilibrium. For if a certain population is exactly right for England under, let us say, socialist rule, and some accidental cause, such as a slightly worse harvest than usual for a year or two makes living a little harder, nature would make the people slightly more fruitful, and this would increase the difficulty of living still further. This would react on the fertility of the people again, and the population would multiply faster than ever, until eventually the population became enormous, and all of it would starve simultaneously, the insufficient food being divided equally. Going back to the population, that is exactly right, suppose instead of bad, it had a run of a few good years. The people would be better fed, and life would be easier, and nature would reduce their fertility, and the population would decrease. This would make life still easier, and decrease the fertility further, so that there would be fewer people living more and more comfortably and getting less and less fertile, until finally the few remaining would become sterile and the population would disappear.

Some socialists say that in a socialistic State parents may have as many children as they like, and they will all be brought up by the State, an experiment tried in Sparta. It is possible that the mortality of the children would then be very great ; but that is not the socialist's notion ; he thinks that the State would bring them up very well, giving them all the same food, same education, and same chance in life. How the population is to be kept down does not appear.

Until socialists show how to limit population pressure they can make no progress ; and when the population principle is properly understood, the evils that socialism is to cure will be gone, so there can be no need of socialism.

Socialists may argue that this treatment of their panacea is begging the question. They will say that the principle of population is not accepted, and it is therefore not their place to deal with it. I am assuming it is set up, and inviting them to knock it down if they can, and they are not called upon to refute every theory that may be set up, and especially not called upon to refute an old theory that has been before educated men for more than a century, and is discredited not only by the general public, but by political economists who are specialists in such matters. This attitude may be just if the discussion is intended to convert an exponent of socialism ; but it may be still open to convert a reader who is not pledged to socialism on the one hand, or to the denial of the principle of population on the other. Two advocates may argue a case before a judge ; the object of each is not to convince the other that he is wrong, but to convince the judge. I am thus entitled to assume that I have already established the population principle, and I am now going on to show the absurdities of socialism, especially as they appear in the light of the population principle, and some of the subsidiary points that have been brought forward in the earlier chapters. Even if this attitude of the socialists were just, one might ask in all humility, how they are going to deal with cases where the population fortuitously comes to be enormously great in relation to the means of support. Either population depends upon what there is to live upon or it does not. In the last case there is no reason why the population of England in the time of William the Conqueror should not have been forty millions; or why it should not be, say, only one million now. No theory as to what determines the population except what there is for it to live upon has ever been put forward. If the socialist, like many economists, denies this, he must either account for the number of inhabitants anywhere in some other way, or he must assume that it may be anything. We are justified in asking him how Britain could be run as a socialist country if it had a hundred or two hundred million inhabitants·; or how he is going to prevent its having two hundred million inhabitants if the influence, condition, or whatever he thinks it is that settles how many inhabitants there are decrees two hundred million. But we may leave the more

extreme case aside and consider the present inhabitants
of England converted to socialism and settled down as
intended. At present a certain proportion of our people
produce food and clothing or runcitic commodities. In
the socialist State these particular people are to do
much less work, and have much better remuneration, the
remuneration being reckoned in good food, good clothes,
and houses and other comforts. But it is clear that
everybody cannot consume more if less is produced.
The obvious reply is that the proportion of people who
do runcitic work is small, and the rest are doing gratular. In the new State, though each person does less,
there will be a far larger number producing food,
clothing, and so on, so that the supply will be greater
than it is now. On the other hand, the supply of
luxuries will be reduced in consequence, which is quite
right, because no one ought to live in luxury when that
is coupled with others in penury. The whole population
will be on nearly the same level of comfort. From
their point of view the main object of socialism would be
the even division of welfare. But this is a very common
ideal, and is not in the least peculiar to socialism.

It is the commonplace of every leader-writer that in
rich countries wealth is, as they put it, very unequally
and very badly distributed. You see luxury and display
flaunting itself in the face of starvation and misery. It
has already been explained that this is not because there
is a fixed amount of wealth or of money in the country,
which the rich have taken away from the poor. The
poor are not poor because the rich have taken their
wealth from them, but because they multiply improvidently, and because they have to compete with those
coming down from higher strata; and the rich are
rich because they have given something to the community in exchange for their riches, which the community wants more. What the rich have given in
exchange for their wealth would have made each one
of the members of the community a little more wealthy
if he had so used it ; but they have used it to increase
their numbers.

But this explanation is based on the population principle, whose truth socialists do not admit. We will, therefore, imagine our country turned socialist, with the proviso that out of pure freakishness they refrain from increasing in number ; the result of general equality, more or less, would be that there would be no thinkers, none to take far-seeing risks, no progress, and no enterprise or development. This sort of result could be got quite easily without socialism. If it were made law that no money or property could be bequeathed, and that none could be given to sons, daughters, or even relations during life, and if such laws could be enforced, we would be in this position in a generation or two. It would clearly be stagnation and degeneration. Few would have any object in doing great things ; and there would be few able to take big risks. The result would be that the community would gradually degenerate ; and if the population kept constant somehow, the people would get poorer and poorer, till it eventually died out, all starving at the same time, the principle of the One-Hoss Shay being applied to a community. Of course, in fact, the population would gradually decrease, and if not interfered with from outside, England would gradually go back to barbarism.

The first count against socialism is that it takes no account of population pressure ; that is to say, it does nothing to remove the primary cause of the evils of society, but is wholly in error as to its nature.

The next count is that it is based on a quite wrong idea of capital and its uses and action. The socialist here shares the ordinary vulgar ignorance. He pictures the world as containing a definite quantity of wealth, which has been grabbed by a well-organised minority. This minority thus has complete power over the rest of the community, and uses this power to exploit them, and to make them do work which is enormously more valuable than the pay given for it ; so that the rich go on getting richer and richer rapidly, while the poor are kept down at the bottom of the ladder.

There is, of course, the notion that the capitalist

makes large profits out of the poor, and that there is a huge fund out of which the hand-worker could receive very much higher wages.

It has already been explained in the chapter on " Capital and Labour," that the average interest is really under 3 per cent. ; and that when any outside event, such as war, uses up capital, so that it is scarce, the rate of interest rises, and the temptation to save is increased, so that more capital is forthcoming. There is then a growth of capital again, until the interest is down to about 3 per cent. After a war, if the people and politicians are short-sighted, the power to save and make up for the lost capital may be taken away by taxes, the proceeds being wasted on unnecessary government work, or on doles to hand-workers, who are out of work owing to the shortness of capital, or because they have been told that after the war they are to be better off than before it ; and ignorant trade union leaders may have injured industry to gain popularity by pushing the same fallacy.

Nationalisation is often considered a step towards socialism, because it so far does away with private capital. But no one can say that the hand-workers employed by the Post Office are absolutely contented and happy. Perhaps less is known publicly about the men in the Navy. It is said that a man goes into the Navy before he knows what it really means, and that once he is in, he cannot get out and start at the foot of the ladder in a new trade ; and that the organisation or discipline is such that he never has a chance of making himself heard. There may be, and perhaps there is, a very serious evil, which is not allowed to cry and get heard. Surely this is what must occur under socialism. Then, during the war and after it, the railways and mines were practically nationalised. We know, therefore, that working under government instead of under capitalists does not make men happier or more content, and it certainly does not make them more reasonable.

If the government increased the pay of its hand-workers, of course there would be great competition for work under it, and a superior class would eventually turn the present class out. But the socialist may say that is because only part of the industry of the country is nationalised ; if it were all nationalised all remuneration would be increased.

There is another curious fallacy which is not at all peculiar to socialists ; that hand-workers are a class by themselves, whose remuneration should not be in return for anything in particular ; it should have nothing to do with what the hand-worker does, but should depend entirely in what he ought to have, what he would like to have, or what the public, or the politicians, or the newspapers, or the bench of bishops think he ought to have.

If we consider a society of one man on an island, he works and gets food. His remuneration depends on his work. If there are two people on the island, they may barter services or the results of services. Every exchange is thought to be for the good of each, or it would not be made. As the people increase in number barter becomes more complicated, and money is invented as a common denominator for exchange. A hand-worker is not a commodity like a table or a cheese; but then no one wants to buy or sell him, he is not property. In slave countries a man was property just as much as a horse or an ox. But the fact that a man is not property does not alter the fact that his work has an exchange value. In a primitive society he may devote it to raising food for himself, or a friend may say, " Come and help me to build a boat, and I will give you more food than you could raise yourself." If he thinks it to his advantage, he sells his work to the boat-building friend on the terms arranged. As society gets more complicated the principles may get more difficult to follow, but they are just the same. The boat builder then sells his boat, if he considers the price offered good enough, and so on. We thus have a society with a million ramifications of methods of exchange or buying and selling ; and every transaction

depends on both parties to it expecting good out of it ;
otherwise it would not take place. Population pressure
makes each kind of worker fit into a degree of comfort
which corresponds with the acquirement necessary for
that work ; and as the acquirements of a hand-worker
are low, so is his state of comfort low. He is naturally
envious of those who are better off.

Not only the socialist, but the trade union leader,
the newspaper writer, the politician, and the more
thoughtless part of the general public, now hold that
though everything else is to be bought and sold according to its value, hand labour is not. It is not to be
paid for at all. The hand-worker is entitled to have
certain pay, and this is not to be earned, it is to be
settled by public dispute, in which politicians, newspapers, labour leaders, advertisers and so on take part.
Employers might have some say in the matter, but they
are grasping and greedy, and must be kept down. The
only people that do not join in the dispute are the hand-
workers themselves. They cannot, because they are
supposed to be represented by the trade union leaders,
but are nothing of the sort. The hand-worker is to
be paid according to the ideas of justice prevalent among
such a motley crowd as this, the rate involving questions
of what the cost of living is, as determined by an
eccentric government department ; what profit the employer is supposed to be making, and what he ought
to make, and what he could make ; and what other
employers do, could, ought to, or might make. But
if the hand-worker's pay is not to be in accordance
with what he does, or the value of his work, why trouble
about all the other considerations? Why not give him
a thousand a year and dispense with his work entirely?
The answer to this absurd question will certainly be
that he is to be paid according to his work. Then why,
involve the government, the trade union leaders, the
newspapers, or the general public in the dispute? On
the average it is quite obvious that hand-workers can
get the value of their work ; if one trade has too many
hand-workers in competition, a few can move off into

another trade ; the rest then exchange their work for
pay, which they want more than they want not to work,
so they get good out of the exchange, and the employers get their work done, which is an advantage to
them, as on the average it enables capital to get nearly
3 per cent., but no more. But the socialists and public
think this is not the real value of the hand-worker's
work ; there is some other and much higher value, and
no one has found out what it is, or how it is to be
ascertained, or how the money is to be got.

The odd thing is that it is hand-worker's wages alone
that are to be settled altogether apart from their market
value. Brain-workers of all sorts, capitalists and landlords, are to get their market value and no more to
begin with, but their receipts are to be cut down to pay
the hand-worker his excess over market value.

But a still odder thing is that it never occurs to
people now that it would be just as simple to interfere
with trade. If the hand-worker had the wages that he
earned, and no more, his cost of living could be reduced
by fixing the price of all the articles he wants. They
are all made by capitalists, and it is out of the enormous
differences between the cost and the selling price that
the capitalist is making his fabulous hoards. Thus, if a
hand-worker gets two shillings for doing something to
a coat, and the tailor sells the coat for four pounds,
the capitalist is making three pounds eighteen, and the
coat should really be sold for just over two shillings.
More reasonable people may admit that the cost of
material, of other hand-work, of works, of brain-workers,
of machinery, of insurance, and a few other items, should
be taken into account ; but most people imagine that
the wholesale maker gets the four pounds, and the
difference between the few items of cost that they happen
to know about and the retail price is maker's profit.
The socialist certainly believes the maker gets a huge
haul out of the four pounds, and should be made to
disgorge it. Why not, therefore, fix the price of the coat
at, say, two pounds, by law, so that the hand-worker
gets the full value of his money ; that is to say, he pays

for hand-work only when he buys the coat, and the price of living is reduced. All foods, clothes, and, in fact, all commodities could have their prices fixed by government boards, councils, arbitrators, newspapers, and parsons, with a bunch of socialist agitators ; all talking, as controllers.

It is obvious to most people that fixing prices is nonsense. The French tried it in old days, and our politicians exhibited this kind of folly, of course, with others during the war. If the price is fixed higher than the market value, there are several results. The public buys less ; and those that do buy, lose. Someone, say the producer, makes abnormal profits, until competition of other producers shifts the profit elsewhere. The extra price either goes in wasteful duplication of manufacture or handling, or the goods are sold surreptitiously below the legal price. If the price fixed is too low, it does not pay to produce the article, and it disappears. During the war meat had a high fixed price. On Saturdays butchers often had meat they could not sell. The poor could not buy it cheap, so it was buried. No doubt it was often given to the poor ; but it could not be sold cheap.

There are cases of special prices controlled. Thus the government may fix the price for carrying a letter at any figure, say threepence. As it has a monopoly, the public has just to put up with it. The result is that fewer letters will be sent, and this will increase the cost of the department per letter, and may soon bring that up to threepence. A further increase may then be made, until the postal service dwindles away and has to be shut down, all communications being made by telegraph or telephone. Similarly the government may over-pay railway men. The result is that fares and rates have to be put up, and the traffic falls, and road motors take a larger and larger share. If the over-payment is considerable, and goes on long enough, the railways eventually shrink and finally disappear.

The brain-work of the works manager, of the banker, of the merchant, of the admiral, of the composer ; the

21

product of the ecclesiastic ; the skill of the juggler ; the attractiveness of the chorus girl ; the courage of the bull-fighter—and everything else that is remunerated, has its value settled by the haggling of the market, just as the price of everything that is sold is settled by the law of supply and demand. Why it should be imagined that the services of a particular though numerous class should not be paid for according to their value is never explained. The idea of fixing wages, apart from value of work, is just as silly as fixing prices for goods.

The third count is a development of the last ; it is that the socialist is quite wrong in thinking a community can exist without capital. The railways of this country, for example, represent, say, a thousand millions of capital. Suppose the State stole them, and stole all the works, docks, buildings, roads, and, in fact, all that it could steal. The shocked socialist may say he is a moral man, and a socialist would be a moral community, and would not steal anything. The owners of the railways, and so on, would be paid full value. Though it is a little digression, we may follow this out. If the government now nationalised the railways, and paid the present shareholders out, they would give them some government security such as consols, or a special stock, or they would issue a loan and pay them with the proceeds, or they would raise either the principal or interest by taxation. If the railways paid as well under State management as before, the obvious course is to hand the profits over to the old shareholders. This is a simple solution, but it assumes that the State railways will pay ; and in that case, of course, the hand-workers are getting none of the benefits of socialism. In any of these cases the old railway shareholders have just as much as they had before. They can indulge in lark-pie, purchases at Christie's, large cars, and all the sinful extravagances which railway shareholders affect now.

But we have not considered the taxpayers. Suppose the tax is levied on the old railway shareholders ; they then get interest, but they have to pay taxes to provide

the interest, the cost of collecting the taxes, and the cost
of paying the interest ; they therefore get less than
nothing for their shares. If all the capital of the
country is acquired, and the interest is not paid out of
the profits on capital, the old owners are paid interest,
but are taxed so highly that they have less than nothing
left. If the socialist is honest, therefore, he must either
use the capital, so as to yield the same profit as before,
so that the fabulous fund out of which the hand-worker
is to be helped disappears ; if he is dishonest, or what
is more likely, honest, but foolish, he will have to tax
the former capitalists, which amounts to stealing their
property.

It is difficult to follow out such changes because,
if society becomes socialist, the demand for commodities
would change very much. If the rich have their property
stolen by the State, and if those who have control do
not get rich, there will be no rich people left. This will
throw out all those now employed in direct service and
doing gratular work. The socialist will say, with reason,
that these people will not be idle.; they will do runcitic
work, and the result of that will be that we will each
do a little work, and that will be quite enough to feed
and clothe the community and give everyone the simple
but ample fare which is all he really needs.

But suppose the difficulty of the State acquiring the
capital is overcome. The problem may not be so
difficult as it sounds, because so much of the capital
may be rendered useless by practically all gratular
supplies being wanted no longer. The State now owns
all the means of production of food, clothes, and simple
necessities. We may take the railways again. They
would have less traffic, but they would still be needed.
At present a railway company owns property in plant
which is always wearing out and getting less and less
valuable. It must meet this, either by putting aside
a sum every year to keep everything in repair, by writing
off the capital gradually in the books or by accumulating
a sinking fund. It might pay all the balance of revenue
over expenditure as profits each year, and issue more

capital at intervals to keep its plant up. This would
be a very clumsy method, but it would make the shareholders realise that continual saving is necessary, a
continuous supply of new capital being really needed.
The simpler method of saving inside the concern, and
putting part of what would otherwise be dividends to
a fund for repair and for purchase of new plant is used,
as this prevents the share capital increasing continually.
But the company has to exercise self-denial and save
just as much as the private taxi man, who is a capitalist
on a small scale, has to save. If he drives and cleans
his car himself, he may consider all his earnings, less
the cost of petrol and garage rent and any motor tax,
as profit, and spend them as his income ; but his car
is wearing out and getting obsolete, and needs repairs.
He must, therefore, always be saving money to repair
his car, and to make up the money needed when he buys
a new car and sells the old.

Who is to settle whether the public is to do without
things they would like in order to lay a new permanent
way between, let us say, Widnes and Walsall, now
garden cities? The control will be in the hands of
committees of the average intelligence and acquirements,
practically of hand-workers. Either there will be no
well-informed people, or they will not be in any sort of
power, because all are to be equal with equal chances ;
that is to say, any one person has just as much right to
control railway finance as any other. If the matter is
in the hands of committees of those corresponding to
the present hand-worker, there will be no saving at all.
The ordinary hand-worker never saves. Even during
the war, when hand-worker families were making, in
many cases, from twenty-five to fifty pounds a week,
there was in nearly all such cases no notion whatever
of saving. If people will not save when the advantage
is so obvious and immediate, they will not save to put
down a new permanent way from Walsall to Widnes.
The committee that deprived its supporters of any comforts or pleasures in order to renew the line would be
voted out at once.

Of course, it may be said that this is a libel on the socialist administration ; it will be in the hands of wise, competent and far-seeing men, who will have no self-interest to serve, or who will not serve it ; but how is this to come about? Socialists spend all their energies criticising existing society, and do not go into details as to organisation. At present governments in all countries are in the hands of people who are much above the average intelligence. In this country, for example, the hand-workers are so numerous, and well-informed people so scarce numerically, that the average intelligence is that of a fairly good hand-workers; but even the House of Commons is enormously above that level ; and the House of Lords is typical of what is called the educated opinion of the country. The complaint of our legislators, made in this book, is that they are incompetent, because they have no special training in their work, and their personal are opposed to public interests, and that, even if they were competent, they have not a free hand. The socialist complaint is that they are too much above the average, and that the control ought to be much more democratic. If the present governments are bad, it is pretty obvious the socialist controls will be infinitely worse. The State may start with capital in its hands, but the capital will soon ooze away between its fingers, and the society will starve—or give up socialism.

The next count against socialism is that it wages war against the great man. By the great man is not meant an amuser who writes plays, music or novels, or acts, or plays the piano ; nor a man who addresses crowds and becomes a " leader of men " ; nor even a soldier or sailor ; but a man who has ability and grit a long way above his fellows, and uses it to advance civilisation. Socialism provides nothing for this sort of merit, in fact, it will not tolerate people who are above their fellows, and will not grant them any adequate reward. If there is no reward there is no motive, and people will not take the trouble to think hard, or to work hard, if they get neither material advantages nor credits; and either raises them above the dead level of mediocrity, that is the essence of democracy in all its forms. Human knowledge would thus gradually die out, and socialism would lead back to savagery. Of course, it never will do this, because socialism is a principle in defiance of human nature, and has no future.

The counts here made are those arising specially out of parts of the subject of this book. There are many others, but they have already been put so much better by other people, that there is no need to repeat them here.

It may be asked : Who are the socialists? What do they want? and Why are they socialists?

There is the student socialist, of which Marx was a type. He discusses capital, wages and so on, and finds that in society, as at present constituted, there is poverty, crime, misery and despair. He sees that a few people are very rich. He then assumes that what he calls the capitalist system is the real cause of all the evil. It is not necessary even to read a book to see that there is great misery in the world. But to show that the misery is due to capital it is necessary, at least, to describe a state of society that would be happy in which there is no capital. By capitalism is meant the development of the industrial system of the West during the last century or century and a half. Are people supremely happy all over Asia and much of Africa? And how about the whole world in the past, of which we have some knowledge as regards Europe for a couple of thousand years, and peeps into other places at other times? We do not hear of any non-capitalist millennium. It is clear that "capitalism" is not the general cause of misery. If the main cause of misery now is capitalism, and there was just as much misery without it before, the introduction of capitalism must have done away with just as much misery as it itself produces. It is therefore neutral as far as producing misery goes; why then remove it?

The Marx type of socialist really writes for students, and presumably for people with some knowledge of social matters. As contributions to the study of economics such work is quite valueless₁; but a book like Marx's becomes a sort of Bible to socialists. It is big and looks impressive, and they quote bits of it, but do not read it.

The movement really depends on the other end of society. The majority of human beings are poor, and they feel want, and see a few of their fellows rich and luxurious, and making themselves masters, in fact, getting infinitely more out of the world. They feel a deep sense of injustice, and very naturally, being human beings, they are envious. This state of things has been going on ever since the earliest times of which we have any records, and have, no doubt, gone on for ages, about which we know nothing. The miserable have always been more numerous, so that all societies have always consisted of the fortunate few controlling the unfortunate many₁; and stability has always been preserved by organisation of the governing classes. There have thus always been openings for the demagogue who tells the poor that they are being ill-treated, and that if they will push him up he will do all sorts of things for them. The demagogue can always find something that causes the trouble, and can shout to have it down. It was very often monarchy, or a particular king, emperor, or " Tyrant." Another time it would be the nobles, or the priesthood, and so on. Now the demagogue has a much more telling cry : " Down with the rich." It may be urged that a demagogue of any sort cannot do much harm₁; his absurdities can always be exposed by sensible, moderate men. But sensible and moderate men do not address crowds, for they would have no effect if they did. Crowds do not listen to sensible men. The suppression of poisonous opinion has always been an unsolved problem. In old days force was used. It increases the trouble. Now we try gentle reason, but it is little better. The pen is mightier than the sword, but it is nothing to the jaw-bone of an ass ; and there seems to be no way of fighting the demagogue, labour leader, socialist, or whatever he may be. The demagogue and his ways have been discussed already. That vociferous socialists are not really sincere, and mainly want to push themselves, is shown by their addressing the ignorant masses instead of the well-informed. If one had, after much research, discovered a new system of medicine, he would put it before the medical profession. If the discovery was a new foundation for mechanics or chemistry he would again put it before specialists. A man who professed to know a new way of curing disease, and shouted to the multitude that he would cure all their ills, would rightly be set down as a quack.

He would also be looked upon as a quack, if he would not take his own medicine. Why do not the noisy socialists go and found a socialist colony, and show the world how it works and how good it is? It may be that they know it has been tried over and over again, and has always failed.

The noisy advocate does not wish to be an ordinary socialist himself; he wants to be at the top. Can anyone imagine Lenin or Trotsky taking their places in the rank and file and being butchers' assistants? Of course their real object was to be at the top. Many of the socialists know quite well that socialism will never come in their time, though they may think it will some day, to them, making a fuss and stirring up misdirected discontent among the badly-off is merely a means of advertising and getting prominence.

That the hand-workers, in fact the majority of human beings, should be discontented, is natural. They are badly off, and see a few very rich and comfortable having what is in comparison a splendid time, and lording over them. There is even such a thing as divine discontent; but that is discontent with ourselves, not with other people. What is needed is that after all these centuries people should realise how poverty is their own fault, not other people's.

The misdirected discontent of the hand-workers is also stimulated by another kind of socialist, the poser. He is not a hand-worker himself, any more than the

ordinary labour leader often is, but he comes from the
middle, generally the upper middle classes. He may
be partly influenced by a generous sympathy for those
who are worse off through no direct fault of their own ;
but his attitude is chiefly due to the wish to secure
admiration from ordinary people round him. In some
curious way ignorant people have come to think there is
something brainy or clever about socialism. Some types
of socialists are known as intellectuals ; and socialists
generally are supposed to have made a special study
of something or other, no one can say what. Women
are especially apt to think a young socialist is clever,
and to form an admiring circle round him. This type
of socialist generally wears a red tie and dresses badly,
so that people will think he is superior to conventions.
He often wears his hair long, or goes without a hat to
attract more notice. He is very often not a self-support-
ing man at all ; he is young, and lives on an allowance
from his parents ; or he lives on inherited money. This
type of socialist does not do so much harm directly,
because he does not often write much, or effectively ;
and he does not address crowds of hand-workers often.
Apart from being a mere humbug, and what he himself
would call a social parasite living on the community, he
does harm because the illiterate say that their theory has
the support of many educated men, and give him as an
example, especially if he has been at a University, say
Oxford. The ordinary hand-worker does not in the
least realise what an incompetent and pernicious prig
Oxford can turn out. It may be too much to expect
young fellows at a University to have much sense of
responsibility. They do not realise that the little gratification of vanity from posing as a socialist is not a
mere harmless weakness, like an acquired taste for the
whole tone scale, or the latest form of self-advertisement,
or self-expression in art or poetry ; it is helping to
increase the unhappiness of the poor by leading them
to believe they are ill-treated. A little modesty ought to
teach young people that until they have shown that they
can earn their own livings, it is out of place for them

to tell the world how to live. Of course they may reply that we pay four hundred a year to enable a man who cannot earn a decent living to help to govern the country.

We now have the woman politician, generally a socialist. She poses as a friend to labour. She has lived all her life on the earnings of men, and is quite unable to make her own living; but she preaches socialism. It never occurs to such busy-bodies that they are themselves the very people they hold up as idle rich, or parasites living upon the community in meddlesome idleness.

It will be said that all these people are quite sincere, and that when people are sincere their motives are good, and everything they say or do should be treated with great respect. We are apt to think those who differ from us in opinion and act on their opinions, and those who do what we consider wrong are actuated by low motives. Human nature is such that nearly everybody does what he thinks right. A man who gives way to anger, temper, or the various lusts of the flesh, may know that he is doing wrong, and go on doing it.; but ordinarily people think what they do is right. For instance, a burglar, if asked quietly, would say that he found himself with no money. He was in a world of human beings, none of whom would give him honest work, or help in any way. There were fabulously rich people, who had no end of money; much more than they had any right to, and infinitely more than they could use. He had a wife and children who cried out to him for bread. They had just as much right to bread as the rich or the unemployed. All the world was against him, and he was quite right to remove a little of their ill-gotten wealth from the people who would never miss it, especially as he took a sporting chance in his adventures.

The fraudulent trustee begins by borrowing a small amount without leave. He wants to make a little money, as he knows of a splendid investment ; he will put the borrowed money back in five days and all will be well.

As he gets deeper into the slough he still persuades himself he is doing right. Luck is dead against him ; but it will turn. These are extreme cases, and many will refuse to believe that either the burglar or the fraudulent trustee can persuade himself he is doing right. A retail murderer may easily think he is doing right. Lytton's *Eugene Aram* is a good study of this. Wholesale murder, as in riots, insurrections, revolutions and war, is always considered right by those who engage in it. Another kind of example may be noticed. Few people are better qualified than barristers to form impartial judgments. In arguing each does his best for his client, and puts a case forward. At the end it is almost invariably true that the winner thinks the judge is quite right and the loser that he is wholly wrong. The most marked development of this sort of bias is the case of ordinary opinions. A man chances to adopt some opinion, and then sets to work to prove to others, but especially to himself, that he is right. This phenomenon has been discussed already. But there is an even commoner development in another direction when advocating some view or opinion advances a man. In such cases the man is certain to become convinced that the cause, or whatever it is, is right. The sincerity of anyone who gains personally by his advocacy is always to be looked at with the greatest mistrust. It is very difficult to believe in the real sincerity of the various kinds of priests that have flourished since the earliest times. Their beliefs pay them. The Society of Friends have no paid priests ; but in other cases, profession of special beliefs and pushing of particular dogmas is paid for ; and sincerity is open to suspicion. In fact, doing what you think is right and thinking what you do is right are very widely different. If demagogues were genuinely sincere they would try to persuade capitalists and well-informed people. If they could show the majority of the upper middle classes, for example, that the hand-workers are badly treated, a change would be made at once. Every serious man who is well off would only too willingly part with his property if that could abolish poverty. But putting a case to the well-informed would not advertise or help them on, so they, the adventurers, harangue the hand-workers. In one sense these people are sincere. The men you see ranting at little knots of loafers outside the public house are sincere; so are the Hyde Parkers, the talking trade unionist, the labour leader, the labour member, the socialist member, the Fabian, the Ruskin College young man; so was Danton, so was Robespierre, so is Trotsky, so was Lenin, so is the Devil.

Harm is done by the newspapers which have taken to reporting the debates of university societies. The crude or naïf notions of a lot of immature students are not in themselves worth the notice of grown-up people; but the papers give the ignorant the idea that these, especially the Oxford students, know, and that their ideas on the questions of the day, which generally concern the discontent of hand-workers, are important. The fallow mind is poor enough; the callow fallow mind is poorer still. Cambridge does not appear to turn out a special type of prig of its own; but not very long ago, when one of the greatest social teachers of the day, Mr. Angell, was ready to give a lecture, the young duffers would not give him a hearing.

CHAPTER XXI

WHAT HOLDS THE WORLD BACK?

IN an earlier chapter a good deal was said as to how it comes about that the principle of population pressure, simple and obvious as it is, is not understood. But the bonds that hold the world back may also be discussed from a different point of view, and deductions from some of the apparently irrelevant chapters may be made. Some of our fetters are fundamentally instructive. The main subject of this book, population pressure, is obviously due to our instincts. Love of life is an even stronger instinct. Other strong instincts are pride, contention, credulity and belief in leaders. Thus belief in the supernatural is the result of ages of development throughout which men were afraid of the dark, misunderstood the apparent resemblance of death and sleep, thought their dead fathers were still present, and imagined that nature was controlled by beings with men's passions and vices. The belief in the supernatural is not the result of any experience of it in the past. The days of miracles are not over, but they are partly over, because credulity is getting less.; and Hume might say that people are not such liars as they used to be—apart, of course, from politics and journalism. But instinctive credulity seems to be nearly as strong as ever. People who believe in Biblical miracles, witches, spooks, fairies, dragons, magic, second sight and such absurdities are merely giving way to their primeval instincts. We are so accustomed to Christianity that we do not think it odd that apparently able people should embrace it; but, when we see scientific men professing full belief in the existence of spooks, we are apt to be puzzled. The fact is they are giving way to their lower instincts, just as much as if they succumbed to sexual excesses or gluttony. The beliefs themselves are not acquired instinctively, of course; instinct provides the credulity and the wish to believe absurdities; much as heredity in a consumptive family does not provide the tuberculosis, but only the tendency. Of course, in many cases there is a further motive. When a man believes in the supernatural, it is generally because he was brought up to it, and his reason was to some extent warped during childhood. People whom he trusted gave him an account of the world that his increasing experience always confirmed, so that he trusted them more and more. They abused his confidence by telling him all sorts of strange things that he could not put to the test. Then he grew up, and never examined into his religious ideas. Women are even more apt to indulge in all varieties of superstition because they are less developed than men, and are in that respect less removed from our primeval ancestors.

When we see scientific men of position posing as believers in spiritualism, and letting themselves be hoodwinked by conjuring tricks, it is not difficult to realise that they are merely succumbing to hereditary or race weakness. When they make money or reputation out of their creeds, we are apt to take a low view of their morality as well as of their mental power.

The charge that they make something out of it, and are therefore probably insincere, may be brought against priests of all kinds; but the case is not the same as that of a man who has a livelihood already, and takes up some form of superstition and makes notoriety or money out of it. When it is said that a parson makes money out of his creed, the question is, what money? He might have gone into any other profession and made an income; and the only money he can be accused of making is the difference between his income as a parson, and what his income would have been in another profession. Parsons do not make much money in their profession ; but they are accorded precedence in all sorts of ways, which is the equivalent of much larger income. Their work is also light ; it involves little brain work, little anxiety, and little physical exertion; it really merely occupies time. Anyone ought to be able to make more in his own profession than if he had gone into another ; and the case against the parson of making money out of his creed is not so strong as it seems at first.

But it seems anomalous that society should pay a large and expensive section to preserve and advocate superstition, generally of a particular kind. If you believe alcohol is deleterious you avoid it, if you are sensible enough; but you do not think of paying a man to tell you that it is bad for you. Still less, if you have an inherited leaning to alcohol, do you pay a man to keep telling you that it is very good for you. Priesthoods are really only a survival. In early tribal days the little tribes or bodies that survived were those that obeyed their leaders, as that was the only form of discipline in those days. It was difficult to believe a great chief was dead. Even now, anyone who loses his parents, when he deals with their effects, can hardly realise they are dead, and feels he would like to carry on everything as they would still like it. A room is arranged in a particular way, and his mother's piano is quite useless, but he feels that to re-arrange the room or to get rid of her favourite wedding present would hurt her. There is also a room full of obsolete and valueless treatises on making sundials, which his father prized and would let no one touch, and he, as a child, regarded with awe. He cannot bring himself to get rid of them as waste paper. What wonder is it that tribal men thought their dead chiefs existed somewhere as spirits ! The belief in " spirits " and the super-natural generally thus helped to preserve the authority of the heads of the tribes, increasing discipline, so that the superstitious tribes survived. But superstition was apt to go farther than necessary. The king and priest might be one until superstition went so far that a separate class of priest sprang up, demanding power and control for itself. If weak it would work under the temporal power, if fairly strong it would work as rival, and if strong enough it would control the temporal power. A class of men could thus arise who cultivated credulity, because it lived upon the credulous. The history of the Middle Ages is mainly a wearisome account of man's blind groping for a thousand years in the darkness into which he was thrown, not by Christianity, but by priests.

When we contemplate a modern bishop we see an elderly man in ridiculous clothes that suggest hurdle-racing, more than maintaining particular dogmatic notions, often coupled with a ludicrous self-importance. He is really only a survival, but the question is how much harm he still does. He has had to compete with other parsons to get into his position, so he must have much ability of the necessary kind, unless he has got on by mere favouritism. To begin with, he knows his creed is false. Tribal instinct, if that is the right name, makes him ready to believe, but his intellect makes it impossible. For example, he will pray only for what may happen, or what he thinks may happen in any case. If a woman has typhoid fever, he will pray that she may recover health; but if she has lost a leg, he will not pray for a new leg to grow, like a lobster's new claw. He knows enough about the body to know that a new leg will not grow, so he does not stultify himself by praying. He does not know enough about typhoid to realise that its course is just as independent of prayer. Again, he will pray for alterations in the weather, because he knows nothing of meteorology, and thinks the weather prayed for may come. But he does not look out for queer curls in the isobars or isotherms in next day's paper, and say, " I prayed those wigglements in." Still less does he expect to see in the explanation under the chart, " The abnormalities are caused by farmers, footballers, fishermen and holiday makers praying for different weathers at the same time." If you ask him, because you want to know, what a soul is, he will tell you it is the immortal part of you.

Yet he and all Christians stand up every Sunday and say their bodies are immortal. None of them accepts his belief as fact in the least. He will maintain it, argue about it.; fight for it, and perhaps die for it ; but he knows it is wholly false—or he would—if he were serious enough to think about it.

Our bishop is just another example of one who is familiar with all the leaves, twigs, and small branches of his subjects, but knows nothing whatever of the trunk or roots. He has never considered the mystery of our life seriously. This is shown by his being an exponent of the local form of credulity. There are so many creeds, and so many kinds of religious development, that the chances of anyone that really studied them, selecting the particular kind that happened to be local, are very small; but all our parsons would have held quite different tenets if they had been born in other places, or at other times. People with logical minds are apt to get very impatient with parsons, and say no one can be a priest of any sort unless he is either a fool or a knave, or they write such biting indictments as Morley's in *Compromise*. But a parson is seldom a knave, and he is a fool generally only in the way most of us are fools, that is in not having logical minds. Those who know any parson personally, generally find him different from other men; he is something between a woman and a child in many ways, with a dash of the actor and the self-advertiser.; but at the same time extraordinarily kind and self-sacrificing, and doing locally a great deal of what he considers good.

But the church or churches of to-day have very little power left now. Their teeth have been pretty well drawn. To realise the harm they have done we have to know that they have been the chief force keeping civilisation back during the last couple of thousand years. The church has always been an organisation for getting control and power into its own hands, and its method has always been the encouragement of ignorance. A large class, whose existence and whose main business depend on their being illogical, and on letting

22

instinct choke down any reason that might begin to show its head, naturally developes to its highest, what has already been discussed as the feminine mind. This involves absolute trust in authority; and the notion that a collection of information as to what other men, just as foolish as ourselves, have said or claimed to have thought is knowledge. The storing of all this stuff depends on memory, and not on any sort of reasoning. Education has been in the hands of the clergy or priesthood from the time they played for power; and it has thus always been along feminine lines when it has been allowed to exist at all. Though the churches do not still oppose all knowledge, for fear the hollowness of their pretensions may be exposed, education is still not only directly under their influence, but it suffers under an incubus of foolish tradition. The feminine or memory mind thought anyone who had learnt a dead language knew something. A man who understands one or two dead languages is still regarded as a scholar; but a commercial traveller who speaks half a dozen that are living is nothing of the sort. Sometimes a scholar is more than a mere dead linguist; he has read a good deal of the matter written by people when civilisation was in its babyhood, and thinks they were intellectual giants because they lived long ago. The remains of direct clerical control are seen in the older universities, which are still essentially clerical, and in our public schools, where it is still considered proper that the masters, especially the head masters, should be parsons, and the head mastership is often a step to a bishopric. Coming lower down, we have seen the question of mass education diverted into a low sectarian dispute about silly points that are of no real consequence at all, while any discussion of what the children were really to learn was put aside.

To get any idea of the effect of the religious instinct, and its product, the priesthood, we must try and imagine where we might have been if it had been suppressed, say, a couple of thousand years ago.

Knowledge has been growing rather freely for a

couple of centuries, but the great and rapid advance has taken place in the last hundred years. The advance made between the beginning of our era and, say, 1800, might have taken a very few centuries, so that we might have been up to our present state of civilisation about the sixth century. People might even have understood the population principle in the time of Mahomet. In that case Attila and Bleda might have been carrying on a war with poison gas, or they might have been nobodies doing quite useful work, such as minding machines for putting creases in Americans' trousers, or if their natural evil bent had play, they might have made gramophones or machines for working pianos. Mahomet would have flourished by preaching on the follies of fashionable society, or by the modern methods of the advertising parson. It is impossible to form the least idea of what society would have been now if knowledge, which has little or nothing in common with what is called "learning," had flourished more than fifteen centuries ago. War, poverty and misery would have disappeared, and that is about all that can be said, but surely it is enough. Of course there is a good deal of absurdity in imagining modern civilisation in the sixth century. It is very difficult to see why civilisation should have developed suddenly after so many thousands of years. Civilisations have developed at various times in various places, and have died down again, very often by being over-run by hungry outsiders. It would be gross exaggeration to say that all civilisation has been kept back or prevented solely by priesthoods. No doubt they have always had great reactionary influence, whatever the creed has been. The overthrow of civilisation by the ignorant hungry has nothing to do with priestcraft. We think our present civilisation is permanent; but some writers have feared that it may be swept away by the ignorant, massed under the influence of priests. It is much more likely that it will be swept away by ignorant, hungry people acting under the keen stress of population pressure, as has happened over and over again in the past; the difference being that the hungry masses will not be outside peoples, but our own proletariat and poorer classes inflamed by socialists and other demagogues.

It is not fair, in any case, to blame the priesthood for all the evil they have done. They are the result of the state of mind of the people. Every people has a government that corresponds to its average foolishness; the government is the result of the foolishness, and the foolishness is the result of the government's actions. Again the newspapers, especially the daily papers, of a people represent the average ignorance and superficiality of its readers; and they live by pandering to it and fomenting it. The same action and reaction go on in other directions, such as the stage, fiction, music and pictorial art.

But our giving way to the primitive instinct of credulity as to the supernatural has given the priests power to keep the world back thousands of years. We still have a heritage of evil in our systems of education; a subject which demands discussion by itself. In addition to this, the churches are opposed to any teaching of the truth as to population pressure. This is not because they know anything about it, or have in any way studied the subject, and found that Malthus was wrong. What happens may be shown better by one actual example.

A man whose brothers had died of consumption, and who was consumptive himself, married a delicate woman. The parson, who knew them, as they were village folk, married them without any reserve. They have had several children in four years, including twins, and they are told that the children are gifts from God, and that He would not have sent them except as a blessing; so they should be very pleased and have some more. Apart from the crime of encouraging the multiplication of consumptives, this doctrine makes people who have children they cannot support imagine they are a kind of public benefactor, deserving outside help in return for their self-sacrifice in producing children. The clergy are thus doing their best to increase the misery of the poor by encouraging one of the worst forms of immorality. We sometimes hear of the horrible things that go on in the squalid overcrowded cellars and garrets of the very lowest, where numbers of people of both sexes and all ages are crowded together with no chance of anything like decency. I know very little of this, and would loathe to know any more. Does the sleek ecclesiastic, who deplores the decreasing birth-rate to fashionable congregations, realise that he is doing his best to increase such social festers? Is he really so very very good? If, by my influence, I tend to cause or increase crime among the lowest, am I really so very much better than the criminals?

Everyone who has any favourite theory or principle that he would like to get accepted, but cannot, falls back on education. He thinks the present generation cannot adopt his ideas because they have not had the right sort of education; and that education ought to be modified and put right, and the next generation will then naturally adopt his views. This is a dream. Each generation settles the education of the next, so there is no chance of getting education altered unless the existing generation can be directly converted. As already explained, education has been developed entirely by the clergy, and though they have now little direct power, they have left a tradition. There is in addition a special type of mind which appears to be developed by schoolmasters and professors. A professor is really only a high grade schoolmaster. This may be largely due to the schoolmaster always dealing with the immature mind. Like the parson, the schoolmaster spends his life on a pedestal above contradictions; and very few human beings can stand that. But there is another influence which is not generally realised. Suppose a perfect system of education were devised and started. At the end of the first course there would be at the top a number of able and competent young men. Most of these would go out into life, but a small proportion would stay as schoolmasters. Something would determine which went out into the world and which remained as pedagogues. The most practical would go out into the world, and the few with the school-master type of mind would remain as teachers of the next generation. It may be assumed that the pay in teaching is as good as in other walks. The next set of students would then be taught in a slightly more peda-gogical ways; and this would increase a little each generation until education was just as academical as before. There is thus no hope of good educations; it always has a tendency to academic equilibrium.

It might be thought that education has nothing to do with the theme of this book ; but it has. It is important that people should be brought up to think about as many matters as possible, and especially about those that concern the happiness and welfare of humanity. It is not that population pressure as here expounded should be accepted; that is not the point ; what is needed is that all such matters should be dis-cussed intelligently. All class feelings; all hatred and envy of the rich; all national animosities ; and all discontents; with their outcome of wars, revolutions, strikes, crime, poverty, disease and misery, generally depend on ignorance; and all our ignorance depends in the first place on the apathy of the well-educated classes.

Education, like other subjects, suffers because people study all sorts of developments and minute points, but do not go to the root of the matter at all. If you ask what education is for, you generally get a vague but impressive answer. It is to lead a man out into a higher life, or it is to bring out all that is in him, or to enable him to realise his higher self, or something of that sort. Probably the bald truth is that we do not know what to do with young people from eight to twenty or so. They are a nuisance at home idle, and there is no way of utilising them ; so the only thing is to have them educated. But there is no reason why the education should not be of some use, being designed with some reasonable object in view. This might be fourfold. First, to enable the boy to earn his own living, because if he cannot do that he is of no use,

Second, to make him understand his body, and how to keep it healthy.; for he is of little use if his health is bad, or he lets himself die early. Third, to make him a good citizen. He ought to know something of sociology, economics, government, and so on. If we were generally educated in that sense there would be no wars, no poverty, no class feeling, and no nonsensical capital and labour disputes. Fourth, to enable him to enjoy his leisure, when he has earned it. Present-day education has none of these aims, unless it is the fourth. The classical school pretends that people learn Greek and Latin as boys, and learn to love their literature. This is, of course, all nonsense. Very few boys ever learn any Latin or Greek to count, even after years of toil, because it is so ludicrously badly taught. If one thinks of all the men he knows, the idea of any of them reading Plato or Horace in the original in the evening after a heavy day on the stock exchange, or at a government office, is ridiculous. Teaching classics has always been a perfect farce. People are waking up about education now.; and we have got so far that there is a rival to classics in the form of science. Others advocate mathematics. We may thus have our future sailors primed with a knowledge of the theories of the benzene ring, and novelists with trilinear co-ordinates at their fingers' ends. It is very easy for an outsider to make fun of conventional education.; but it is probably useless for him to suggest any improvement. But in connection with the main subject of this book it is fair to point out that human unhappiness is largely the result of ignorance. It is not that we are ignorant in our own departments, but that we are not only ignorant outside them, but we do not want to know anything. Present-day education still partly aims at making people interested in old books in dead languages. In this it fails ludicrously. It also aims at making them logical by training them in man-made illogical ancient grammar. Again, of course, it fails. It aims at making them fond of reading worthy books by a course of what is called " literature." Again it fails. If you think of most men of your acquaintance, taken one at a time, you will realise, that outside his own special work the average man knows nothing in particular, and does not want to know anything in the very least. People do not want to know ; but to be amused. Occasionally he has a hobby, and occasionally a man does good work in two or even three directions like a modern da Vinci. But the ordinary educated man of to-day has no real desire to know anything, least of all about sociology. If you look at the people going up to business in trains, the men are all reading daily newspapers. If one finds anything in a newspaper about the one or two things he understands, he finds the writer is ignorant₁; but he is apt to think the newspapers are sound in the hundreds of other subjects he does not understand. But if everyone finds the papers are at sea on the questions he knows about, it is best to realise they are inaccurate, superficial, ignorant, and partisans on all subjects. They thrive by saying what their readers will like, not what is true. Even their news is all distorted₄; and the majority of it is ephemeral stuff of no importance. There are columns about sensational cases, self-advertising people, talk of politicians, and anything that may hold a feeble attention. And as even that sort of stuff needs too much mental work on the part of the reader, he is treated to a back page of process blocks of stage and society people, chiefly grinning women. The business girls in the trains either chatter or read papers which have less news, less balance, and several pages of grinning women. But many of the girls read novels. That men as a rule know nothing outside their business, and do not want to know₄; and that women are, if possible, even less anxious to study anything, may be the result of our eduaction, or it may be a fault of man. It seems as if education must have something to do with this₄; and that our absolutely complacent ignorance is to be laid at the door of our educational systems.

So far we have been discussing the education of the well-to-do₄; the education of the overwhelming

majority of our population was expected to raise them
intellectually, to rouse interest in all branches of knowledge, and to do all sorts of wonderful things. Teaching
every person to read has not taught him to read what is
good. He uses his ability almost entirely to read newspapers and seditious stuff.; that is to say, matter
specially concocted to be bought because it flatters
his prejudices and his vanity, and tells him his troubles
are due to the wrongdoings of others, instead of being
the results of his own faults.

Again, it is very easy for an outsider to find fault,
and his fault-finding may be quite superficial. The
four aims of education may be looked at in connection
with the average hand-worker. First, it should enable
him to make his living. There is something attractive
in providing everyone with an education which will
enable him to rise to opulence or, more important, to
distinction. But the populace cannot all be heroes in
Smiles' biographies,; and the educated toiling millions
will stay toiling millions. If a boy is going to be a
motor-driver, a lime-burner, or a french-polisher, there
is no use teaching him his trade at a board-school.
In old days trades were more general, and a journeyman
knew more, and apprenticeship was the way of learning.
Now work is all tending to need less and less skill and
less and less knowledge. Instead of being a fitter or
a turner of the old school, the boy becomes a machine
minder, and the machine does one or two operations
automatically, and he does monotonous work which needs
no training, no skill, and no intellect. Women and
young boys can do it almost as well. What is education
to do for a man in this sad case? and it is now the
sad case of many millions. What is called mass production would have been a great benefit if population
had stood still, as we would all have been so much
better off, that the hand-worker could have had very
short hours. But as things are, it merely enables more
people to live on a given area, at first in the same degree
of comfort. But the degree of comfort of any stratum
of society depends on the training and mental equip-

ment needed to keep a place in it. If the training and mental equipment are very low, the scale of living will be low. Though technology is going forward very quickly, and much more knowledge is needed by those directing works, the tendency of modern methods of manufacture is to degrade the great mass of the people. There will soon be very little skilled hand-labour.

We are for the moment discussing education.; and the question is : How can education, State-aided or not, occupy any reasonable portion of nine years of a boy's or a girl's life in teaching him or her to make a living by watching an automatic making nicks in the heads of wood-screws?

The next part of education was teaching the child about its health and its body. This might occupy a little of the nine years very usefully. More time might be given by a girl; she might learn all about bringing up babies and small children. Just now we have much attention devoted to infant welfare, parental aid, and so on.; and kind women, with hearts full of sympathy, devote themselves to educating their less fortunate sisters in rearing healthy children. But most of the children are doomed to die either as infants, or, at any rate, without being parents. They die largely as infants ; and they must and will die so, just as long as we remain ignorant of the principle of population. As long as the birth-rate is too high for a community of long-lived people increasing slowly, these women are merely keeping children alive so that they die a little older, probably in greater misery. If selected children are helped, they are raised, and the others are worse off than ever in competition with them. It is difficult to see, therefore, what education can do for women in the humbler classes until the principle of population is understood.

The next part was citizenship. Of course school-board education might educate hand-workers to understand something about economics, capital and labour, government, wages, trade, and so on. But this is useless just now. An education involving a study of all branches of sociology would be very valuable to the well-to-do classes, because it would lead them to take interest in such subjects. It is not that a knowledge of present-day economics or sociology would itself settle matters ; but that it would lead able men to study such things more, and we would eventually solve the problem of society, whether on the lines of this book, or in another and better direction does not matter. The great point is that the world is full of misery because we do not study the conditions with any real interest. There would be no use teaching people who are going to spend most of their lives watching such things as screw-making machines, with the idea that a few millions of them could evolve some new social order by the use of their brains. The only real good of any education of this sort is that it might enable them to see through the pretensions of the politician, and especially the agitator or " labour leader."

Whether any system of education will enable a man who has watched a screw machine all day to enjoy his leisure more is doubtful. The present system, beyond enabling him to read, does nothing. The screwer may have recited Browning with a cockney accent, but he drops it. There are many highly educated men among the hand-workers. When I was an apprentice, I asked a man with whom I was working why a part of a paddle engine was called the " entablature." He gave me a lot of instruction in architecture. Knowing him better, I found he knew some German, had read some mathematics, and was musical. Another time I left an alarm clock to be put right, and a man brought it up in the evening. He was much interested in poetry, and especially Ossian. He explained Macpherson's share in the modern version, and argued that Homer's work had been " Macphersoned." After an interesting evening, he asked for fourpence for " fettling " the clock and left. These types are certainly not board-school products. They are very common in the North, especially among miners.

There is another source of general ignorance and misinformation which depends on our instinct for hero worship and on our mental indolence. There is a tendency to believe that once a man's name is known, he is an authority on every subject of the day. Some men became publicists. Somehow they get their names known, and they then write on anything that is a topic of discussion either in the papers, in magazines or in books. Others make a position, and are at once listened to with respect on quite mundane subjects about which they know nothing in particular. If anyone is eccentric enough to want to know something about education before selecting a school for his son, he will get : " How I ought to have been brought up," by a well-known Admiral or Field-Marshal. If he wants to understand the war, or talk about it, he will read : " How I would have run the war if I had not been God," by some popular novelist, with a preface by an actor and an introduction by a pushing ecclesiastic.

The novelist is one of the most serious dangers. He uses his fiction to disseminate all sorts of erroneous ideas, and can make everything come right in a story. Then he becomes a general authority, and lectures the world on matters of which he knows nothing. Fiction might be a splendid vehicle for the administration of mental drugs which people will not take in any other way; just as jam is good for covering a dose of nasty powder; but the powder is prescribed by a competent medical man, not selected by a confectioner.

The instinctive hero-worship that comes down from primitive times, when the tribes that were loyal to their leaders survived, also makes us believe in politicians, and figureheads of all sorts. It has often been pointed out that as a country gets more democratic and ignorant, it believes more in men and less in measures.

CHAPTER XXII

LIMITATION OF FAMILIES

THE only course Malthus suggested was the use of moral restraint. Moral restraint meant marrying late, or at least having few children simply by exercise of strong self-control. Malthus is often looked upon as the founder of artificial limitation of the family. This is absurd, of course; none of the modern methods was known in his day.

Marrying late, and exercise of self-control, have been known for ages to have been practised by people for their own personal benefit; but practically by those only who are high enough in the scale to be capable of taking long views. Such a prudential check as moral restraint of population—to use Malthus expressions—never could appeal to the proletariat.

Not only do late marriage and Malthus' moral restraint demand moral courage that is rare; but they tend to have very evil effects. It has long been the custom for people of the comfortable classes to marry later; and recently families have been artificially limited a good deal; but the artificial limitation has not yet altered the average age of marriage. Leaving artificial limitation out for the moment; it is clear that late marriage and celibacy give rise to secondary evils that are very serious. To begin at the small end, a girl is physically ready for marriage at, say, seventeen, but she marries about ten years later. The life of a girl in the comfortable classes from childhood to nearly thirty is merely expensively wasted time. First she has to be educated. This really means that parents do not know what to do with their children, and have not time to look after them, so they send them to school.

A system has developed by which the schools pretend to educate the girls very highly; and they give them a bad and expensive imitation of boys' education, which itself is useless. There is some excuse for wasting a boy's life from childhood to twenty in school, because the parents feel that he has to make his living, and believe that education will fit him for the struggle. It does not, of course. Girls' education fits them for nothing in particular. Like boys', it is essentially training the unthinking memory on matter which is quite valueless when remembered. In addition, girls have hundreds of pounds spent on accomplishments such as dancing, reciting, drawing, painting, and playing the piano or fiddle. The dancing is useless, because new dances have come into fashion by the time the girl comes out, and none of the rest of the accomplishments is ever wanted. Then, when she leaves school, the girl has ten years of waste life before her. She may have a " good time " for a little, until that palls; otherwise she goes in for Art with a big A, or pretends she is going to make a good living as a professional musician or in literature. Recently she has been told she is going to have a career as a doctor, barrister, engineer, or something, and it takes her many years to realise that there is no such career in which she is of any real use. All this time she might have been developing her mind and body if left to herself. If she does not marry, she is apt to be disappointed and soured ; if she does, all this time has been wasted. For ten years she has been sexually starved, and has been exposed to temptation all this long time. She may have been taking what she calls her " work " very seriously, perhaps over-working her brain at some women's college, but she always feels that a man may come into her life at any time, and that she may " scrap " her " career " at any moment quite suddenly. One of the most difficult problems for well-to-do parents is to find out what to do with girls from school to marriage.

In the poorer classes the girl works from childhood upwards. She helps her mother, and looks after her brothers. Her school is merely an interruption in her work. When she leaves school she may go out to work as a typist, a shop assistant, a domestic servant, or a waitress, or she may go into a factory. Again, her work is mainly filling up time until she is married. She may not have to wait as long as her more wealthy sister; but population pressure insists that she shall not marry at the physiological age. This delay probably does her system harm. It would probably be untrue to say that girls in the poorer classes get into trouble more often. There is everything in favour of their doing so. They are much more mixed up with young men and boys, and have more opportunity and greater temptation; but, on the other hand, they are not so idle. The general feeling of sexual morality seems to be much higher in the lower middle, and the upper hand-working classes.

The effects of late marriage in the case of men is much more serious. The scourge of prostitution is almost entirely due to population pressure. This involves the unspeakable degradation of a number of women and the white slave traffic; and it spreads virulent and disgraceful diseases. It may be urged that if population pressure disappeared there would still be all sorts of sexual irregularities and vices. There would, no doubt, still be great tendencies in that direction, for men seem to be, unlike dumb animals, frequently naturally immoral sexually. This may be the result of the evolution of a partially reasoning animal, coping with the population pressure in the dark; and in that case it will take a long time to change. But under present conditions, as it seems impossible to do without such vices as prostitution and all sorts of sexual immorality, there is no serious sound public opinion against it; only sensationalism and hypocrisy. If population pressure were less, and it were not only possible, but even not difficult to suppress prostitution, public opinion would soon change, and would become so strong that the immoral would be social outcasts.

The limitation of families, in addition to late marriage

in the upper classes, reduces the downward flow into the classes below, which are not only receiving additions from above, but also producing more people than there is room for, and sending them down further all the time. At the bottom we have unlimited and irresponsible production of feeble children, high infant death-rate, rotten physique and low mental power and unspeakable misery. Though population pressure gives rise in the upper classes to the serious secondary sexual evils that have been mentioned, limitation of offspring is gradually and surely spreading there. It is in the lower middle and lower classes that the greatest trouble lies r; the lower you go the more serious the evil.

It might be supposed that the matter is quite simple, and all that is necessary is to preach limitation of off-spring, with the idea that once it is understood, population pressure would fall and life would be easy. There would be fewer hand-workers, so they would demand, and of course obtain, higher wages, and would live comfortably. Any stratum of society that found life uncomfortable would immediately shrink until the demand for it increased, and it could get proper consideration, or it would shrink out of existence. We should then have a sort of millennium. Bradlaugh and Mrs. Besant started a crusade of this sort in the seventies. Their way of treating the subject was very coarse, and they naturally made themselves very unpopular among the respectable people of those days. But their ideas were crude.

Imagine the practice of marriage at the physiological age, and limitation of offspring to be general in any community, say, in Scotland, or in the Partially United Kingdom. The patch fallacy is always ready to creep in, so let us begin with the case of Scotland. The result would be that the upper classes, to begin with, would not send so many down into lower classes, or into England. As they would not have such large families to provide for, life would be easier, and some of the incentive to hard work would be gone. People even from England might come into Scotland and compete with them.

The upper classes in Scotland would thus gradually become infiltrated with Englishmen. They would, we will assume, fall in with the new Scotch practice and marry early and limit their families. In course of time more English would come in, until the Scotch upper classes were composed chiefly of Englishmen. Jews need not be discussed, but it is obvious that they might then get a footing in Scotland. Another change would occur, too. Much of the work done by the Scotch upper classes is in competition with England and other countries. This work would tend to move out of Scotland.

Consider the poorer classes next. The Scotch people of the abyss first would tend to disappear. They would realise that as they cannot support themselves they cannot support children, and if they were sensible, a supposition we will make for this occasion, they would die out completely in one generation. But Scotland would then be a better place for the submerged than England, or any other country where there is irresponsible multiplication, and especially where it is coupled with legal or charitable relief. There would thus be the same population of incapable paupers as before.; but they would practically all be English, and especially Irish. They would give up having children on coming to Scotland, and though they would have no descendants, their places would be taken by immigrants as soon as vacant.

Going up through the numerous grades of handworker, we find the same phenomenon differing in degree. Take a particular grade of hand-worker. The first point is that there is a better chance of rising into a higher stratum, because the people in the higher stratum are having an easier time.; the next is that each grade of hand-worker is competing with English hand-workers at the same trade, and if the Scotch hand-workers get at all slacker, the English workmen will come into Scotland, and the Scotch workmen's jobs will gradually shift into England. There are thus two tendencies.; one for the Scotchmen to rise to the top, not of other countries, but of their own; the other is for them to disappear altogether, or commit race suicide. Race suicide is supposed to be a terrible crime; but it is not easy to see who is injured. The Scotch would not be injured, because they would not be in existence. Whether the rest of the world would mourn the disappearance of the Scotch is another matter. It is to be hoped they would, and they ought to.; but they might not. The criminality of race suicide is more likely to appeal to Irishmen. They would argue that it is an awful thing for your posterity if you have no children; and that childlessness is apt to become hereditary.

It is probable that the main result would be that Scotland would have a population with the Scotchmen generally at the top, and more immigrated Southerners as you go down the scale. Whether restriction of family would, in fact, tend to make the upper classes less vigorous is doubtful. Ambition is so much stronger in proportion to parental instinct in educated people, that it is quite probable there would finally be a permanent population in Scotland in which all the upper layers were of Scotch origin, and the rest English. The upper layers would then be permanent; and the rest would always have the birth below the death-rate, the number being kept up by immigration. The total population of Scotland would be somewhat less; as, even if the upper classes worked as hard, and retained their energy and vigour, the middle and lower would get slacker, so that the production of the country would fall, and it would not be able to support as many people.

There are many other effects of limiting offspring that must be mentioned. It is said to be bad for the health of women to have few children or to be childless. This may be true, but it is obviously worse that children should be born to die of starvation and misery than that women should suffer a little in health. Apart from that, women would suffer much more from mother-hunger. Whichever way things are, it always seems to be the woman who suffers.

It is probably better in most cases for people to marry young and have their share of children young. The mother especially is not too old for her children, and instead of leaving a long, abnormal gap in her life, between, say, eighteen and twenty-eight, and no time to herself again until she is old, she has leisure in middle age, when she can utilise it and enjoy it.

The case of Scotland was taken because it gives a clean-cut area without isolation. Directly we take the Kingdom the patch fallacy comes in, and we cannot help thinking of it as isolated. Though we have sea all round us, we are one of the least isolated peoples. We are more dependent on other countries for food than any other people ; in fact, we may rather regard England as a workshop or town, making things in exchange for the necessaries of life.

Let us imagine an isolated country which practises family limitation. There is no poverty at the bottom, because the poor all disappear in a life time. There is no poverty in the class above, and life is not such a severe struggle in the upper classes.

Though an isolated civilised country cannot exist, it may be discussed as a kind of ideal case to see what the tendencies would be. There are two large questions to be considered : what the effect would be on the people in the country, and what relations such a country would have with the outside world.

Beginning with the brain-workers; the tendency would be to reduce competition. Whether it would be reduced very much it is difficult to say ; it certainly would not be increased, and it looks as if it would fall perceptibly. This is a very serious matter. Industry is usually discussed as if it depended simply on capital and hand-labour. The popular idea is that coal is in the ground, and capitalists own it ; all they have to do is to pay miners to get it up, and pay them too little for their work. Then the capitalist employs hand-workers to fetch iron ore, and other hand-workers to make it into cast iron and steel, again underpaying them and making huge profits. Then the steel is made into

everything from a watch spring to a bridge, or from a
telephone magnet to an Atlantic liner, purely by hand-
workers who know practically nothing. But this is all
nonsense. The whole development of industry depends
on technology and organisation. Both are necessary,
and both need a high type of brain, which has been well-
trained, and has gained much experience. If the brain-
working classes find life easier, they will surely get
slacker. The result will be that they will fall behind
in their knowledge of technology·; and they will lose
initiative and enterprise on the one hand·; while the
anxiety of organising a large concern, and dealing with
the idiosyncrasies of human nature, on whose understanding good management of men depends, will out-
balance the good, and industry will become slacker and
slacker. The result will be that the population decreases, a matter in itself of no moment, while poverty
disappears altogether, and the island is occupied by
people who are all comfortable in their various social
strata. There may be a tendency to get slacker and
slacker·; this, of course, means that as long as the
runcitic and gratular consumption remain the same in
proportion, the population decreases until the land will
support it with the reduced vigour in cultivation. But
this is not the important tendency of slackness. If
the brain-workers get slack, generation after generation
may get slacker, the effect being balanced by reduction of population, until the island is finally peopled
by a primitive type of people with no brain-workers.
The arts will then have disappeared, and the small
population will be ignorant.

This is only a possible result. It is not known
whether making life easier for brain-workers tends to
lessen their keenness seriously. It must be remembered
that, as pointed out earlier, there are three main human
motives, hunger, sex hunger, and vanity·; and vanity is
far the strongest. It is almost certain, therefore, that
the upper strata, at least in our imaginary isolated community, will be fairly energetic. But as one of the three
motives is lessened right down the society from top to

bottom, it is not likely that the people in any stratum will be quite as keen. They may keep in the same classes as at present, but with a smaller number in each, and much less competition ; the first question is whether the relations of the classes as to number and degree of comfort will remain the same. Suppose the population is as low as half the number it was in non-limitation days ; then only half the food need be raised, and half the runcitic products generally. These will be produced by the same proportion of the people as before, working less hard. There is no reason to suppose that there would be a hand-workers' millennium. There will be no poverty as we understand it.; but there will still be competition to get to the top. Brain-work is much harder than hand-work ; and the brain-workers will therefore always command a better return. The broad result of limitation in an isolated community would not be any sort of Utopia. Man would still be the same animal. He would have all the follies and vices that he has now. But the whole of the present lowest stratum of society would be non-existent. There would be no hard struggle for life anywhere. It is probable that after a time a family would be considered a mark of wealth.; and the upper classes would have larger families, and the lower would be childless, or nearly so. It would be a mark of success in life to be able to afford children, and to bring up and educate them well. People who had families they could not afford would be regarded as immoral and foolish, as they ought to be now.

But we have been discussing a community that is completely isolated. As a first step from this condition, suppose the community imports, say, tea, tobacco, and a few other things.; exporting some goods in exchange ; and that it has a gold standard. Its money will then be comparable as to value with that of other countries. Suppose a case of tea of a certain standard size is worth £10 in Europe, and suppose the best thing the islanders can make is a pump, and that the standard price of a pump is £10. The outside world who supplies a case of tea may get paid either by receiving a pump or £10 in gold. If there is much gold in the country, the payment will be in gold ; if little, it will be in pumps. If one can be made and sold for £10 in our community, and is also made and sold for almost the same price abroad ; and not only the hand-workers, but the whole staff, and everyone connected with the production of the pump, are better off, while doing the same work, it might appear that all the salaries and wages must be higher, and that the cost must be much above that corresponding to a sale price of £10. The answer is that the value of gold rises, or in popular language, prices are very low. It is assumed, for simplicity, that there is no restraint of international trade. The result is that there is an almost isolated community, which confines its dealing with outsiders to buying a few goods like tea, which cannot be made at home, and paying for it in pumps, or any other manufactures. The result of limitation of offspring is that there is no poverty, people being well-fed and well-clothed and comfortably off, with reasonable leisure. This comes to the people apparently in the form of normal pay, but very high value of money, compared with runcitic goods.

At first hand-workers in other places will argue that if wages are the same in the two communities, there is no good in moving. Wage-earners nearly always consider the amount only of their wages, and not what they will buy ; so that it will be a little time before they realise the advantages of migration. But people higher up in the scale will want to move in as soon as population pressure has been reduced. As we are dealing with changes that must be slow, we may assume that the hand-workers also will see that it would be wise to migrate.

If they are allowed to come in as they like, the community is not isolated, and we have the imaginary case of Scotland, already discussed. If they are not allowed to come in, we have the case of a community allowing no immigrants. In the present state of the development of civilisation that means that the people must be prepared for war against others, and perhaps even generally against the rest of the world.

We have the idea of the inhabitants of parts of the world proposing to keep them to themselves already; but the notion is not well developed. Australia and New Zealand may like to keep out both Japanese and Chinese. This is largely race feeling, of course. The United States is already in a very difficult position. The Indians are dying out, and there is no acute problem as to them. But the negro question is very trouble-some, as the negroes are there, and the United States or their forbears brought them there; and they cannot be sent back. There are also a very serious Chinese, and a still more serious Japanese question on the West side of North America. But these are essentially race difficulties. South Africa opened its gates to Chinese hand-labour, but only on condition that the Chinese should not stay there; again a race affair.

It has probably occurred to many in Australia and New Zealand that the inhabitants might be better off if they stopped all immigration altogether. On the other hand, employers of all sorts, including the smallest shopkeeper or farmer of any sort, thinks he will be better off if he is supplied with cheap hand labour; so there is a large and important part of the people anxious to have hand-workers coming in.

In a new country like Australia, or especially New Zealand, which can be developed very quickly, as capital soon gives a big return, population pressure may be small for quite a long time. The people have the habits acquired in old countries of marrying late, and in some cases of having small, or at any rate not large families. We might have had good examples of communities in which population pressure was reduced, while population volume increased rapidly; the happy state being due to the easy rapid development of new countries. Un-fortunately both colonies are democratic, so the govern-ment is controlled by the ignorant—well meaning, no doubt, but ignorant; and the development of the colonies is checked by all sorts of foolish legislation intended to benefit the hand-labourers at the expense of the rest. Both colonies, whose staple products are food and wool, and in the case of Australia, metals, which are in great demand, restrict their external trade, and thus check their own development. In spite of their restraint of their own progress, these colonies are going ahead very fast, as the natural resources are so great·; and there are already signs of the beginnings of immigration and race troubles. Chinamen are, or were, allowed to come into New Zealand for a time only.

Australasia, in any case, cannot give us any idea of what an isolated country would become if the population question was understood. One main difference, and it goes to the root of the matter, is that the hand-workers there all believe that they and the capitalists are in competition, and that the employers make their profits by underpaying, and so on. The result is that they are always discontented, and therefore unhappy. Getting good wages does not make people happy if they think they are being robbed all the time, and that they are badly and unfairly treated in all sorts of ways. Running the government and passing all sorts of humorous laws, intended to benefit the hand-workers at the expense of capital, may salve the imaginary wounds a little, but the main effect is to keep things back.

There is a growing desire among the Chinese, and still more among the Japanese, to settle in Australasia. As long as this desire is rather small, the Japanese and Chinese can be kept out, or let in temporarily on terms·; but as soon as such a matter becomes important enough to be a national affair, say, in Japan, war will be threatened. Obviously Australia and New Zealand could do nothing. England could not protect them.

It would seem clear that the wisest course in Australasia is to develope as rapidly as possible, so as to be numerous enough as to men, and rich enough to stand up to an Eastern country before there is a well-developed idea of any sort of invasion. It may, however, be considered a little presumptuous to try to teach two important colonies their business.; so we may go back to teaching the world in general, as that is everyone's prerogative.

A community that limits offspring must therefore be completely isolated as regards immigration, or must suffer a continual influx of outsiders. The first condition means war in the present state of civilisation. But ideas of war are changing rapidly. Consider the position of the world with, let us say, a large island in which the population pressure was reduced. With the notions of to-day, a nation in which population pressure is high would contain a large number of enterprising, energetic people wanting to move into better places. They would want to move to the island. The islanders would refuse to let them come. The nation would argue that it suffered from over-population, and it must, as a nation, secure an outlet for its excess of people. This was one of the ideas at the back of the minds of the Germans when they went to war. Such a nation would go to war with the island, and insist on an outlet for its excess population. As urged in the chapter on war, there is every chance of war being a different affair altogether in a short time. It may consist largely in hampering trade·; but it is more likely to be mere killing off of the enemy, men, women and children of all sorts and ages.

If the warlike nation understood the population principle it would not go to war, because it would realise that emigration is no cure for population pressure, as it lessens it for a short time only, and that often so little as not to count. No modern nation would go to war with the set object of reducing either its own population, or of making more room in another country so as to send emigrants there and give them good openings later. Though war was originally a population valve, that has never been generally understood. The lapse into war would begin with the nation getting envious. Newspapers would say that it was absurd that people on the island should have such easy lives, when they were mentally and morally so inferior to their readers. They would add that the islanders thought that because they lived better they were inherently superior people, and despised and disliked their neighbours, and they should be taught a lesson. Popular feeling would thus be worked up against the islanders until it broke out into war.

In discussing the limitation of offspring and its effects, it has been assumed that the result, in an isolated people, would be smaller populations living more easily, more morally and more happily ; the proportions in the different strata of society remaining practically as they are now in ordinary cases. This may easily be wrong. It is quite likely that the standard of living would increase more among the hand-workers than above them. Even in ordinary civilisation in England the income of the poorer classes has gone up much more in proportion than that of the richer, though agitators are fond of saying it is the other way round. Mr. Mallock has pointed out that the moderately well-off have increased enormously, and not the very rich, as popularly assumed. It is very likely that the condition of the hand-workers would go up still more, under the new conditions, as the change would be greater and greater the lower we go down the scale, as growth of families is already more restrained at the top than at the bottom, improvident multiplication increasing gradually all the way until its maximum comes among the miserable at the bottom.

But whatever the result is as far as relative comfort of the different strata of society, the point to be seen clearly is that limitation is not a general cure of all evils, acting at once ; because it cannot become general all over the world at once; and as it gets more common among enlightened people, they will still be hurt by the competition due to the population pressure of the backward. What is wanted is a social sense, or a feeling that will make people think of their fellows in general and not only of themselves. We want a public opinion according to which a man with a large family is regarded as putting a burden on the community to satisfy his own selfishness. On the other hand, somebody must have offspring, or the race will die out. It is likely that having families will become the duty of the well-to-do and rich, a tax being levied on children, beginning fairly low, but increasing very rapidly with the number. This would tend to improve the race quickly, as the stock would be bred from the best instead of, as now, chiefly from the worst.

The law of diminishing returns applies to the produce of land. If you make fewer locomotives they do not come out cheaper; in fact, in manufacture the tendency is for larger output to yield increasing returns. We can imagine a community which has practically no land produce, and is really a sort of large workshop. Britain has a good deal of land produce ; but as the land produce is small in proportion to that of other countries, it may look as if reduction of population pressure in this country would not do much good.

Suppose we understood something about population, and limited families sensibly. As a result of our knowledge we would also reduce all doles very gradually to zero, so that there would be work for all, and no incompetent idlers living on the rest. Under the head of doles is here included all poor-relief, organised " charity " and government aid. We might then reduce all useless government activities, such as armaments and fighting services, all the departments for interfering with industry, most expenditure on education, and on professional religionists. It may be said that such views on armament and fighting services are extreme ; and that the right thing to do with education is not to stop it, but to remodel it so that it does not consist practically in training only the memory, and storing the mind with knowledge which has conventional, but no real value. We will, therefore, consider two changes only, limitation of families, and stoppage of maintenance of the idle and unfit at the expense of the active and fit. The stoppage of doles would at once make the community better off, because we would have some million more people working, and producing, with the same consumption as before. There would be a

temporary fall of population pressure, so limitation of
families need not be adopted at once. But after a little,
when the population had increased up to the point that
people had come down again to the present standard of
comfort for each kind of work, limitation would be
adopted.

We may consider two communities or countries, one
like Britain, which depends partly on its own land,
and largely on foreign land, ; and one like Denmark,
which does not use all its own land for itself, ; but
exports land produce in exchange for manufactures
and other goods.

Suppose both are in such a state as to population
pressure that people in each grade of work are in the
same state of comfort as in those grades in other
countries. These grades are not high enough, so in
both countries they reduce population pressure by limiting families. The result in Denmark is easily traced, ;
with the same amount of work they produce more in
proportion, ; as the land is not pressed so hard. It may
be urged that the people would get lazy ; in fact, they
might get lazier and lazier, while they reduced the
population more and more, making life easier and easier,
until the whole country was very sparsely populated.
This assumes that Denmark is peopled with the theoreti-
cal economists' man, whose sole motive is enlightened
selfishness. As was pointed out at the beginning of
this book, man's motives are primarily his own survival
and survival of his race, ; but these primary motives
soon disappear, or rather they do not count when they
are easily gratified. The ruling motive is actually pride,
chiefly in the form of vanity, coupled with a strong desire
to do right. In addition, when the question of limiting
families is fully understood, population pressure will
not disappear, it will merely be reduced. People will
still want to have children ; all that will happen is that
they will not have children when they see they cannot
bring them up at their social level.

In Britain, on the other hand, reducing population
after all the lazari have been abolished, does not make

life much easier, because land produce is in much smaller proportion.

It may be urged that we are considering countries, and there is no reason for considering countries as opposed to mere districts. This is not a lapse into the patch fallacy; the reason why two fighting groups were chosen is that, as already explained, if life is easier in Denmark or Britain, people will want to come in from places where population pressure is great. Though this would not do the places any good, the people there would think it would, and might go to war if their emigrants were not allowed to come in. If, instead of Denmark and Britain, we consider Britain alone, and think of the districts·; when population pressure is generally reduced, there will be a slight movement from the manufacturing to the land districts. Similarly, if we consider not Denmark and Britain alone, but the civilised world ; when population pressure is reduced, population will fall more in the manufacturing than the land countries.

Returning for a moment to Denmark and Britain, let us think of them by themselves, imagining Denmark to export land produce to Britain and to import manufactures in exchange. As Denmark now produces more cheaply, it will give more produce in exchange for manufactures ; and the result will be that even if England were purely manufacturing, with no land, and therefore no increasing returns, it would get the full benefit of increased returns if land producing countries reduced their population pressure.

This emphasises the importance of getting people to attend to elementary economics, and to do away with all restriction of foreign trade. It brings home to us again that a government is responsible to outside countries as well as to its own ; and that if our colonial governments restrict our food supply under the impression they are doing themselves good, they are ignorantly and quite unintentionally doing us a serious injury. Similarly, all the land countries that restrain their exports of food are injuring all the manufacturing countries. It is quite true that the manufacturing countries which stop exports by taxing imports are injuring all the food countries ; but Britain, at any rate, is not a universal enemy in that way, though we are always on the verge of lapsing into restraint of trade.

CHAPTER XXIII

THE FUTURE

FOR the last century or more there has been much talk of making life happier for the more lowly.; but nothing has come of it. The lowly are better off, but that is in no way the result of the oceans of ink and wastes of paper that have been used up ; still less is it the effect of the still greater output of oratory or talk.

The fundamental reason is that people do not study sociology. They think they can settle difficult questions without any thought or knowledge,; and they do not realise that other people have given any real thought to them, and may have sounder views.

There are some particular fallacies or wrong ideas that prevent advance. Perhaps the oldest and most serious are the notions, first, that the rich are rich at the expense of the poor, and second, that governments are good, and can help the poor and put things right.

The unreasoning hatred of the rich is based on incurable human weakness. When we see men better off we feel that we are just as good, or according to our conceit, much better, and it is unfair that they should be richer. We also think what a lot of difference a little of their wealth would make to us, and how little they would feel the loss. No doubt this feeling has existed as long as man ; or at least since any ideas of property were developed. The hatred of the rich by those who were not well off was very marked in Palestine some two thousand odd years ago. Thus : " The rich man hath done wrong, and yet he threateneth withal.; the poor is wronged, and he must intreat also." "' .What agreement is there between the hyena and a dog? and what peace between the rich and the poor? As the wild ass is the lion's prey in the wilderness ; so the rich eat up the poor. As the proud hate humility ; so doth the rich abhor the poor." Turning from Ecclesiasticus to Enoch, we have : " Those, too, who acquire gold and silver, shall justly and suddenly perish. Woe to you who are rich, for in your riches have you trusted ; but from your riches you shall be removed ; because you have not remembered the Most High in the days of your prosperity ! Woe unto you, sinners, who say : ' We are rich and possess wealth . . . our barns are full.' They shall surely die suddenly."

Throughout the New Testament there is the same under-current. In the parable the crime of Dives was simply that he was rich. He may have made his money in return for great services to the world. He is condemned to everlasting torture. Lazarus, whose merit was that he presumably would not work, but lived on other people, goes straight to Abraham's bosom. Dives is not even allowed to send warning to his brothers, who are also rich. They may as well as not be hard-working, kind, God-fearing people, who have not the least idea that it is a deadly sin to be rich. They had been brought up to regard both David and Solomon as estimable. But they must suffer torture for ever and ever simply because they are rich, without any hint that they are doing wrong. There is infinite injustice and infintie cruelty towards the rich. This is very extraordinary when we remember who it was who spoke the parable.

Then, again, we have : " Go to now, ye rich, weep and howl for your miseries that are coming upon you. . . . Behold, the hire of the labourers who mowed your fields, which is of you kept back by fraud, crieth out : and the cries of them that reaped have entered into the ears of the Lord of Sabaoth." Here is the envious assumption that the rich become so by paying unfair wages.

From the envy of the rich, coupled with human conceit, arises the notion that the rich have become so at the expense of the poor. It is a short step to the theory that there is a limited quantity of money or wealth in the world—to the uninformed money and wealth are the same thing—and that the rich can possess it only by taking it from the poor. The next step is also simple.; it assumes not only that the rich have taken the money from the poor, but that they have stolen it. This string of nonsense has been the stock-in-trade of the common demagogue, ever since there has been a common demagogue. Doubtless the demagogue of the earliest civilisations flourished on these fallacies. There were common demagogues then, of course, just as there were other parasites. The same string of nonsense is the stock-in-trade of the common demagogue of to-day; whether he is a labour leader, a socialist, a syndicalist, a democratic politician, or, in short, any popular kind of reformer.

The demagogue not only battens on the misery of the have-nots, and uses it for his own advantage; but he himself is largely the cause of it; as he persuades them that they are treated badly by the rich. It is said that the Devil opens his favourite gambit with : " It's very hard." But the demagogue is not content with stirring up the jealousy and envy of the poorer classes; he will cause revolution and bloodshed if he thinks it will push him up.

For this ability he depends on the universal belief in the power and beneficence of governments. History consists mainly of accounts of two closely related phenomena. Population pressure causes peoples to fight one another and kill off the surplus.; and to rob one another of food or wealth, and to get slaves. And population pressure makes the poor envy the rich, and want to rob them. The only way to rob them wholesale is by getting the government into the hands of the discontented. The government is an organisation existing for the benefit of those who control it; and it is difficult to overthrow it, because the rebels are not organised, and have very little chance of beginning to organise. The government, though an organisation, always involves inside forces of destruction. The king or president balances the powers of the various interests next him. In old days he carefully played the priests against the lay lords, and balanced one interest or class against another, so as to keep in his own hands the power of tipping the balance one way or another. He murdered, assassinated, robbed, lied, cheated, and committed any other crimes that he thought helpful. Machiavelli has given us some of the methods of autocratic government with delightful frankness. The tendency of government is to enlarge its sphere, so as to glorify itself and make more patronage ; and it tends to go on until the majority of those governed cannot stand it any longer; or until population difficulties, which come more in waves as the society is primitive, bring the government into trouble.; as the government is blamed for the badness of the times. The demagogue is always telling the poorer people that they are being robbed and ill-treated by the rich, and that the rich have the government in their hands, and are using it as an engine for oppressing them. He says that if he is put into power they will end all this, and the poor will become rich, or, at least, the envied rich will be made poor, which tempts them more. If the government is democratic he may get in peacefully.; but generally throughout history the demagogue has found insurrection and revolution the normal course. No doubt revolution tempts him most. He hopes to get in on the top of the wave, and become the head of the new State. He thus plays for big stakes. The fault of history is that it is written by men who have no knowledge of sociology, and often have all sorts of prejudices of their own. Neither is school history honest; such people as Buckle or Lecky might never have written. One of the most prominent prejudices at present is in the direction of saying that the rich have always oppressed the poor. But apart from that, men and events loom large, while the conditions of which the men and events are the results are not mentioned and not known. The mathematician who told the historian he might as well let bygones be bygones, no doubt felt that history had little to do with the facts of the past.

The whole of history, or of the more serious kind of history which is not concerned with court scandals, or the methods of fighting primitive battles in primitive times, is mainly on account of the effects of population pressure in producing wars of all kinds ; and of the instability of governments, which are continually being upset by the cheap and ignorant talker, who uses the misery of the poor for his own advancement.

The evils man suffers from are, and always have been, made much worse by the talker, public speaker or orator. He is the same pest whatever he is called. He appeals to the crowd, and works upon the weakness and unreasoning sentimentalism of the crowd mind. In old days, when writing was very laborious, and there was no way of making many copies, public speaking was naturally the most important way of putting ideas forward. In those days the audiences would naturally include all the educated. The natural result was that oratory developed into a fine art, and the talkers became very important. A man became an orator as a means of self-advancement, just as he does now. He did not start with some theory, scheme or doctrine which he had studied, and train himself in talking to be able to communicate his ideas-; he began by cultivating talking, and when he had found his mouth he embraced any theme he thought would make him popular and successful, outside his legal work. Demosthenes became an orator simply because he saw what a lot of kudos he might get. He went in for Philippics because he thought it would pay. When he had to fight against Philip he ran away. Cicero was of the same kidney; a man of enormous vanity. There was no opening for the demagogue then, as the body of the inhabitants were slaves ; and nothing could be got by haranguing them about their very real ill-treatment or by starting revolt. Poor Spartacus soon came to grief. The talker has survived printing, which did away with any need for him. He now addresses crowds of uninformed people, who come together because they agree or are ready to agree with everything he says. People who disagree do not come, or are kept out if they try to get in. Anyone who has found his mouth and made himself known, becomes a talker on any subject that he thinks will advance him. A woman goes into an empty church and addresses it from the pulpit, and realises she has the gift of talk, so she takes up Bradlaughism as a means of advertisement ; then she thinks Buddhism will bring her more notoriety; finally she devotes her tongue to talking nonsense to the Indians. Again, the women who succeeded in making themselves notorious talkers in the suffragette outburst, now go on talking along all sorts of other lines that will continue their notoriety. Women may be more dangerous agitators in the future than men; they often have a better flow of language, because that type has such colossal conceit that there is no self-consciousness; their nonsense is more emotional, and appeals to their crowds; and they are reckless because they know, that being women, they will never be punished.

Though some of it is merely useless, nearly all public speaking is harmful. Sermons in England are a sort of excrescence on the service, preserved solely to gratify the vanity of the parsons. They generally merely waste the time of the congregation. Every now and then a parson uses his pulpit to hold forth on secular matters which he knows nothing about ; and if he is fashionable, and has some sort of ecclesiastical handle to his name, the daily papers often report him, and some harm is done. Whether the pulpit has much power in maintaining the hurtful influence of the priests in Ireland or not, the whole effect of sermons for harm is fairly small. The influence of the churches on the development of sound knowledge on all sociological matters is against progress, as it always has been; but its effect gets less every day. The church will probably lose any influence it still has by the admission of women. It is supported mainly by women now, and they support it because women like men in what they consider positions of authority.   In the near future the rector may be any middle-aged woman.   Her husband will not be an assistant parish worker, he is more likely to be a local tradesman.   When women parsons are common, ladies will cease to attend, and their example will be followed by all women, and the real support of the church will be gone.

Speaking in a national assembly is mere obstruction of business.   It does not affect the members themselves, as they have already settled how they will vote, and may be away in committee rooms or elsewhere while the talking goes on.   It is merely self-advertisement addressed to the public through the papers.   The board of a limited liability company is not generally very efficient, but it has sense enough to carry on its discussions in private.   When politicians stump the country they throw all ideas of truth and honesty to the winds. They promise that their parties will do all sorts of good things that are entirely outside the power of any government.; and they tell the wage-earners lies to flatter them, to make them feel that they are treated ill, and that this party or that will put them right at the cost of the State.   They will set man against man, and class against class, to gain a little popularity for their contemptible selves.   Limehousing is a straight road to the highest political honours.   It is odd that though many people are intensely interested in politics, there is no method of determining the magnitude of a lie. It has been said that a study becomes a science only when exact measurement is possible.   To make politics a science, we want a means of measuring mendacity. When a politician tells the hand-workers that after the war they shall not go back to a position as bad as that in 1914, he is stating what it is obvious to well-informed people and even to him is not the fact. During the war the country lost much capital, and the only way to recover was to produce more and consume less.   But the mere departure from truth is not really a fair measure of a lie.   Though much commoner, a lie has something in common with a quaternion. The fact is stretched or squeezed up, and turned in a new direction ; and a lie is a ratio, too, namely, the ratio of the harm done to the hearers to the good to the teller. In this case the denominator is the good to the teller.; the merely personal consideration of being popular with the hand-workers, getting their votes, and keeping in power. This is a very petty and contemptible little denominator. It is almost a vanishing quantity compared with the numerator. The numerator is the discontent of the hand-workers with fair wages, which is fostered by a statement by a man they consider of high authority. The result is to help strikes and preposterous demands of one section of hand-workers, to increase dissatisfaction all through the hand-working classes, and to make them all expect higher wages than are possible. More than this, it helped to get wages, hours and output settled in such a way as to hamper the whole industry of the country, and to hurry us into a state of scarce capital, high cost of living, and general unemployment, with its accompaniment of violence, riots, and a general tendency towards mad revolution. The political lie, in which the politician does immeasurable harm by flattering the lowest prejudices of the ignorant, in order to gratify his own little personal vanity, is thus a fraction with a very large numerator and a little pigmy denominator, and is as nearly as may be an infinite lie.

Akin to the harm done by the politician is that of the ordinary labour agitator, syndicalist, socialist, and the like. If we are ever to reach a state of perfection, one of the first steps onward will be to give up public speaking of all kinds. The " leader of men " is generally a fanatic, or a fool, or both, who stirs up the crowd by appealing to the crowd mind. He does not lead them anywhere that makes them better, or does any good. Another change that must be made is to outlive the belief in governments, and to curb their power so that they do not interfere with industry, and, in fact, do only those few things that must be done

by government, and must therefore always be done
badly. As public speaking has not abated at all since
the invention of printing, there is no chance of its dying
out for many a century. As men have believed in
beneficent government since the dawn of history, and
have always indulged in bloodshed with the object of
changing one bad government for another; and as,
in spite of the experience of thousands of years, they
have greater faith in governments than ever, there is
no hope of improvement in that direction.

It is easy to despair of the present generation, and
to pin one's faith on the effects of education on the
next ; and it is easy to think that the educators will
adopt one's own view, as enlightened people, and instil
it into the young. There is no chance of this. We have
had education of the richer classes for thousands of
years, and we have had education of everybody for
some generations, and what is the good of it? The
public school university man knows nothing of social
questions, and cares less. Whether his education consists in much more than applying his memory to the
retention of useless material, because everybody else
does it, is for experts in education to say. Turning to
the poorer classes, it is a commonplace that they are
enabled to read newspapers ; and that is all. They
buy the papers that flatter their vanity and prejudice, and they imbibe false ideas and accept nonsense as fact, just as newspaper readers in higher
classes do.

To anyone who has understood the population principle as a boy, and has lived with it through a long
manhood, there is nothing more dispiriting. There
appears to be no hope of people ever understanding
what is really wrong with the world ; and until it is
understood, nothing is of any use. No alteration in
government can be of any avail. No difference of
attitude of capital and labour can have any effect.
No developments of industry can do any real good.
All the changes that are usually called advances merely
enable a larger number of people to live in a given

set of degrees of comfort and of misery. All advances and discoveries in academic science are to him merely interesting intellectual amusement. They are of no value in lessening human misery. Science is a pleasant incitement to competition with intellects like his own, but bigger. Invention and industrial advance is much the same. A new machine, a new chemical process, or a new industry is of no value to the world. Success in life provides for his family first, and also satisfies his vanity, but that is all ; it is of no real use to the community.

We are just a world of funny people, taking ourselves and our useless work very seriously, and thinking we are of some importance to others than ourselves and our dependents:; and if our funniness was not itself a source of pleasure, life would be dreary and hopeless as regards everything but one's own family and friends. The best course, perhaps, is to devote energy to such matters as art or music, which have nothing directly to do with improving the condition of mankind.

Man has existed, say, four hundred thousand years; and the simple fact that he exists in virtue of having children, and what obviously results from that, has never yet come home to him; though, by division of labour, he understands all that is to be found in the Bodleian, the Royal Society's and Patent Office libraries. Will he realise that he exists by having more children than an average of one for each adult in another half-million years? Probably not if he wants not to know.

But a new hope has arisen lately ; and the solution of the problem is now developing, and after four thousand or so a change seems to be taking place in a single century. This is not due to Malthus, or to any books like this one ; and it is not due to any sort of enlightenment on social subjects; it is due, as all other advances are due, to enlightened individual self-interest. For about seventy years the limitation of families has been practised. It began in the middle classes, and spread both up and down; and it will gradually extend until it changes the whole of the relations of society. The limitation of offspring, and the means, form the greatest discovery man has ever made. But no one knows the discoverer, and such matters are mentioned only with bated breath.

INDEX

For Product Safety Concerns and Information please contact our EU
representative GPSR@taylorandfrancis.com
Taylor & Francis Verlag GmbH, Kaufingerstraße 24, 80331 München, Germany

www.ingramcontent.com/pod-product-compliance
Lightning Source LLC
Chambersburg PA
CBHW070543270326
41926CB00013B/2184